THE BOOK OF MAC
REMEMBERING MAC MILLER

DONNA-CLAIRE CHESMAN

PERMUTED
PRESS

A PERMUTED PRESS BOOK

ISBN: 978-1-63758-068-4

ISBN (eBook): 978-1-63758-069-1

The Book of Mac:

Remembering Mac Miller

Cover photo by Karen Meyers

Cover design by Tiffani Shea

Permuted Press, LLC

New York · Nashville

permutedpress.com

Published in the United States of America

1 2 3 4 5 6 7 8 9 10

First Edition

For Malcolm

Table of Contents

Cast of Characters

Josh Berg (recording and mix engineer, producer)

Justin Boyd (friend and photographer)

Just Blaze (producer, "All Around the World")

Clams Casino (producer, "My Team," "One Last Thing")

Karen Civil (digital media marketing strategist, friend)

Quentin Cuff (tour manager and dear friend)

E. Dan (friend, engineer, ID Labs founder)

Nick Dierl (friend and publicist)

Eric G (producer, "2009")

Aja Grant (pianist, Phony Ppl)

Benjy Grinberg (founder and president of Rostrum Records)

Chuck Inglish (producer, "Wear My Hat")

Craig Jenkins (music critic, *New York Magazine*)

Big Jerm (friend, producer, ID Labs cohort)

Will Kalson (friend and first manager)

Kehlani (singer)

Wiz Khalifa (rapper)

Marc-André Lauzon (Mac Miller Memoir Twitter page co-founder)

Cody Lee (Mac Miller Memoir Twitter page co-founder)

Thelonious Martin (producer)

Phonte (rapper of Little Brother fame)

Rapsody (rapper)

Sap (producer, "Donald Trump")

Sermon (blog era titan)

NADIRAH SIMMONS (editor-in-chief, *The Gumbo*)

SKYZOO (rapper)

SYD (front woman, The Internet)

THUNDERCAT (bassist, producer, "Inside Outside")

CASEY VEGGIES (rapper)

VIC WAINSTEIN (friend and engineer)

IAN "REX ARROW" WOLFSON (music video director)

Introduction

On the day Mac Miller passed, September 7, 2018, I penned a personal letter to him. What followed was a year-long endeavor to honor Mac's music and memory entitled *Year of Mac*, published in the digital hip-hop magazine, *DJBooth*. I had been writing about Mac Miller's music for years, but I did not know I was writing *The Book of Mac* at the time. Looking back on this opening letter, it makes perfect sense that my original parting words to Mac were the catalyst for this broader project. This book is the byproduct of over two years of writing, reflecting, and crafting interviews in adoration and celebration of Mac Miller. I hope you enjoy it.

Thank You, Mac Miller

I did not want to have to write this, or anything like this, ever. Now that I am writing, I cannot imagine doing anything but, and that is a gift you gave me. Ever since you were Easy Mac with the cheesy raps, ever since you flashed brilliant grins on *Blue Slide Park*, you gave me the gift of language and poetics in a way no one else ever has. I was seventeen and scared in a hospital bed, and you had my back, man. You and your punchlines and Big L impersonations and parties on Fifth Ave took my mind off brain tumors and possibilities of chemo, spinal taps, and surgeries. You took me to Pittsburgh and you rolled me a blunt, and you made me happy again.

I was seventeen and thought my life was over, but with *Blue Slide Park*, you showed me all the ways life could be lived. I was woefully depressed and didn't know the first thing about proper therapy channels, medication, or admitting I had something deeply wrong with me, and you got me excited about life again. In the hospital—and no one knows this, but since we're one big Most Dope family now—I watched videos of you freestyling and tried to craft my own 16s whenever my room was empty. It was so grounding and therapeutic. When I hit the flowstate while the nurses were away, man, I thought I was finally anxiety-free. Here's the thing about me rapping, though—I wasn't very good. But you sure were.

Then the surgery happened, and I was okay, and you were okay. I played *Blue Slide Park* as we left Columbia Neurology behind us. And we kept smiling like we do, like you said. Then the winter of 2015 rolled around, and I shut myself up in my bedroom, drew the shades, and wrote a letter. You know how it goes. On the emotional readiness scale, I would consider myself Tinkerbell. I feel too much too fast and then I implode. The beauty of *Faces*, then and now, was that it was twenty-four laborious, abstract, and deranged songs. You went from tripping to screaming to breaking down love and drugs. You had the words for me when I was my most confused.

In the winter of 2015, I had this itch to kill myself, but I also had this convoluted spirituality. I wore a Kabbalah bracelet and a Star of David, and you must get it because you titled your album *The Divine Feminine*. In 2015, I wasn't sure if I was supposed to live or die, so I tested myself. I put myself in dangerous situations and through dangerous acts and drank dangerous amounts just to know. If I was supposed to die, I would. I made it into a game because I had to. I gave myself "the *Faces*-rule." The tape came on and I gave my mortality a stress test.

This was all terribly ritualistic, and I was at my lowest, but every time the project came to a close, I was still alive. I had vivid, graphic nightmares and stopped sleeping. *Faces* gave words and sounds to my nightmares, and when I realized I could finally explain myself, I realized I could survive. Thank you, Mac, for reaching out from whatever plane you were on when you made *Faces* and showing me there was a life left for me to live in a kindred, cosmic sense that only made sense to us.

I lived, man; we did it.

Even soundless, Mac, you gave me my words. You gave me my life, man. I wrote myself out of 2015 with *Run-On Sentences: Vol. 1* on in the background. It was February, and I was still sitting in pitch darkness, but I was finally back at that poetry business. I was writing the best poems of my life, and the first publication credit I ever earned was for a piece I wrote to "Birthday." The poem was about living, some-how—just like all of your music and your legacy will be about liv-ing, somehow.

I lived, man; we did it.

In 2016, my life was feeling like it was mine again, and like clock-work, your music was right there with me. It was uncanny—it *is* uncanny—how we've managed to live through everything together year-to-year. It's a Jewish thing, I think. In 2016, I was in and out of love and you were very much in, and I was feeling on top of the world somewhere in Bushwick, and you had it all figured out too.

And then when life didn't ask and pulled the rug out from under me, in the pockets of *The Divine Feminine*, you were still there, still understanding. I returned to *GO:OD AM*. I learned what fight and recovery sounded like. All these years, man, and you kept teaching me what life could sound like if I just gave it some time and elbow grease. When I began to settle into the reality of my depression, to accept that this is how I am going to have to live every day, *Watching Movies with the Sound Off* was the record that showed me exactly how sadness could be beautiful and beyond reproach without being glam-orized. Your language was always fucking thrilling, but *Watching Movies* unlocked something in me that colors everything I write.

You made "I Am Who Am," which I've vowed to get tatted down my arm just as soon as I know this writing thing is going to work out. You made a song about the Jewish Diaspora and how you don't want to be chosen, you just want to be left alone. You made a song talking to a void, while talking to yourself, while talking to me, while I talk to myself, and it was slick and avant-ish and brilliant. You made my favorite song, Mac, the one I play for people who want to get to know me.

In 2017, my grandfather passed away. The same day I found out about his passing, I bought a three-foot painting of you because I was distraught and that seemed like a reasonable coping method. As I'm writing this, I have that piece of art framed in my living room right beside me. I look up at it whenever I have a writer's crisis of faith. Some people have an everything-artist. Some people have a mentor-artist. Shit, Mac, you were *a light*. You were transcendent to me.

Then there was *Swimming*. You didn't release that album, Mac; you gifted it to me. 'Nother year, same shit. One-to-one, you and I. It was 2018, and I was fucking terrified, man. I was scared and excited and at peace. All at once. I woke up in the middle of a panic attack damn near every day; some days I didn't know how to help myself. *Swimming* was the first album I put on every morning. I mumbled bars to myself when the breathing got tough. All of the nameless evil that plagues me lived on *Swimming*, in this stunning, heavenly package I could never have articulated without you. People might think you saved my life, but you did something so much more important: you showed me exactly how I could save myself.

In 2018, I found out you read my writing—a lot of my writing—and you liked it. That means the world to me. At the time of writing this, over thirty people have reached out to me to see how I am. I'm happy to be part of your legacy in that way, to be known in my corner of the internet as That Mac Miller Girl while you go down as a legend who touched so many people's lives.

Thank you, Mac. Thank you for your love and for reading my writing. Thank you for teaching me that I can keep living so long as I keep writing, so long as I keep creating. Thank you for explaining the Jewish Diaspora to me in song. Thank you for *Macadelic*, an album that sounds like my specific brand of day-to-day. Thank you for growing with me and showing me that I am not crazy. I promise on everything, I am going to write my heart out for you, just like you showed me time and time again for a decade.

There truly has never been a motherfucker iller, Mr. Miller.

2010

K.I.D.S.

"I just started rhyming every day. By fifteen, I was sure this is what I wanted to do with my life... Bars, bars, bars, recording. I just fell in love with everything... *Kids*, the movie, that is real shit... That's what I wanted my mixtape to do: tell it from the perspective of a real-ass, regular-ass kid."

—MAC MILLER[1]

1.   Mac Miller, "YRB Mac Miller interview & freestyle," interview by *YRB Magazine*, filmed August 30, 2010 in New York, https://www.youtube.com/watch?v=aAmjZ_p_PwQ.

QUENTIN CUFF (tour manager and dear friend): I went to the same high school as Jimmy [Murton] and TreeJay. Jimmy and TreeJay were good friends with Malcolm. We weren't that close, just acquaintances through school. My senior year, I saw on Facebook there was this person named Malcolm McCormick, but the [profile] picture was Big L. So I thought Mac was Black. He would get into these rap battles with people on Facebook forums—he would just write a whole verse battling back to another person. I thought that was cool; here's this Black dude from Pittsburgh that was an online battle rapper.

I met Mac at a party. [He] was freestyling in Brandon's kitchen. I was seventeen, Mac was fifteen. After hearing his raps, I was a fan of his music. He spilled beer so I gave him one of the extra shirts I had, and we became friends after that.

WILL KALSON (friend and first manager): I knew him from when he was a little kid. I went to school with Miller [McCormick, Mac Miller's older brother] my whole life. So I knew Malcolm from a young age, hanging out in Point Breeze, playing basketball. He would be down at the courts causing a scene 'cause he was ten, eleven years old. He was a memorable person. When I was a sophomore in college, my friend Brian [Beedie] had started to rap. We had been good friends since high school. He sent me Malcolm's music because his little brother was one of Malcolm's best friends at the time. We were messing around, recording songs, and at the same time, Malcolm was messing around and recording songs.

IAN "REX ARROW" WOLFSON (music video director): The first time I met Malcolm, I was shooting a feature film in Pittsburgh, and a good friend of mine who was in the film recommended Malcolm as someone who could play the role of a high school drug dealer. Malcolm showed up to my house dressed for the part: a polka dot Yankee baseball hat and a hoodie that said "Pimps, Moneys, Hoes." It was quite an introduction. It turned out my mom was his Sunday School teacher eight years prior. Classic Pittsburgh thing. He was in my film for a brief scene, and then we reconnected a year later. That was when we shot the first music video we ever did.

Big Jerm (friend, producer, ID Labs cohort): I met him, probably, through MySpace, honestly. It was probably 2008. He was sixteen, and I think he might've heard stuff I did for Wiz [Khalifa]. He was still Easy Mac at the time and I didn't really take him seriously at first. He got a beat off me back then for something off *The High Life*. A little later, I interned at ID Labs as an engineer. Around 2008, 2009 I would see Mac around, working with other people. We kinda connected, and he was persistent, so we started working like that. We became closer, and I understood that he was more talented than I originally thought. It just evolved from there.

E. Dan (friend, engineer, ID Labs founder): My first experience with him was him coming in and trying to give me a turntable—like a CD turntable—for studio time. I'm like, "Dude! Where are you even getting this shit?" My homie that was doing sessions with him is like, "Oh, he gave me a TV last week." I'm like, "What!" We're not a pawn shop, you know? So my first impression of him was, "Who's this kid giving me stolen shit for studio time?" I accepted the CD turntable, which may or may not have been legally purchased, but then the next session ... He showed up and paid, via PayPal, from Karen's photography business. It was like, "Alright, with this kid!"

Rex Arrow: When I met him, he was sixteen years old and my feeling about him was that he had an infectious personality and that he was a great person, but what could I actually learn from someone that's nine years younger than me? It was a decade of discovering that it really doesn't matter how old someone is, you can learn things from every person. With Malcolm, I could not see him for six months, and the moment I saw him, it was always "How are things going in your life?" It felt like no matter where he was in his career, he would always take the time to actually catch up and there was always a moment where he would take himself outside of whatever was going on in his life to listen to your problems and to just be a friend.

WIZ KHALIFA (rapper): First time I met Mac was probably at ID Labs. He was just a young kid, still in high school. I probably just graduated. I could see the potential in him. I [could] see him working hard. I was impressed with how he was putting [his career] together. I always enjoyed his music. Being from Pittsburgh, we have a certain sound that we all carry. To hear him coming up and being consistent with the sound, it was like he was ahead of his time. He knew exactly what pocket he was in.

BENJY GRINBERG (founder and president of Rostrum Records): I had been working with Wiz for a couple of years, and I had moved from New York back to Pittsburgh because I couldn't afford to live in New York anymore. I was trying to get Rostrum off the ground—and I was intent on getting Wiz off the ground. I moved back to Pittsburgh and was spending essentially every day with Wiz at ID Labs where we recorded. I just started seeing Mac around. He would have his own sessions, or he would just show up and hang out with people.

Every once in a while, he'd say, "I have some new music, you wanna hear it?" We would sit in the second studio room, which was tiny, and he'd play me a couple songs. I would give him a little bit of advice. It was arm's length at that time. I don't think either of us knew where it was headed. He was just looking for some advice, and I was happy to meet up with him, listen, and tell him some moves he should make. We did that more and more, and it developed into a relationship that solidified into him coming over to Rostrum.

RAPSODY (rapper): It was 2010; he and Khrysis and 9th [Wonder] had connected on Twitter and they were actually on tour. It was the first tour they did, and they were traveling in a station wagon and it was the core crew: Mac, Jimmy, TreeJay, Q, Clockwork. He came to the studio, and he just worked! Mac has always been who Mac is from the first day I met him to the very last time I saw him. Always been this fun, energetic kid who was filled with so much love. That's just what it was, and you feel that soon as he came in the door. He loved hip-hop. You knew he loved the music, and he was gifted, and you knew he wanted to have fun with it and share that positivity.

He went right to work. He talked to 9th, he joked. We recorded "Extra Extra" that first visit that he came. And he left, and I think maybe two or three days later, he hit 9th like, "Yo, I wanna bring Rapsody on the road with me." Just like that! Nobody really knew me at that time from a can of paint, so from day one, you just knew what kind of person he was.

Skyzoo (rapper): The first time I heard him was when he and his team reached out to me to get a verse. This was 2009, MySpace days. I got a message either from him or his manager, a dude named Will [Kalson]. I can't remember who reached out. I checked what they were doing and was like, "It's dope!" You could tell he was young. I think he might've been seventeen. He had this hunger to him. This excitement. When you're young, you just wanna rap. You just wanna go, go, go, go all day. He was at that phase of his evolution as an MC. He was dope! I gave them my email and they sent the record, and we did ["Pen Game."]

We kept in touch on MySpace, and then my debut album came out. A week or two later, he dropped the record. I was like, "Oh, word, good move!" I knew the strategy behind it. So that was cool! I would've done the same thing. Mac hit me and was like, "Yo, we just dropped the record. Thank you so much!"

Fast forward a year later, South by Southwest, at this point . . . Mac is outta here. You know *K.I.D.S.* . . . I'm walking down the sidewalk and across the street is Mac with a crowd of fans, talking to them. He sees me and runs across the street in the middle of traffic. "Yo, yo, yo, Skyzoo! I'm Mac! I'm Mac Miller!" He was like, "Yo, we finally meeting! We was talking for a year on MySpace." So we dapped it up and [exchanged numbers]. Every time Mac would see me, he would say the same thing: "I was seventeen with a Skyzoo verse! Can't nobody tell me shit." It was a testament to the way he looked at me as an MC. I thought that was cool. Obviously, seeing his growth as an MC, as a musician, as an artist, was great to see.

WILL KALSON: When I met him, I don't think he had put out *But My Mackin' Ain't Easy*, yet, but he had been working on it. I just thought it was fun and funny, and I just saw instantly he was gonna be a star. I don't know if other people saw that yet, but I had a feeling about him. His early music was *fun*. It was hilarious, but he was actually *rapping*. He was fucking around, but he wasn't. It was serious. I was impressed as someone who was already very, very into hip-hop.

HOW MAC MILLER TAUGHT
ME TO BE COMFORTABLE
IN MY QUEERNESS

Some time ago, when I was much younger and a lot less well-read, I imagined the queer life to be a depressed one. All media taught my baby gay self was that the life of a lesbian was tragic, and all my family seemed to telegraph to me was that I would never find peace while queer. As I spent ages eleven and twelve coming into consciousness of my queerness, I vacillated between great highs and greater lows. I felt the joy of finding an answer to my feelings and a community for my yearning. I also quickly realized that who I was did not fit the mold of my Russian-Jewish culture. Giddy moments wherein I could finally place my affections were replaced with shame. For the better part of my childhood, I felt so guilty. I was so tired of myself—my queer self.

How is it that I was tumbling through pre-adolescence and already exhausted? The burden of self-discovery and self-affirmation was already weighing on me. I knew fully I was gay on a family trip to Maine where I read a lesbian novel—Julie Anne Peter's *Keeping You a Secret*. I checked it out from the local library to confirm my suspicions. While reading the book, everything came into almost laughable focus. It was the "of course" moment of the decade. It was also terrifying. As I churned through the pages of *Keeping You a Secret*, I came to realize I was different in all the "wrong" ways.

I wish I could tell my harried younger self the things I would later experience. Your fiancée will read the same novel on your lap, and you will giggle at how trite the work's dramatics are. You will love yourself. You will be free, clutching the Star of David around your neck and gazing past her eyes into your happy life together. Instead, I was twelve and afraid. I thought being gay was an emotional death sentence. In the novel, the family abandons the protagonist. In my own life, already familiar with my parents' homophobia, I realized bitter solitude was a genuine possibility.

Of course—I have to say "of course"—I had my music. Most importantly, I had Mac Miller. Vividly, I remember the moment queerness changed for me; it was Malcolm's doing. I was thirteen or fourteen, on another trip with my parents, listening to "Knock Knock" and other select cuts off *K.I.D.S.* At the time, most of Mac's music centered on his youthful wiles, his desire for women, and the grand fun of being a young man. The way Malcolm's music was structured, images of pursuing women were presented as punchlines. Or they were just plain sweet in their innocence, as on "Senior Skip Day":

> "Supposed to be in class but I ain't goin' / Let's chill on the couch / See what's on the telly / Girl, we won't leave the house"

Every mention of a girl was met with spry candor. Mac was a grinning ladies' man. His aura was infectious, and it made me feel good. "All the pretty little girls come and flock with me," Mac rapped on "Knock Knock." "And I like my rhymes witty, all my dimes pretty," he continued on the second verse. I remember running around the beach in blue strappy sandals, earbuds firmly in place, knock-off iPod in hand, feeling like I could just lift off and fly. The world was mine. *This* was what it meant to like girls: this endless fun and jive.

My self-hatred and fear were replaced with the notion that liking girls could be a carefree and fulfilling exercise. I had spent my youth petrified, knowing that the moment I came out to my family, our entire dynamic would change. But here was this rapper who seemed to have as much zeal and pep and gleeful lust as I did, and he sounded over the moon. Mac Miller—especially in his early work—sounded thrilled to be alive and in like with every passing woman. He became my own personal wingman. Whenever I'd dwell on my Otherness, I'd recall Malcolm's joy and make it my own.

> "Mirror, mirror hangin' on the wall / Who the flyest white boy of them all? / Got your girlfriend screenin' all the calls / She bubblin', we fuckin' then you cuddlin'"

—*"The Spins"*

Mac's happiness also took the form of a wellspring of confidence. Every line about a woman was met with an equally pulpy line about himself. For a relentlessly-bullied oddball, listening to Mac Miller made me feel unstoppable. While in school, my queerness was maligned, but in my own Mac Miller-filled world, my queerness was celebrated. It was a mirror effect. He was the most fly; I was the most fly. He was worry-free; I was worry-free. All the girls flocked to him; perhaps all the girls would flock to me.

Surely, this young man had no idea what it meant to be a repressed queer kid, but he did know what it meant to have a good time. That's what I needed: the promise of good. Everywhere I looked, my shame was affirmed. I had no models for queerness. Every book I read ended in misery. With Mac Miller, liking women was a source of joy and laughter. In his happiness, I found solace. I discovered the queer existence could very well be a happy one because there is no shame in liking and loving women, whether you're Mac Miller, or me, or from any other walk of life.

That day at the beach was special because it marked the moment I realized my identity did not inherently mean punishment. Mac Miller's seemingly endless cad-like persona gave me the gift of forgiveness. The project of me loving my queerness began that very day when I took flight with *K.I.D.S.* as my fuel. I gave myself the budding gift of self-love.

At one point on "The Spins," Malcolm makes a playful (if not tacky) joke out of oral sex: "She gave me head with my concussion." Not his best bar, but to this day, I rap along with smooth, bubbling delight. Malcolm did not show me *how* to be queer, but he did show me I could be queer *and* happy. He showed me shame was a waste of time. Guilt, too, was a pittance. Mac Miller gave me the foresight to begin rejoicing in my queerness, and so I did.

QUENTIN CUFF: When Mac was a sophomore, I started hearing his *But My Mackin' Ain't Easy* tape. Jimmy has verses, TreeJay, [locals]... That's when I was like, "Yo! This dude has bars!" I started working with him when he was in the middle of doing the project with Beedie as The Ill Spoken. Him and Beedie were doing that project [*How High*], and Will Kalson was managing the group. This was before E. [Dan]! *But My Mackin' Ain't Easy* are the inaugural bars before *Jukebox*.

The maturation was so crazy. I was like, "Man! He has something." He was allowing me to say my ideas, and he would take some of them. The shift between Ill Spoken and *Jukebox* was he produced multiple beats on *Jukebox*. He had this massive keyboard he would make beats on, and it wasn't some crazy technology, but he was making crazy-ass beats on this keyboard. That's when I understood where he could go with his music. I thought his hooks were fire. And he had bars!

NADIRAH SIMMONS (editor-in-chief, *The Gumbo*): I love soulful hip-hop songs, and I can't remember what tape it is off the top of my head [*The High Life*], but he sampled "Just My Imagination," and I was just like "Wow! This white dude is sampling this old, classic song, and doing it justice." Then, just seeing the way he interacted with dudes so early on in his career. He's on a song with YG, and he's hanging out with Chance [The Rapper] and bringing Chance on his tour. Something about him just having respect for the culture... The fact that he, and it's so weird to say "was," so respectful and he was so in tune, and he was a student of the genre and of the culture. That sold me.

PHONTE (rapper of Little Brother fame): 9th [tells me] he got this "Kool Aid & Frozen Pizza" joint, and that joint is going up! I had never heard of him, so I pulled it up on YouTube and I see it's him rapping over the Lord Finesse "Hip 2 Da Game" instrumental, and I'm like: "What the fuck!? Are you serious!?" In a good way! I was like, "How old is this kid?" It would've been one thing if he rapped over a hit-hit. That "Hip 2 Da Game" record was no big, monster record. Even by underground rap standards. It was a dope joint, and if you were a head, you knew it, but it was no big record everyone would've known. The fact he chose to rhyme over that blew me away.

SKYZOO: Man, he was super generous and welcoming. Super cool. Stayed humble always—I'll give you a story on that. 2011, me and my DJ, DJ Prince, were in Pittsburgh doing a show. The show was on a Friday, and we were supposed to dip out. There was a *huge* storm back in New York, to the point where they shut all the travel down. We got stuck in Pittsburgh. We had to extend the hotel a couple nights; we didn't know when we were going. We met some people at this clothing store/record store. We got cool with them, and Sunday night was the VMAs. They were like, "Yo, come kick it at the crib, we got the VMAs, we gon' be hanging out." I was like, "Word."

Me and my DJ go to the crib, as soon as we walk in the door . . . Mac's sitting on the couch rolling an L! Mac looks and he's like, "What the fuck is Skyzoo doing in Pittsburgh on a Sunday night!" He was like, "Yo, we could've been fucking hanging out. Come sit down, have a drink, here's an L." We was drinking, watching the VMAs, and he just kept looking at me: "I can't believe Skyzoo is in Pittsburgh on a Sunday night."

RAPSODY: It wasn't about celebrity or how big he was becoming at the time; it was just two people that were homies that had love for each other, just wanting to make dope music. It was just raw like that. I remember he was like, "You want some hummus, man?" He was like, "Rap, how you don't eat hummus? You gotta try this." I went and tried it, like, "Nah, bruh. I'm not fucking with no chickpeas." Those are the memories I remember. And just watching Most Dope. How much love they had for each other; they were really brothers. That's what I remember: him always joking. The dude never stopped laughing.

QUENTIN CUFF: Definitely magnetic. He had all the confidence in the world in his talent. Things just happened for him quickly, bro. He had a destined path of what he was supposed to do in his life and in his career. I still don't think [I've] met anyone that has dedicated that much time to music, or been close to anyone that talented. His personality ... He was just hilarious! We hit it off from a perspective of liking similar albums—we connected on listening to OutKast and [watching] comedy movies.

WILL KALSON: He transferred to [Taylor Allderdice High School] his junior year. That's when he changed his name [and] started to take things a lot more seriously. I knew I wanted to keep working with him. I knew that Malcolm was gonna do big things. I *knew* it. He was just focused, even in high school. He didn't care about school—all he cared about was music. He just had the drive to do it. *The Jukebox* was supposed to be a prelude to the *Class Clown* album, but he changed projects by the minute. He was such a creative force, always coming up with new ideas. Constantly! He was always excited about them. When I was in college, he would hit me up on iChat all the time, and he would play me songs.

QUENTIN CUFF: Mac had a studio setup, and he let us come record once or twice. A month after that, Mac was pretty much like, "Yo, I know you're trying to rap and shit, but I'm trying to take my stuff more seriously and if you would help me ... I feel like you have a good mind for ideas and music business ideas." I didn't know what the fuck I was doing—we were learning stuff together. He allowed me to be part of his career, his life, and [to be] his friend.

WILL KALSON: One of my most vivid memories of him is the way he would look at you while he was playing you a song. He tried to look you right in the eyes to see how you were feeling about it. He wanted to know what you felt about it, good or bad. It was important to him, for everything to be—I wouldn't say he was a perfectionist, necessarily, but he was a very, very hard worker. He had what it takes. He had the work ethic.

K.I.D.S. was an exciting time because he was working on that mixtape the summer after he graduated high school. We knew that shit was gonna happen, because his views on YouTube were going up, and it was all organic.

We were going down to ID Labs every night that summer. This was the old ID Labs. It was pretty small, but it was intimate. He was definitely in talks with Benjy and Rostrum, and they were trying to work things out, but to me it was clear either way: With or without a record label, he was gonna take off. It was his choice to sign to Rostrum; he wanted to do that. We were just having a lot of fun in the studio every night. At that point, E. Dan and [Big] Jerm had fully embraced him. When he first started going around ID Labs, they were like, "Who the fuck is this kid, coming in here trying to act like he runs the place?" But that was just his personality! They realized how talented he was and what a good heart he had.

HEALING POWER

There was a point in my life where I was so paralyzed by fear that I could barely leave the house. The thought of going to the grocery store set off a bone-deep panic in me. When I eventually forced myself to step into the store, my body tensed. I got dizzy. The lights blinded me; I sweat through my clothes no matter how many layers I was wearing. As soon as I got home, I hid under the covers, sometimes crying, sometimes panting. A ten-minute trip to ShopRite knocked me out for an entire day. It was the fall of 2018, and I was at the height of my unmedicated mental health struggles.

My anxiety that October was peaking. I knew deep in my bones that what was wrong with me was more complex than what I knew of at the time. The symptoms of my depression were abnormal and manifested themselves physically and wantonly. My anxiety took many forms, and my triggers seemed endless. I was fixated on taking my own life. Somehow, though, I had some fight in me, some energy rattling inside, telling me there was more to life than how I was miserably living. This energy, too, manifested in many forms and without warning. I lived for this energy as I lived for the patches of sunlight kissing my cheek on a cold, windy day.

Energized days—stable days—were few and far between, but over time, I found a way to summon them. I had to. My crippling fear of leaving the house was starkly contrasted by my need to get out of the depressed hole I had dug in my apartment. Outside is healthy, running errands is therapeutic, and you cannot live life cooped up. You'll go mad. I know this. I lived it. When getting in my car on a Sunday morning to run errands would make me nauseous, I found there was one solution to ground myself and get me through the simple tasks: Mac Miller's 2010 breakout, *K.I.D.S.*

Malcolm's fourth mixtape, and the one that would put his name on the map for all time, saved me. There is a spry energy to the tape. His youthful face adorning the cover; his jeering voice spitting sometimes passé, sometimes involved raps; his cad-like reflexes; his joy—it flipped on a light in my spirit. It is impossible to feel anything but unfiltered happiness as Mac raps his breakfast order on "Senior Skip Day." You feel like *the man* when he details his sexcapades on "The Spins." You feel *alive* as Mac walks you through his life as a fly Pittsburgh teen. It's not about retreading your old memories; it's about stepping into Malcolm's moment and living life to the fullest alongside him.

The first time I ventured to the bookstore by myself, I spun *K.I.D.S.* as I swept down the highway. I had spent the entire morning talking myself up. I cannot stress enough how the simplest tasks, even the ones I enjoyed the most, choked me out. The thought of getting out of my cave and seeing other people made me ill. When stepping into a public place, my vision immediately blurred. I lost my ability to speak. Whatever space I was in got dark and tight. The walls collapsed on me, and I was beset with the need to throw up.

None of this happened when *K.I.D.S.* was on. None of it. The drive was a breeze, a blast. The sun beamed and the trees were turning colors. Liberated from my dark apartment and taking in the sights of a windy highway, I felt at peace with myself. Walking through the store with my earbuds in, I was too preoccupied with Malcolm's world to get sick. His bubbling and classic beat selection, his wordplay, it was all so enchanting. *K.I.D.S.* wormed its way into my psyche and put out all the fires that lit within me each time I left the house. I browsed the store until the tape came to an end. Then I played it once more. I stayed out all afternoon, listening to *K.I.D.S.* again and again as I did the simplest things I could never bring myself to do: Order a drink, sit alone in a cafe, chat with strangers.

K.I.D.S. has a hidden healing quality. Unlike any other project in Malcolm's deep catalog, *K.I.D.S.* is untouched by vices or murkiness. The darkest moment is a eulogy to his "Poppy." The mixtape is a bright light, an encouraging nudge, and welcoming smile. You find yourself lost in the way Mac laces up his shoes, how he rides around town searching for fun. That afternoon, that fall, "Traffic in The Sky" became my anthem. The hook ("I ain't got a damn thing on my mind") puts life into perspective. As Malcolm watches the clouds, you feel your own stress melting away. Suddenly, the anxiety becomes auxiliary, and you start to wonder why you paid it so much attention in the first place. You snap out of it and snap into life, reminded that it's worth living.

When you're depressed, they tell you to practice smiling and saying nice things to yourself. The goal is to internalize the good until it replaces automatic negative thoughts. *K.I.D.S.* is "the good" of life distilled. Every bar and every beat speaks to the highs of our human existence. Something as basic as "Kool Aid & Frozen Pizza" is elevated. From *K.I.D.S.*, we learn to make our own joy out of the most mundane things. Life becomes bearable. Where happiness can be considered "corny," Mac finds a way to bring joy to the mixtape circuit without coming across as constructing a cardboard kingdom.

K.I.D.S.' simplicity is its biggest victory. Malcolm does not waste time proving himself or vying for anything. He simply loves to rap and wants to share his goings-on with the world. There's a purity in his approach, which cannot be manufactured. Immediately, people believed in Mac Miller, the artist and the young man. His conviction and love of hip-hop were infectious. There was no grandstanding. In 2010, hip-hop was being sucked into Mac Miller's orbit. Sure, the tape was *just* Mac Miller, and you could take him or leave him. But admit it: You took him, didn't you?

Eight years later, it was *K.I.D.S.* that got me through the fall of 2018. *K.I.D.S.* got me out of the house, got me taking care of myself. *K.I.D.S.* carried me to the finish line while I searched for a doctor who finally diagnosed me with Bipolar II, among other things. The tape brought me back to life on days where I outright rejected living. The tape taught me how to smile in the face of discomfort. And the tape kept me smiling as I drove to the pharmacy to pick up my first dose of anxiety medication. *K.I.D.S.* was there for me as I got my life together. That's what Mac Miller does—he smiles and he saves.

QUENTIN CUFF: I came up with the acronym, but in retrospect, I don't think that was the coolest acronym... We were just smoking weed at Miss Karen's house in Mac's old room, and me, him, TreeJay, and other homies would be talking about a bunch of different concepts. *Mac Miller's Day Off* was the only alternative name. We realized reality is much more serious than a Ferris Bueller [movie]. What Mac had to say on "Poppy" and "All I Want Is You"... it was a lot darker than *Ferris Bueller's Day Off*. I'm not saying *K.I.D.S.* was dark; it has a lot of bright moments. It was obviously the *New Hope* in his trilogy. It was what let people know this guy is a jedi. To his fanbase, he's the chosen one. It also did have darker moments, especially on "Poppy" and "Traffic in The Sky," they're very mature.

SKYZOO: I loved that he flipped the *Kids* movie because it's one of the dopest fucking movies. What it also says is—Mac probably didn't see *Kids* when it first came out. *Kids* was my life—to an extent, I lived like that in high school. For Mac to be so much younger and go back and dig into the crates and pull that out and introduce it to a bunch of kids his age, that was the coolest shit to me! It's gonna make kids go back and do the research.

That was Mac! He was so about the culture and hip-hop. He respected it; *K.I.D.S.* showed you that. The beats he would freestyle to, the instrumentals he would pick, being a Dilla-head. All that shit was him reaching back because he respected the culture so much. It speaks volumes.

QUENTIN CUFF: Everyone played their part. I would try to place as many beats as I could, even though I didn't know what A&Ring was. "Good Evening" was a beat I found. I felt like it was a huge thing for him to be sampling a record Drake sampled. B [Dot] Jay also made "The Spins." I found both of those beats. I'm pretty sure Will found Wally West and the Lord Finesse beat.

The intro to *K.I.D.S.* was epic. The same way [Mac] put My Morning Jacket in the "Nikes on My Feet" video, he had an ear for shit I didn't know about before him. He put me on to all the Brainfeeder stuff before we became friends with Thundercat. He was a real fan with music as a whole.

Sayez has two different joints on there: "Paper Route" and "Outside." Me and Mac were listening to beats at my old apartment. I watched Mac hear seven of those beats and start writing immediately and just [start] making incredible music. Willisbeatz ["All I Want Is You"] is a friend of Mac and his older brother. The person [Dru-Tang] that produced "Cruise Control" is Mac's friend from childhood as well.

I heard the Drakes [of the game] and *Kush & OJ* had already been out, and we knew what we were up against. There's a direct correlation between "The Spins" and "The Thrill" by Wiz. Both Empire of the Sun samples. With "Good Evening," there's the Drake [influence]. But there wasn't no rapper that was seventeen years old doing a "Kool Aid & Frozen Pizza." He's doing a "Poppy." We're doing an eclectic mix of sounds. It was just original. [Mac] wasn't trying to be anyone else or imitate anyone else. He had his own flow and wave.

E. Dan: My initial impressions were skeptical. Jerm had just started working at the studio. I just happened to hear [Jerm] working on something [he] and Mac had done. It was drums Jerm cooked up and this guitar stuff Mac played. He was singing the chorus, rapping, and it was super groovy. I'm like, "This is really good!" It was right around that time Benjy swooped in and got involved and signed him. The other side of that, too, was I was really, really busy with Wiz. That all culminated in the "Knock Knock" session. Then we knocked that song out, and it was fucking awesome, and we loved it. I was like, "This kid is so much fun to work with." Immediately, I was into it from that moment on.

QUENTIN CUFF: Whenever Mac signed with Rostrum, he got an unlimited budget to work at ID Labs. E. Dan had already shown him love by recording for pretty much free after Malcolm had went through phases of selling TVs for studio time. Benjy came in and was like, "I believe in this too." Everyone at ID Labs started to believe in Mac. That's where the turn in *K.I.D.S.* happened, because you have E. Dan going in there and doing the final touches on the album, and they make a song like "Knock Knock." I believe Benjy found that sample. Once [Benjy] got all-in on Mac, he helped refine what songs had that tempo, what would go.

BENJY GRINBERG: It was the beginning of *K.I.D.S.* recordings. He sat me down: "I'm working on a new tape, and I wanna play some of the records for you." When he played them—early versions of some of the records—I was like, woah! These are way better than what I had heard before! The amount that he had progressed in that little time was impressive. And the music was dope. Fuck. That's what turned the tide for me to say, "Maybe we should be looking at something a little bit deeper."

QUENTIN CUFF: We had this natural relationship with the guys at Rostrum. Benjy liked his music and [is] the reason Wiz did a verse on "Cruise Control" on *High Life* for free. Artie had sent out the songs to get more people listening on all platforms. After that, Benjy was like, "Hey, I would be interested in helping you guys release music." At that point, it was a no-brainer, because we had a great relationship with them. Benjy is a good guy that made a lot of key decisions at the beginning of Mac's career that put us in a great position as a team.

E. DAN: ["Knock Knock"] was, in fact, the first time I remember us working together. We had met before that because he was in and out of the studio. The setup at that studio was ... It was a rectangular building with a door in the front and my room was at the back. The only bathroom in the entire place was in the larger control room, which I used. So, people would have to come through there to use the bathroom. You meet a lot of people. That was probably the first time I met Mac: he wandered back there to use the bathroom. Talking to him in later years, apparently, he was intimidated, because I was the man in Pittsburgh with a studio. He had just signed his deal with Benjy at Rostrum. It was our first time sitting down to work on anything together.

It was actually Benjy who found that sample. I remember him sending me this YouTube link, like, "Hey, this might be something cool." We got in there and I played [the sample] for Mac, and Mac being Mac, he was enthusiastically for it. As he was with any idea, I would later learn. I just started in on the sample, looped it up, and started adding tons of sounds to it. Oddly enough, I just pulled that session up the other day. I couldn't believe all the shit I had tucked behind the sample of that. There was a piano and three or four synths.

We just started layering this thing together, and Mac was such a goofball at the time. He came up with that goofy chorus really quick, and then we had the bright idea to get everybody in the studio—Jimmy, Q, Tree, Nomi, and one or two other people—to stand outside of the booth, and I brought the mic out. I had them all yell the parts in the chorus. The "Hey!" and the "Let 'em in!"s. In the course of three, four hours, we knocked out the entire song. The only thing I remember adding, after the fact, was just a little arranging on the bridge. That was how it went down.

BENJY GRINBERG: Mac was nonstop. Every day—this was the whole time we worked together—he always had his mind on what's next. "What song can I write today? How can I do it differently? Who should I be working with?" Everything. There was no Plan B for him. This is what he was doing.

THE HUMBLE MAGIC OF
THE MUSIC VIDEOS

There's no denying 2010's *K.I.D.S.*, Mac Miller's fourth mixtape, was his breakout moment. *K.I.D.S.* stole our hearts with its youthful cadences and fun-loving spirit. Whether we were traipsing about in PJs smoking weed alongside Malcolm or tuning in to the simpler times of our lives while listening to the tape, *K.I.D.S.* was a special moment in Malcolm's discography. The project was arguably the peak of Mac's first creative renaissance, how he went from his early days of being known as Easy Mac into the fully formed Mac Miller, officially capped off one year later by *Blue Slide Park*.

The magic of *K.I.D.S.*, however, smartly extends beyond its shelf life on wax. Teaming up with Rex Arrow, Mac's dear friend and long-time music video director, *K.I.D.S.* was accompanied by a series of videos: "Nikes on My Feet," "La La La La," "Kool Aid & Frozen Pizza," "Don't Mind If I Do," "Senior Skip Day," and "Knock Knock." Each video expanded our perception of Malcolm as a creative, but more importantly, they made us feel—if only for a moment—that we could be Mac Miller. Scenes of him grocery shopping in PJs, lacing up his sneakers to go vault around town, skipping school to drive around getting high, all added up to a relatability factor ingrained in Mac's music to this day.

There's a storytelling magic to the *K.I.D.S.* videos. They capture Mac at the height of his youthful essence. There's an overwhelmingly homegrown spirit to these songs. These are not videos meant to flex on us, but rather, videos meant to humanize Mac, man of the people. More than accompaniments, these videos are required viewing for potential fans. First, you're drawn in by Malcolm's smirking raps, and then you fall in love with him by virtue of the access his videos gave us into his world. They're all-in on the minutiae of being a Pittsburgh teen. The music videos break down any barriers between Mac the artist, Malcolm the young man, and Mac Miller fans.

We open with Malcolm begrudgingly getting out of bed in "Nikes on My Feet." The room is littered with empty bottles of Hennessy, Sharpie drawings on the furniture, and stains on the sheets. There's a bong in the bed, as well as Mac's few trophies at the time and a picture of Mac and his mom. All of these personal touches work together to simultaneously fame-up Mac and establish him as one of us. The bottles suggest he's living the high-class rapper life, but the fact that he's in his childhood bedroom reminds us he's still just a kid. Within the first thirty seconds of "Nikes on My Feet," we strike a delicate balance between a budding star and an ordinary kid with ambitious goals. If we didn't think so before, we now know for sure: Mac's one of us dreamers.

"Nikes on My Feet" may be the second in the self-described "A Day in the Life of Mac Miller" series—part one goes to "Another Night," a single off 2009's *The High Life*—but it is the first official visual chapter of the *K.I.D.S.* story. Released on June 1, 2010, the story we're getting here is one of humanity. Everything Malcolm does in "Nikes on My Feet" is tempered. When he holds "stacks" of cash, it's mostly singles. When he whips a fresh car, it's probably his mom's. The crew he's touting are just his best friends gathered for an afternoon of fun shooting a little music video. There's nothing flashy to this star-on-the-rise. It's just Malcolm. That's why the video succeeds.

"La La La La" was released just a month after "Nikes" and was shot and edited by Dan Myers. Here, we're taking a quick break from the day-in-the-life approach, which makes sense if only because "La La La La" wound up as a bonus track on *K.I.D.S.* The video is nicely simplistic, with Mac and Co. sitting on a stoop kicking rhymes with their laptops open. For a short bonus song on an otherwise seminal project, "La La La La" is nothing flashy. As the anticipation for *K.I.D.S.*—released on August 13, 2010—grew, "La La La La" added a nice gust of oxygen to the fire started by "Nikes on My Feet." Our narrative of humanity, and now humility, continues.

We return to the day-in-the-life motif with "Kool Aid & Frozen Pizza." Where "Nikes" ends with Malcolm fading out of frame and everyone piled in a car, driving home, "Kool Aid & Frozen Pizza" finds Mac and a gang of people on the basketball court. We're back to understanding the grip he has on Pittsburgh's rap scene. Released on July 26, 2010, nearly two months after "Nikes," this video already feels more polished. The colors look more natural, more true-to-life, with a touch of saturation to emphasize videos as art pieces. The framing is more intuitive. The whole of "Kool Aid & Frozen Pizza" has more life, as liveliness is the goal of *K.I.D.S.*

This time, instead of paying attention to the small details, we pay attention to the various settings Malcolm leads us through. We get the streets of Pittsburgh, the clothing store, the park, the basketball court, the convenience store, and more. Before, Mac was showing us what, exactly, filled up his life—weed, cigs, friends, and booze. Now, he's showing us where, exactly, his life unfolds. We go from relating to Mac's indulgences to relating to his city-wide playground. Who among us is not a regular at a corner store? Who among us doesn't have memories of the park, the court, or walking downtown with a too-large pack of friends? Mac taps into these shared memories for "Kool Aid & Frozen Pizza." He may be showing us his life on screen, but we're seeing two visions: us and Mac. It's always been us and Mac.

To close out the day-in-the-life series, we have "Don't Mind If I Do," which opens on Malcolm's infectious smile. The first thirty seconds are spent on a vocal sample, during which we watch Mac messing around and cheesing. Then, suddenly, we're on a boat cruising along the water with a bunch of girls. We quickly gather that this is a day in the life of a rapper who's made it, that this is Malcolm's image of success. This pairs well with Mac singing, "Tonight might be the night I make it" to open "Traffic in The Sky," which plays over the introductory piece of the video.

Once again, to get the full weight of this video, we need to pay attention to the details. This time, I draw your attention to Mac's facial expressions. While he's cooling on a boat, we see him break character. His smile peeks through not a minute into the video. Mac's playing around. He's not some materialistic artist doing it all for the money—it's all for the love. Mac is *still* Mac even with the lavish lifestyle he's visually purporting. As the sun sets on the water, we transition into "Don't Mind If I Do" and the craziest pool party Mac's ever thrown. This video is meant to illustrate Mac at his most successful—and true to his nature, the image of success is all his friends gathered around him.

"Don't Mind If I Do" sustains the spirit of *K.I.D.S.* The best-produced video in the day-in-the-life series, it still has its roots in humility. Mac thinks big, but he thinks for himself. Watching him party and grin, we feel so kindred to Mac. An army of people with their thumbs up, that's Mac's vision of success. Sustained love, that's Mac's vision of success. Two days after the release of "Don't Mind If I Do," *K.I.D.S.* dropped to great fanfare and acclaim. It went on to become Malcolm's breakout hit, and the first project to anchor him to his fans' lives.

The videos didn't stop. Next up, on October 22, 2010, we got the iconic video for "Senior Skip Day," which was the clear *K.I.D.S.* standout. "Senior Skip Day" takes the day-in-the-life series and truncates it, packing all three *K.I.D.S.* episodes into one video. We get Mac waking up, Mac around town, and more of Mac's vision of success (lots of women lining up for his attention). There's something peaceful about this track, about watching Mac buy ingredients for breakfast in his pajamas. After the splendor of "Don't Mind If I Do," it's nice to see Mac back at home, just *being*.

"Senior Skip Day" takes simple concepts and stretches them to their emotive ends. There's nothing to unpack. Everything is on the table for us to pick up and treasure. And yet, the video and song endure because they showcase Mac at his then-happiest—just enjoying himself at home with not a care in the world. Watching Mac dance in the grocery store, the ease of it all, fills us with glee. How can we not root for the kid? The story of "Senior Skip Day" is one of endearment. We had already found ourselves in the videos leading up to *K.I.D.S.*; "Senior Skip Day" simply ices that cake.

Mac chose "Knock Knock" as his final *K.I.D.S.* video and his final chance to flex his creative chops with Rex Arrow. Part time-piece, part party, "Knock Knock" stands as Mac's most creative video to the date of its release on November 22, 2010. Mac and Rex play with color, narrative, lighting, the works. We get some of the same settings from the day-in-the-life series, reminding us that Mac wasn't going to switch up no matter how ambitious his visuals had become. We also get Mac hosting a warehouse party. This story is less about success and more about growth.

"Knock Knock" strikes us because Mac goes from being one of the guys to appearing as a full-fledged artist. Delivering fresh scenes and new color schemes, the video acts as a pay-off for all the time we spent relating to Mac Miller in previous videos. Though we see less of ourselves in the visual, we now see Mac Miller gearing up to take flight. Because we've been bonded to him across the preceding music videos, we don't mind seeing less of ourselves in his visual work. Instead, we cheer him on, for he is exploring himself and flexing his creative muscles. "Knock Knock" sets the stage for the music videos to come too: how Malcolm will play with narrative, color, and perspective for the rest of his career.

The primary story of *K.I.D.S.* is easy to follow—a young man leading us about town while chasing his dreams. Yet, the videos accomplish a different kind of story as well, one of an artist earnestly looking to relate to his fans while simultaneously looking to be himself. Mac makes even the most banal moments seem cool and acceptable. We watch him get out of bed, for goodness' sake, and we're enamored. The story of the *K.I.D.S.* videos is one of establishment and invitation. That is, establishing there is no line between Mac and his fans. He invites us into his life and vice versa. We leave these videos realizing we're in this together, us and Mac, and we will be forever. At the end of the day, we're just some motherfucking kids.

Quentin Cuff: The videos with Ian [Rex Arrow] made *K.I.D.S.* what *K.I.D.S.* is.

Rapsody: Before I even met him, I saw the videos and I just thought he was dope. He came out at a time when, you know, he took [hip-hop] back to the essence and core of what it was. For him to break through during that time, I thought it was dope. Like here's this kid and "Kool Aid & Frozen Pizza" comes on, and it's an ode to [Lord Finesse] and you're like "Wow! This is dope." For a kid that young to appreciate it, and he could go! He could spit. He had flow. That's what drew me in at first, like this was different. He didn't care about what was trending. Then when you get to meet the person, that makes you fall in love with the music even more. It's a direct reflection. You know it's not fake. With Mac, it was real! What you saw was what you got. We were drawn to the genuine person that he was.

Rex Arrow: When Malcolm first played me ["Knock Knock"], we both kind of jumped to "It would be cool to do something that was kind of a throwback." That sort of slowly evolved, and the idea of mixing black and white, and color came in. I had done some dance stuff in college, and musical theater in high school. I was like, "Look, man, it may sound strange, but I think it would be cool if we kinda did something that felt a little *West Side Story*." It was a cold day in November. We shot the whole thing in one day, which is crazy to think about now.

The moment he wrapped his head around it, he was 100 percent down. From the black and white stuff, to him sort of lucking into finding this varsity style [jacket] that he found a week before, it added the perfect element to the video. He was a total champ about doing the stuff that was more dancy. When we moved into the studio to do the color stuff, it was amazing to watch him perform. He jumped into that character, and there were forty, fifty people in that room, and he had them all completely charmed that entire time.

It was one of those videos where we felt like we took a big step forward, and there were a lot of those videos, but that one felt like something special. It resonated with the kids listening to it. And my mom loves that video, for what it's worth.

WILL KALSON: We were just watching his numbers on YouTube go *up*. We were out here charting new territory for a white Jewish kid from Pittsburgh. I don't know if he knew how big it was gonna be. There was definitely an understanding that things were gonna be big.

NADIRAH SIMMONS: I love his videos; it's always his homies with him. The one thing that separates Mac Miller from the blog era was that they stuck with their homies. To see a video and see TreeJay and see Jerm and all these people that he is so tight with, and not only are they on his team . . . They're making this art together, and they're having fun together. It's like "Yo, let's all go hang out and just do what we do, as the people we are."

BENJY GRINBERG: He had the "Live Free" video, which was polished and fun. That [video] had some nice views and helped take things up a little bit. Then we started releasing songs, and every time we did, it would just get bigger and bigger. There was this crazy momentum building. What really helped create the excitement were the videos that he and Ian were making. They were so raw, and fun, and intimate, in a way. People were getting into it. When "Knock Knock" came out, it was sort of an explosive moment as well. Everything was incremental, it wasn't necessarily one moment. "Kool Aid & Frozen Pizza" caught a lot of people's attention. The "Nikes on My Feet" video . . . It was incremental. He kept getting better and better, and the songs got bigger and bigger.

REX ARROW: Every couple of months, he would hit me up, and we would do a video. The momentum was starting to build. I remember the week he had returned from LA, which was his first time in LA, and he had just recorded "Nikes on My Feet." It just felt like such a revolutionary step forward for him and the *K.I.D.S.* campaign . . . Everything just started picking up speed and accelerating, and we couldn't shoot the videos fast enough. It was hard to describe, but we kept feeding off the momentum that he was building. We kept shooting video after video and got more ambitious.

It was exciting! I would be in New York and I would come back to Pittsburgh, and every time I reconnected with him, it was clear he was taking leaps and bounds forward. Whether it be on the recording or production side, even his vision for how everything was going to come together. It was his idea to weave the video campaign together for *K.I.D.S.* as a day-in-the-life video series that we built upon.

"Nikes on My Feet," it's kind of a long build up until you get to the track, and for Malcolm, he kind of wanted to expand into more storytelling. It was kind of infectious, between Malcolm and Q and TreeJay and Benjy; there was just a momentum to just keep pushing things bigger and bigger. By the time we got to "Don't Mind If I Do," we wanted to go bigger than we'd ever gone.

QUENTIN CUFF: There's this guy that passed away; he's a bigger guy that was in a bunch of the videos. He was in the studio whenever Mac was recording "The Spins," and I'm pretty sure he's the one that said, "Yo! You graduated high school today," and that's why Mac says, "Yo, I just graduated high school!" Those candid moments . . . All these rappers have these cool, deliberate adlibs, where Mac had this "Haha!" and that's where the *Class Clown* thing came in. That always stuck with me. He had in his head what he wanted to do.

I used to listen to *Kids'* [original soundtrack] constantly while we were making *K.I.D.S.*, and that's how we came up with the skits. The last little guitar thing that plucks? That's from the OST. This is like a Pittsburgh *Kids*, how Mac is living. He was mature—to an extent. He was also the class clown. *Class Clown* was also gonna be the name of *High Life*, and eventually he changed it. That's another lost title.

BENJY GRINBERG: He was a perfectionist to a certain degree. I have on my laptop eight different *K.I.D.S.* playlists that were [each] supposed to be the final playlist. It happened with every single album, where it's like, "I think we're done," and then by the next morning, I'd have a message: "I just wanna do a couple things . . . ." The next thing you know, the tracklist is different, and there are some dope songs that never made any of the tapes because of that process. I recall that part of the process, when he's getting toward the end. His reshuffling of the deck to get [the project] he loved.

WILL KALSON: Before he signed to Rostrum, I did all his online marketing. I would send all his songs and videos out. I would send stuff out with little to no reaction from the people I was sending it to, but closer to the release, I started to get a lot of responses. It was surprising. I remember the last video I sent before Arthur Pitt took over his online marketing was "Nikes on My Feet," and that just went *insane*. Every blog picked it up—I couldn't believe it. At that time, blogs were everything. It was just a special feeling in the air.

Malcolm was just always good at creating a full project. There had to be a theme to everything he was doing. He never just did things. The sound he was making at the time, although it was a throwback to golden era hip-hop, was fresh. I helped A&R that project a good bit in terms of beats. I did give him the "Kool Aid & Frozen Pizza" beat— the Lord Finesse beat he ended up getting sued for. I would send him instrumentals all the time. In general, there was a lot of cool stuff happening in music too. But this was different and it connected with a lot of kids.

CODY LEE (Mac Miller Memoir Twitter co-founder): If I can remember correctly, [K.I.D.S.] was downloaded off of DatPiff, which was where you'd find all the new mixtapes. That brings back so many memories by itself . . . But I was probably your average fourteen-year-old, browsing the internet on his family computer trying to load my iPod Nano with songs for the next day. I remember hearing songs like "Nikes on My Feet," "Good Evening," and "Knock Knock," and instantly fell in love with the project. I heard "Good Evening" play for the first time in years at our tribute event held at Stage AE, and I remember getting chills as the vocal chops just brought back one hundred memories … I kinda stood there frozen thinking about the times I [spent] listening to that song years ago … That was the magic of *K.I.D.S.* for me.

E. Dan: Oh, it's the one! It's the one that turned so many people on to him and gave him a fanbase. It's all of those things I was anxious for him to leave behind, just some of the innocence and the off-the-cuffness of the lyrics. I think that's why people like it so much—kids his age and younger. It just felt carefree. So I think it was important. I don't think he could've started with *Macadelic*. He had to start with *K.I.D.S.*

Rex Arrow: Music videos are tricky, and he sort of realized that, at least from a perception standpoint, there might be a little bit of an uphill battle. He's a white, Jewish rapper from Pittsburgh. I think the approach was always to take it askew of the center and do things that were slightly irreverent or slightly unconventional, that way at least he could sort of be in his own lane.

Quentin Cuff: He threw [the] rapper persona out the window, and on *K.I.D.S.*, he wasn't trying to be this flex-y person. There was more violent talks on *High Life*, while on *K.I.D.S.*, it was straight lifestyle. For kids in the summer? Not much more can be said. "And I'm gonna make it as a rapper," that's the other thing he would always say.

To hear Mac say my name on "Get Em Up," was … He had said my name on a few other songs from *Jukebox* that mean a lot to me, but him saying that on "Get Em Up," it just charged me up. This dude believes in *me*? It's easy for me to believe in *him*! He's fucking talented. But for him to shout me out, that shit charged me up to the nth degree.

E. Dan: It was such a whirlwind for him. My only other experience in watching someone ascend to any level in the music business was with Wiz, and that was a *long* process. With Mac, it happened so quickly. I realized people were into what he was doing. Then, the more I got to know him, he's just so much fun to be around. So much energy. Especially at the time, the dynamic between us—he had so much respect for me and what I did with my rinky-dink little studio in Pittsburgh. It turned into this relationship where he was a younger cousin. He had this thing with me, where I was this OG character to him. We just had a lot of fun creating. It happened pretty [quickly]. After that first session, it was, "Okay, I fuck with this kid." It just grew over the years.

BENJY GRINBERG: There wasn't a dark side to it. It was, "Isn't this great? Thumbs up!" That whole mentality ran through those first couple of projects we did together. For the fanfare, we started doing more shows and really enjoying it. It was a pure time of progress, of happiness. Everyone grinding together towards a common goal.

The music took it to the next level. The visuals played a big role. Mac hit a new level of creativity. And sometimes these things are just timing. I think it's just a perfect storm of good timing, of kids looking for something like *this*, which I don't think they were finding in anybody else. And the fact that Mac was so relatable. He didn't feel like this faraway star. He felt like your boy, or your little brother, or your friend from school. He just reminds you of somebody you already know. On top of that, he's a very, very, very good artist. All those things coming together, not to mention joining in our team, it was a perfect storm.

SKYZOO: The bigger Mac became, all these other young white kids was hip to me. On a random day, I'd get 150 followers on Twitter because Mac would shout me out. I never asked him for shit; I never wanted shit. It would be cool to make more music outside the one joint, but we got the one joint. The last time I saw him was at the Brooklyn Hip-Hop Festival, and I had my little brother with me. He saw Mac—I think my brother was fifteen at the time—and he's like, "Yo! That's Mac!" I'm like, "Mac's my man!" Mac came over, doing the whole shit: "Do you know who your brother is? Fucking legend!" He was always humble.

JUST BLAZE (producer, "All Around the World"): Sometimes, when you see somebody and you feel the energy . . . You get it. What I can say is, the moment I heard his music, I said, "Alright, I get it!" This kid used to bring me dope music, and Mac was one of the artists he brought me. I don't even know if he knew Mac like that. I actually never asked him about that, but he played me the music and I was like, "Yeah, I get it. This kid might actually have something. Alright, bring him through." I was meeting with new artist after new artist that entire week, and the one thing that stuck out to me was Mac's music. It's not something I can put a quantifiable factor on. It was just dope.

WILL KALSON: It blew us all away, but we didn't have time to dwell on it too much because we were on the road. We first started touring in my '94 Volvo station wagon, my mom's old car. Five deep. Before *K.I.D.S.* came out, we started doing shows. We were grinding and it was so much fun. Those were some of my best memories touring. Those initial tours were so much fun because everything was new—for all of us. It was a special time, for sure.

The K.I.D.S. Tour—that tour was so fucking fun. We had the best crew; we were in the sprinter van, there was no structure, really. It was just on us to get to the venue on time, to get merch set up, and to get ready for the show. There was no one pushing us to do anything. It was a magical time. Just being in that van, being in LA for the first time, with Juicy J in the backseat, heading out to a show. Moments like that were crazy to me and crazy to Malcolm too. We were both really big fans of music. Just spending those moments together . . . Those are times I'll never forget. I have so many favorite memories with him. It was just a really, really, really great time.

QUENTIN CUFF: He appreciates *K.I.D.S.* to this day. He even brought back "Knock Knock" [in his live set]. I go back to that project every year and a lot of the songs sound fresh. My new favorite is "Traffic in The Sky," and I feel like that's aged the best out of any song on there. That song is a classic. "Poppy" is my second favorite. Those aren't even the songs that are Platinum! For [Mac], it was like, "I'm always grateful [for] the start of it," but he had so much to progress and do.

"POPPY" PLANTED ROOTS FOR "REMEMBER"

It's 2010 and you're enjoying your first run through of *K.I.D.S.* You've laced up your Nikes, just like Malcolm, and you've watched the clouds float by while getting high on "Senior Skip Day." There's not a care in the world. The world is yours. And then, Mac hits you with a swerve. Sixteen songs in, Malcolm delivers a eulogy to his late grandfather in the form of "Poppy." The song is as gloomy as *K.I.D.S.* will allow. We go from the vibrant and voice-cracking charm of "All I Want Is You," from the bright nature of the tape overall, to a sparkling and pensive Buckwild beat. Over a Pete Rock sample, Mac devotes three minutes to commemorating his grandfather. He keeps his spirit alive. Mac even brings out his broken-up singing voice as he yearns for everlasting life.

"Poppy" feels precious. It's a candid moment for Malcolm—one that caused him to tear up while recording it—on an otherwise breezy and stressless mixtape. More importantly, "Poppy" serves as an incredible precursor to Mac's touching "REMember" off 2013's *Watching Movies with the Sound Off.* "Poppy" plants roots for the ways in which Mac will go on to memorialize a fallen friend, and placing the two songs side by side, it's clear they are operating in the same canon. Mac's eulogies follow simple rules: There must be singing, there must be long verses, there must be straining against the clock, there must be a normalization of mourning, and there must be a promise of continuation. Both "Poppy" and "REMember" check all of these boxes, making them emotionally satisfying beyond measure.

The first verse of "Poppy" begins in the same manner as the second verse of "REMember." Both opening lines greet death and set a somber scene: "Hello death, it seems that we meet again / You keep taking friends that I'll never see again" and "It's a dark science, when your friends start dying / Like, 'How could he go? He was part-lion.'" In the context of *K.I.D.S.*, we quickly realize Mac is setting aside the motif of joy he's been weaving for fifteen songs to get serious with us, to level with us. Now, we can relate to Malcolm on a whole new level. We aren't simply enjoying the spoils of youth together; we're going down the dark roads together too. "Poppy," then, is critical to the decade-long endearment Mac builds between himself and his fans.

The structure of "Poppy" lends itself to being understood as a eulogy. Mac's delivery is measured; the song feels like a speech given at a wake. The majority of the first half of "Poppy" occupies itself with straining against mortality. "Never leave our heart, never leave our thoughts," Mac says before getting into his wishes. That is, before getting into regrets over his grandfather not seeing him graduate and grow into a man. Mac spends much time on "Poppy" fighting against the inevitability of losing his elders. The eulogy works because it captures the inescapable sense of disbelief.

Even when Malcolm attempts to make peace with his grandfather's passing, he still tries to keep him alive and give him agency. "I know you had to leave, so rest in peace, but please can you watch over Nanny?" Mac pleads with his grandfather as if he were sitting across the table from him. He follows this with a direct address to his grandfather's departed spirit, working towards accepting his passing: "All the prayers I'm saying may bug you / But I'm just checking in on what you up to." Diving into the grey area between life and death, into the space of prayer and the power of spirituality, makes "Poppy" an oddly mature and metaphysical track. This delving into metaphysics will only be par for the course as "REMember" lives on one of Malcolm's most experimental offerings, *Watching Movies*.

Then we have the chorus in which Mac promises to keep his grandfather's spirit alive through his own love and living. Here, we see Mac contemplating the future: "Times goes by, going without you

/ Hope you know, I've been thinking about you / And I know, I know, I know, I know that they took you from your home / But you're in my heart, so I'm never gonna be alone." Mac touches on the symbiosis of memory, too, how keeping someone in your thoughts keeps them alive, and keeps you company. This idea will become the major theme of "REMember," which, from its title, we can gather is all about the importance of remembrance and legacy.

Ten years on, and "Poppy" is the foundational Mac Miller eulogy. As we transition into the graver "REMember," we can look back on the writing and structure of "Poppy" as a clear guide for Malcolm's eulogy to his friend of ten years.

Unlike "Poppy," "REMember" immediately begins with the future. The songs are, ultimately, inversions of each other. Their arcs create a perfect circle of eulogizing. "I hope you're proud of me, dude I grew to be," Mac begins. By opening with the future, Mac immediately invokes the power of memory as a spellbinding and time-altering construct. Remembering his fallen friend allows Mac to bridge gaps between the past and the future, listeners passing either through Mac or through Mac's memories. Here, Mac sets up his growth to be an extension of his friend's life, as if he were watching over him, just as Mac wishes on "Poppy."

Soon after, we enter the structure of "Poppy," with Mac straining to understand death's presence in his life: "This life moves fast, I never knew that." Between "REMember" and "Poppy," we get the sense all Mac wants is everlasting life, but he keeps falling short of feeling invincible, as death clouds his circles. Much like Mac does on "Poppy," he attempts to bend time and fact with "REMember," admitting, "You had a girl, I kinda wish you knocked her up / So I could meet your son and talk you up."

These final lines of the first verse are a mirror of Mac's hoping Poppy takes care of Nanny. Both work to keep the person alive, to address them as if they were still living. Both moments attack our concept of permanence and finality. Moreover, on "REMember," with the invocation of children, we get the sense Mac is obsessed with the legacies of those he loves. On "Poppy," he is Poppy's legacy, but on "REMember," Mac realizes his friend's legacy has been threatened. Thus, in naming the song for his friend's initials, he gives him the legacy of which he was otherwise robbed. Mac's eulogies not only mourn the deceased, they attempt against all odds to extend their lives.

During both "Poppy" and "REMember," Mac normalizes mourning. The mere presence of "Poppy" on a happy-go-lucky tape like *K.I.D.S.* suggests hurting is a fact of life to be acknowledged, not denied. Likewise, as Mac says on "REMember," "It's cool to cry / Don't ever question your strength." By 2013, we came to expect this guiding light from Malcolm, but in 2010, it was revolutionary. To see him build upon the themes and continue to make it okay to be a young man in touch with his emotions is both rewarding and effective. That is, it brings us closer to Malcolm and fosters that unbreakable connection keeping him alive to this day.

Just as with "Poppy," "REMember" ends with a sung segment looking towards the future. "Cause way back then I didn't know shit / And I don't know shit now / And when the whole world is looking hopeless / I'mma still hold shit down," Mac promises everyone. Just as he means to keep Poppy in his heart, he will hold his friend in his heart for all time. Again, we get the symbiosis of memory, how it feeds and nourishes all parties.

In 2010, Mac wrote a touching eulogy and expanded his craft. He repeated the process in 2013, three years wiser and all the sharper with his pen. The connections between "Poppy" and "REMember" are numerous and are to Mac's immense credit. Penning a track like "Poppy" at the height of his first and most care-free creative renaissance, having it lay the groundwork for the ascent of his second creative renaissance, was no easy feat.

Mac not only proved his potential on "Poppy," he braced us for all that was to come in terms of his content and emotional availability. We go from being some motherfucking kids to remembering youth, and the entire time, Mac is with us. Now, we remember him, and the power of memory does its job to keep Malcolm thriving.

Benjy Grinberg: It feels like chapter one. Whereas everything that came before it felt like the prelude, *K.I.D.S.* is when it really *started*. I think, musically, it was a step above anything he had been doing and what anyone else was doing at the time, in terms of combining common themes with great hip-hop beats. This just started, or heavily picked up, the momentum he created. It would snowball into what things happened after, from *Best Day Ever* to *Blue Slide Park* and so forth. This was pushing the turbo button on things.

Wiz Khalifa: A lot of people followed the movement, and they understood he was more than a white rapper, or whatever. He proved himself to a lot of people. Whether it be going to the radio, freestyling, or performing in front of large crowds, people who didn't know his music became diehard fans. He made sure people fucked with his music, as opposed to giving them an option to.

Nadirah Simmons: When he says, "We're just some motherfucking kids," that is my life lesson. Not to be so hard on yourself. Especially in life, in the time that we're in now, with society and the pressures around us, we are so hard on ourselves. Granted, I'm twenty-four, I'm not just a motherfucking kid, I'm also human. I'm just a person. It helped me not be so hard on myself when I disappointed myself. You are only a kid; you can make mistakes. I do have the capacity to make mistakes, and I can grow, and I can learn.

Will Kalson: Good music is timeless. Good projects are timeless, and Malcolm was able to put out a lot of good music throughout his career. Pretty much everything he's dropped is timeless in his own way because he created a theme with each project that will take you back to the moment in time you heard it. He was all about nostalgia, even at a young age. He was a senior in high school and he'd be talking about "Back in the day . . ." I think that kind of carried over into his music.

WHAT IT MEANS TO BE A "MOTHERFUCKING KID"

In 2010, Mac's way of life was that of youthful splendor and carefree antics. It was about being a bunch of "motherfucking kids," living it up in Pittsburgh and beyond. Yes, *K.I.D.S.* was about savoring youth for all time, enjoying the freedom from responsibilities, and having the whole world in front of you. The smallest details of the tape—topping off pancakes with scrambled eggs, skipping school, smoking joints outside, and selling tapes out of shoeboxes—are the loudest and most resonant.

In the crevices of *K.I.D.S.*, Malcolm tells a tale of youth's unending hold on us. Going back and spinning the mixtape, we can't help but smile at the oddities consuming him. The tape is splendid to listen to all these years later simply because Mac, without realizing it, was laying the groundwork for us to take in his music and feel our youth rushing back. Maybe, just maybe, we realize upon pressing play that it never left. Sure, a decade removed from the project, we may not be lazing about eating pancakes at noon, but the spirit of the album remains in our hearts. At the very least, it remains in mine.

Growing up and growing old alongside Mac Miller is one of the most rewarding experiences. We see him mature before our eyes across his discography. Yet, attaching our maturity to his earlier works, too, has a rewarding payoff. The magic of listening to *K.I.D.S.* as an adult comes by way of the differences in lifestyle. Mac spends a majority of this tape running around or rooted in place getting high. The motions of adulthood couldn't be more different. Life sweeps by at an alarming rate, to the point you're unsure if you're even living your own life.

In great contrast, *K.I.D.S.* moves with the flow of life. It's set decidedly in the thick of being. When you bring these two worlds together—the wired tendencies of youth and the somber aloofness of adulthood—the result is a hearty laugh. I find myself giggling at the ways in which life has changed, how we're all growing up, and how, as cantankerous as we feel, there's still some time to smile and enjoy what life has to offer. There's a hunger on *K.I.D.S.* for the spoils of youth. For the ease of it. Malcolm makes a big show of having nothing to do, and though my days are now filled with meetings and endless emails, I still feel Mac's hunger to kick back.

K.I.D.S. feels like forever; I am increasingly aware my time on Earth is finite. But as we grow up and our time becomes more scarce, there's something to listening to Mac rap as if he had all the time in the world.

When I hear Malcolm rap his breakfast order on "Senior Skip Day," I think of hungover Sundays, yearning for a greasy breakfast to bring me back to life. *K.I.D.S.* grafts itself onto life as I understand it now. Sure, I'm not as pressed about the shoes I'm wearing, as on "Nikes on My Feet," but I am concerned with the quality of the fuzzy socks I hope to get for the holidays. I don't have time for joy rides through town, but you can catch me jamming out on a drive to the pharmacy. I have random aches and pains interrupting my day, not smoke breaks or hookups or calls from friends to run amok outside. Ten years removed from the tape, ten years older, and ten more years plagued by anxiety, I still consider myself a "motherfucking kid."

I'm a kid in the way I get giddy about the minutiae making life worthwhile. I'm a kid because I still wait by the window for the mailman to drop off a package. I'm a kid because a fresh cup of coffee feels like a cause for celebration. I'm a kid because a sunny day still gives me a reason to smile. I'm a kid because I still have it in me to laugh so hard I cry and fall over, and roll on the floor, and roll into the counter, and laugh at that too. I'm a kid because I've decided as much. Because the forward-pressing of time can't steal my lust for life—that's Malcolm's lesson on *K.I.D.S.*, his warning. It's about safeguarding yourself and your childlike energy; it's about throwing up a handful of confetti every time you find a spare moment to yourself.

The key to survival is finding something small to love about each day. There's no life without the small things. Youth feels so sweet, in part, because the simplest joys are the longest lasting. As adults, we have to realize that if we spend our time waiting for the big things to unfold, we'll have wasted all our lives in anticipation and done absolutely zero living. That is why, without realizing it, Mac's obsession with the playfully finer things in life made *K.I.D.S.* a blueprint for staying young. You stay a "motherfucking kid" by falling back in love with life even after it's done you dirty because there's always another treat waiting in the wings.

With that, it's a pleasure to go back and hear *K.I.D.S.* and see the things that enchant a young Mac Miller: sagging his pants, smoking weed with friends, macking on women. We don't look down on Malcolm for his tastes in life's pleasures—we admire him. How nice it must be to feel genuine happiness from the tiniest things, we think. A run-through of *K.I.D.S.* is a reminder to allow happiness into your life from any and all avenues. When you grow out of *K.I.D.S.* and return to it with new context and aged ears, you hear but one note from Malcolm: You're never too old for joy. You can be a kid forever.

Ten years on, that's the greatest lesson *K.I.D.S.* has to offer us MacHeads: how to stay young forever. Mac showed us youth was about excitement. It was the thrill of a new day that kept Mac Miller and *K.I.D.S.* rolling forward. No matter how cranky and achy and apprehensive about the future I get, no matter how much my time gets monopolized by outside forces, as long as I can find one reason to stay excited each day, I'll remain a "motherfucking kid," always. As long as we follow the path Malcolm laid out for us, we all will.

2011

BEST DAY EVER

"I know that I'm going to be doing two things every day for a long time: touring and making music."

—MAC MILLER[2]

2.   Rob Markman, "Mac Miller Hustles to the Top," *Antenna Magazine*, June 1, 2011, https://antennamag.com/mac-miller-kids-interview/.

BEST DAY EVER DEFINED MAC MILLER'S SPIRIT

No matter where life took him, Malcolm brought his smile. Everyone who ever had the pleasure of interfacing with Mac knew him for his shining character and bright personality. His closest collaborators, like Big Jerm and E. Dan, and fast friends like Kehlani and Casey Veggies, remember his kindness, wit, and smile. While happiness as a mood did not prevail over the last records he made—by 2012's *Macadelic*, we were witnessing Mac heading down a darker road—happiness *did* define his ethos as a man. More than any other release during his first and most carefree creative renaissance, *Best Day Ever* captures that joy and beautiful spirit.

Best Day Ever evolved naturally out of *K.I.D.S.* Even though *K.I.D.S.* was relentlessly upbeat in content and sonic presentation, it embodied the reliable randomness of Mac's daily life. It didn't really have an ethos to it. That changed on this mixtape, which feels like a mantra, its titular track boasting lines to live by: "No matter where life takes me, find me with a smile"; "And I ain't gonna wait for nothing / Cause that just ain't my style / Life couldn't get better / This gon' be the best day ever." *Best Day Ever* bottled up Mac's soul.

More than a mixtape, *Best Day Ever* was a lifestyle. "I get frustrated, but it doesn't last long," Mac said in a 2011 interview with *WheelScene*. "I just look at the people around me and the blessings I have had and I feel snotty to get that upset about anything. I have an incredible life and I am blessed with the ability to be on a tour bus right now, touring across Europe and making music for a living, so there is nothing that I can get that upset about."

Big Jerm remembers the process that led to the mixtape as "just having fun." Indeed, fun encompasses every song on *Best Day Ever*. "Oy Vey" is a wonderfully playful nod to Mac's heritage. "Wake Up" is an infectious and celebratory anthem that opens with Mac saying, "We just having fun, man." On "Life Ain't Easy," Mac reflects on his career and expresses his hope to change the world with his music. These songs carry the lightness of *K.I.D.S.* but also begin building toward a unified message.

"*K.I.D.S.* was a real worry-free, mind-free project," Mac explained[3] ahead of the mixtape's release. "*Best Day Ever* is, like, more things to do, more things to talk about. More experiences, a different state of mind. More mature." For the Malcolm of 2011, maturing sounds like stepping into his own joy and turning it into a way of life. Think of the glee that comes with making "I'll Be There," an ode to his mother, with the venerable Phonte. Think of the way Malcolm opens "All Around the World" with "I got my cup filled up / We came to have a good time so turn my music high / We gonna tear this place up."

Damn near every song opens with a promise of goodness. Take "In the Air" beginning with "Hey, everything good right now" or the first line of "Donald Trump": "Ayo, the flyest motherfucker in the room / Yeah, you know it's me." These affirmations are about more than being self-assured, they are about living in your confidence and thriving as yourself. "Donald Trump" mirrors and expands upon "Best Day Ever" as a series of mantras to live by, particularly on the hook, where Malcolm vows to take over the world.

Years removed from the tape, *Best Day Ever*'s distinct energy can still be found in even the most serious of Malcolm's interviews. "I really wouldn't want just happiness," he told Craig Jenkins in a 2018 *Vulture* profile. "And I don't want just sadness either. I don't want to

---

3.   Mac Miller, "Mac Miller Discusses Creative Process of Best Day Ever, Favorite Collaborations & More," interview by Sermon, Sermonsdomain.com, February 1, 2011, https://www.youtube.com/watch?v=wGe45L1wVB0.

be depressed. I want to be able to have good days and bad days ... I can't imagine not waking up sometimes and being like, 'I don't feel like doing shit.' And then having days where you wake up and you feel on top of the world."

While *Best Day Ever* is all about making the most of life and basking in happiness, it still tracks with the Malcolm of 2018 who says he wouldn't want to solely be happy. The notion of living life to its fullest means accepting the negativity that accompanies being alive. But it does not have to define his life. To this salient point, think of this choice line from "Wake Up": "Now everyday feelin' like the best day ever / Heard it's a long road but it get way better."

Best Day Ever was Mac's first "on top of the world" moment, and he got to capture that spirit forever. "I bring some color to a world that's filled with shades of gray," Mac says on "Keep Floatin'." When Mac stepped into his own light, he was bringing us with him. Every moment of celebration was inclusive. Every smile had us smiling in return. It all comes back to that smile, how bright it was, and how he could not help but share it with the world.

Big Jerm: After *K.I.D.S.*, he got busy and was traveling a lot. I think he was figuring that all out, beyond Pittsburgh. "BDE Bonus . . ." That was originally the intro until E. switched out the beat for the actual intro. I was at the old ID Labs, and I was in the front room making "BDE Bonus," and Mac was in the back room with E., and he heard it in the front. That was the song that triggered everything. It's an Earth, Wind & Fire sample. I had it chopped up for years. I might've sampled it in 2005 or something. I was messing with it in the studio that day and [Mac] heard it. I put the drums on it and then E. played live bass on it, and that was really all—drums, the sample, and bass.

Quentin Cuff: After the K.I.D.S. Tour, we went to Chicago to work with Chuck Inglish. That's when they made "Wear My Hat."

Chuck Inglish (producer, "Wear My Hat"): There's a story where—this is like early 2011 after we first met—he wanted to work. I told him I'm down for sure, and we hadn't really met, and he was a rapper on the up and up. I told him if he flew to Chicago and booked a room at a studio right near where I was staying, we could lock in for a week. It wasn't about charging him. In two days, that man pulled up, and we spent three days together eatin' food and picking each other's brains. I think that was the first time that I took a chance on someone that I didn't know. That's what established our real friendship. We were locked in together. It was like this: "Do you think I'm tight?" "Hell yeah." From there, we just always had these quality control conversations. I think that's what I'll always hold on to the most. When Mac wanted to know if some drums hit, or if he wanted to know if something was cool, I would always hear from him. If he thought it was cool, that shit was tight, but if *I* thought it was cool? That's what's up. I would get calls at all sorts of times of the day. He would switch a number, and you know when a number pops up on your phone and it says "Maybe"? I squint and look at the clock and be like, "Okay, that's Mac."

Or, I'd be asleep, or it be early in the morning, and I get a FaceTime and it's him: "Hey man, I need more drums."

QUENTIN CUFF: Teddy Roxpin, a producer from Boston, was all Will Kalson. Teddy did "Get Up." I remember shooting the video. Mac had specials every year. We would do a show in Pittsburgh every year, a show in Denver on Halloween, and we would always do this Christmas [show] at the Showboat—it's closed now—in Atlantic City. By the last year we did it, they got us like ten hotel rooms and A$AP Rocky was the opener. It was crazy. That first year we were doing that [Christmas show], we went down to the pier and shot that video for "Get Up" at a beach, and it was cold outside.

All those songs were getting done right when *K.I.D.S.* came out. When I look at the tracklist . . . you can track where we were by the different producers. Chuck Inglish has two joints on here: ["Wear My Hat," "Play Ya Cards"], that was when we stopped in Chicago. Just Blaze, we were in New York, and we worked on a few things . . . .

JUST BLAZE: Me and Mac were friends, it wasn't really a music thing. I used to give him studio time at my old studio uptown in Harlem. I actually caught a little bit of flack for it because my partners were like, "Why are you giving this kid free studio time?" I'm like, "Trust me, he's gonna be something." He wasn't the Mac Miller we know now, by any means, not that metrics are any indication of your talent, but he maybe had 10,000 followers. I bring that up because one of our running jokes was: He would never have more followers than me. At the time, I maybe had 100,000. He eclipsed me by far, but it was something we used to joke about. I saw and heard something that was special, so I gave him the early outlet to work on his craft. As a DJ and a music person, sometimes you take the stance of, "It's not about what I can get out of it, but what can I do for this kid?" He would come to New York and have nowhere to record, so my space became his unofficial home.

The way "All Around the World" came about was he played me the demo that he had done with one of his homies. I was like, "The dude who you sample, I know him." It was Jesse [F. Keeler] from MSTRKRFT. It was a sample of a MSTRKRFT record ["Heartbreaker"] with John Legend. I know Jesse well, so I was like, "If you ever decide to use this and put it out, I can get it cleared no problem." It was just helping him with his craft. It was driving me crazy that in the hook of the song they originally did . . . they only sampled what they had available on the original version, but I knew there were other parts of the record they could use. That's what led me to call Jesse to get the STEMS and flesh it out. I called Jesse and had him send me the parts to the original sample. I took their demo and made it into the song that we all know.

QUENTIN CUFF: It's crazy "Donald Trump" was the one to blow up because "All Around the World" was a smash!

SAP (producer, "Donald Trump"): I had reached out to him to work on stuff. I had a friend of mine tell me to go work with him. I had looked him up and thought he was dope, and he was talking about how he had reached out to me before, in the MySpace days. I ended up taking a train from Philly. It was eight hours. When I first met him, he was finishing up *Best Day Ever*, and that same night we had met, we made "Donald Trump." It was pretty cool. Nobody expected it to blow up and do that. You can't really predict that. And we made that record just for fun.

BIG JERM: I think that surprised both of us because, like I said, I met him as Easy Mac. That's all I thought of him as, at first. I think E. figured that out, too, when we all were in together. He would sit down and play anything. I don't even know where that came from. It was just natural to him, really.

Not being able to pay for studio time was the only thing keeping him out of the studio. He would try to trade us computer monitors and random stuff for a little bit of studio time . . . I'm not even sure if he legally acquired these things, but he would show up with random stuff and try to trade it. He had one of those CD turntable things that he traded to E. for a mix, or something like that. Just anything he could do to further his music career, he would do.

SAP: He made you feel excited about everything, you know what I'm saying? Every little thing that was going on, he was just excited. He always kept the energy lit up in the room. No matter what mood you was in, he kinda put you on the same page as him. It was infectious, you know? And it was effortless. That's just who he was. His attitude, to me, was infectious. If you wasn't feeling a session or whatever that day, he would just make you hype about the session. It was crazy. Not a lot of people can do that: bring the best out of everybody they working with by making them feel comfortable.

QUENTIN CUFF: Phonte's on a song, "I'll Be There," which is by Beanz N Kornbread. Will found them.

PHONTE: Me and 9th were working again and he's like, "Mac, he got a joint he wants you on." He sent me two records. One of 'em, he wanted a verse on. I did a verse and the song never came out. I ended up using the verse for something else. The second song was "I'll Be There." The producers on the track [were] these brothers named Beanz N Kornbread. They did the track, and it was this gospel thing. It reminded me a lot of—a similar chord structure as—"Be Real Black for Me" by Roberta Flack and Donny Hathaway. Real churchy kind of thing. One of the Beanz N Kornbread guys did the reference. I listened to it and thought, "Okay, this is dope!" So I did [the song] and sent it back. [Mac] was like, "Man, y'all don't fuck around!"

That was it. I did the song and at the time, I knew my record [*Charity Starts at Home*] was on the way. I was in the process of finishing up. I didn't even charge [Mac] for it. He loved it, and a couple months later, my man DJ Forge [is] DJing the night of Mac's show at the Cat's Cradle, which is a venue [in] Chapel Hill, North Carolina.

He texts me, and he's like, "Man, you got a room of fifteen, sixteen-year-old kids singing your hook!" I was like, "Word? Shit, that's crazy!" That record ended up being a real bridge for me. When [Mac] died, and I put up a post on my IG, it was a lot of cats saying, "That was the first time I heard you."

QUENTIN CUFF: Khrysis ["She Said"], that's another producer we linked with in North Carolina with 9th Wonder, and Jamla and Rapsody. That's where ["Extra Extra"] comes from: stopping there on tour and going out with them.

RAPSODY: It was one of the last stops on the tour. I went out with him for three weeks, and this was at a time where every video Mac was putting up was getting millions of views and he had this song, and I didn't have any videos. So, it's like, let's just do a visual. So we got Kenneth Price, who was our homie at that time, like, "Yo let's just go to the diner and do something fun." What you see is we went to the diner, ordered some food. Mac was being Mac. That video is basically a documentary of an hour or two hanging out with us. Joking and rhyming. We wanted to be as natural as possible. It was a vibe for us, more than anything. You just see two kids at the time having fun and living their dreams.

BIG JERM: "Snooze" or "BDE Bonus," [they] just came together so quickly. I always like when that happens. Like it's meant to be. Everything comes together the way it's supposed to. "Keep Floatin'" was cool because Wiz did his hook first, maybe six months earlier. It was for *Rolling Papers*, and I don't know what happened. It was just sitting there, and Mac found it, and Wiz said it was cool. I thought that song was never gonna come out, and then Malcolm heard it and made it into something cool.

QUENTIN CUFF: [*Best Day Ever*] was a segue, and it was an exciting time because everyone was getting acquainted with Mac. On that [mixtape] is where the experimental sounds came in. Songs like "Down the Rabbit Hole" are 100 percent a total psychedelic and eclectic take. It's like, "Let's take people to *this* place." It was something we always felt was special.

BIG JERM: He might've said "Oy vey" to me because, I'm not gonna say we fought, but you know. From being around Malcolm a lot, he was kinda like my little brother in a way with the music stuff. So we would always mess with each other. So it was like he was annoyed with me; I did something that made him say "Oy vey." He came with that sample too. ["Oy Vey"] came together from there.

QUENTIN CUFF: Then you have "In the Air," which is, *Jesus.* I don't think "In the Air" even has drums. Those songs are crazy. "Play Ya Cards" was good . . . Working with Chuck Inglish was just an honor. "Snooze," to me, that's a classic song. Damn. "Life Ain't Easy," another crazy song. The optimism in all these records! He had already seen success so there's not a lot of anger or sadness. To me, it was an alley-oop. He wanted to call it *Best Day Ever*, which, I think, came from the success of *K.I.D.S.* and being high on life.

March 3, 2011, is when he released "Donald Trump." Rostrum was the label; they took care of pretty much everything for us logistically. This is tripping me out because we went on the Incredibly Dope Tour! That was January 13 until February 20, and then it extended to May 21. Between February and March, we had to have shot the "Donald Trump" video and dropped it. The way Rostrum had us dropping things just kept the momentum so crazy. Mac had three or four projects within the first two years, and that's not including *High Life* and *Jukebox*.

SERMON (blog era titan): [Me and Mac didn't meet] until the beginning of 2011. That's when he was on his first major tour across the country. He came to Seattle for the first time. I met him at the hotel they were staying at, which was not too far from the Space Needle. The venue he was performing at that night was called The Vera Project. It fits four hundred people and it was sold out. A lot of energy. When I got to the hotel, I got to meet everybody—Q, Clockwork. Then, me and Mac were kicking it by ourselves in a room in the hotel, on the first floor. He played me *Best Day Ever* before it was slated to come out. That was the coolest moment of my blogging career. He was just a happy and positive person. He was just thankful to be in Seattle, thankful to be on tour, and to be able to experience everything that he'd done thus far. Even though it was the first time we met, it felt like I was meeting someone that I'd known for years. It was a natural connection.

"BEST DAY EVER" AND "WEEKEND": MAC MILLER'S GENRE OF CELEBRATION

"Life couldn't get better."

—"Best Day Ever"

Of all the threads connecting Mac Miller's discography, his lust for life and celebration deserve attention. *K.I.D.S.* established Malcolm as a rapper chasing life's thrills through remarkable bars. As his career progressed and his life changed, Malcolm retained his passion for life. He was always a ray of light, always laughing, always looking to make those close to him happy. Smiling was Mac's ethos. In his music, Mac's perpetual cheer transformed into a unique genre of celebration evident on 2011's "Best Day Ever," and fully matured by 2015's "Weekend."

Mac Miller celebrated life for all it was worth, through good and bad times, always with remarkable honesty. Per its name, "Best Day Ever" captures a spirit unadorned by strife. In 2011, Mac was celebrating the success of *K.I.D.S.* He was celebrating his work ethic. He was celebrating his family—Most Dope and otherwise. He was celebrating beating the weary notions of paranoia, as in "Best Day Ever," which takes the time to acknowledge the negativity lurking around the corner; however, the track is too preoccupied with the present to give in to anxiety about the future.

"No matter where life takes me, find me with a smile," Mac sings on the hook. His voice, though never perfect, carries a wonderful and toothy sincerity. This pairs well with the opening of the second verse, which mirrors the first, beginning again with the confessions of a workaholic: "I never take a day off" transitions into "got a couple full weeks without a good night's sleep." These details of the more demanding side of being a full-time artist elevate "Best Day Ever" two-fold, the two bars showcasing Malcolm's ability to weave intricate themes into the happiest of tracks. He's not just providing us with vapid positivity. "Best Day Ever" becomes a sly and self-aware cut, for as much as Malcolm is celebrating, he is equally highlighting his struggles. Though in 2011 he had far less to be worried about than in the following years, Mac still takes the time to display how the fruits of his labor require actual labor. It's a validating moment, and the song can rightfully be seen as a hard-work anthem—one of many ("Here We Go," "Malibu," "Insomniak," among others) he wrote.

Mac Miller celebrates life by being present. As sweet as "Best Day Ever" sounds, the track does not sugarcoat life. The second verse, though playful, shows signs of Mac's trepidation about following the path to fame. While he's throwing a party, he's still keeping a watchful eye on himself. Perhaps this makes the party all the more fun, all the more earned. For one, we are able to celebrate Malcolm because we believe him when he calls himself the hardest working kid in music. We can celebrate, too, because we know what's to come. Understanding Malcolm's untimely end makes his celebratory moments all the more important. We don't stop smiling because Mac never stopped, even as he matured and his music grew more sophisticated and heavier with the burdens of adulthood.

"If we gotta fight, I'll be down for the war," Mac says to conclude the second verse. While he would confront battle after battle in the coming years, he would also be rewarded with many moments of triumph and causes for celebration. "Best Day Ever" planted necessary seeds for Mac Miller to continually understand what it meant to appreciate life as he grew older. These roots spread and flowered fully in 2015.

"Best Day Ever" is a prelude to 2015's "Weekend," which props itself up as yet another celebratory hard-work anthem, battling the truth of Mac's demons. By 2015, the list of his vices had grown. He candidly documented his battles with addiction and depression on 2014's *Faces*, and 2015's *GO:OD AM* was his wake-up call. It was the album he was meant to make at the time, wherein he proves himself to be a sparkling rapper with a real eye on his future and getting clean.

"Weekend" was *GO:OD AM*'s celebratory single, a moment of reprieve from the hedonistic bangers ("Break the Law") and dire moments of self-reflection ("Perfect Circle / God Speed"). It was Mac's opportunity to reflect on his career and his relationship to fame, and to pat himself on the back, within reason—always within reason— just as he did on "Best Day Ever." Naturally, his circumstances had changed, but the spirit of 2011 finds itself on full display here.

> "I got a little bit of money fillin' my pockets / Roll around like I run this shit / I got a system filled up with toxins / I've been broken-hearted, now it's fuck that bitch / Getting high to deal with my problems / Fucking bitches, getting drunk as shit / But these bitches getting obnoxious / They nothin' to me though, I love this shit"
>
> —*"Weekend"*

Malcolm alluded to the work required to pursue happiness on the verse of "Best Day Ever." The first verse begins with a laundry list of problems, but is quickly abated as we dive deeper. As the problems pile up, so too does Mac's need for release. The allusions to the necessity of celebration coupled with the disciplined work ethic ("Go long days, longer nights") of "Best Day Ever" are realized on "Weekend" when Mac, alongside Miguel, declares: "Everything good by the weekend," later adding, "We going out tonight, yeah we going out tonight, like fuck it."

The hook carries an oddly similar energy to "Best Day Ever." Both choruses catalog the base need to celebrate the self and unwind, no matter what is happening around us. Much like the hook of "Best Day Ever," the party of "Weekend" feels earned. There's an irreverence to both songs. We *are* going out tonight. Life *could not* get better. Mac is demanding joy. He is summoning it and rooting it in place. Life shall be good. It is Malcolm's mandate.

The second verse of "Weekend" follows the second verse of "Best Day Ever," too, in that both get darker and reveal Malcolm to be overworked and deserving of his own party. "I been having trouble sleeping / Battling these demons / Wondering what's the thing that keeps me breathing / Is it money, fame, or neither?" Mac questions. We're a long way away from him struggling to sleep because he's buzzing with creative energy. By the time we hit the hook, again, Mac's party feels earned. Celebration feels more like a necessity for living than a flourish. He makes celebration feel crucial. By the time Miguel's outro arrives, and he's promising us everything will be all right, we realize the party is the only way to come down from the perils of working too hard. The party is the salve for all the horrors that accompany making big dreams come true.

By making the party feel like an essential ingredient to living, Mac Miller creates his own genre of celebration. Where celebrating yourself can often feel gluttonous, he makes it feel like a welcome and essential thing. We exist in a culture that rewards hustling to death, but this genre of celebration rewards us for taking time off and basking in ourselves. Perhaps this is why it feels so good to lose yourself in the candy of "Best Day Ever" (or the measured debauchery of "Weekend") because Malcolm urges us to enjoy all that we've worked for without guilt. That's the true victory of this brand of celebration music: It's guilt-free enjoyment we all deserve.

Big Jerm: I probably should've felt more pressure, but everything was so new for all of us. In Pittsburgh, that never happened before. Wiz's *Kush & OJ* came out and then *K.I.D.S.* that same year. All of that was unexpected for me. I was appreciative of everything, but I wasn't sure of where it was at. I probably could've taken it more seriously, looking back. It was just fun! Nobody was thinking about money stuff. At the time, we were just having fun and that was probably the best part about it, honestly.

I recorded 90 percent of [*Best Day Ever*] too. It was pretty carefree back then for everybody. I don't think he felt like there was pressure yet. He didn't really start feeling pressure until after *Blue Slide Park* got some bad reviews. At this point, it was just: go to the studio, see what happens, and have fun.

Quentin Cuff: I felt like it was easier for him to make music once people liked him. There was pressure after *Blue Slide Park* because there was hate. Whereas with *K.I.D.S.*, it was everyone saying that was their favorite shit, bro. Everyone was saying, "Tape of the year!" People were talking about it! It spoke for itself. Most of the people we respected and liked were rocking with it. Bow Wow was like, "I was trying to sign you to Birdman!" We were like, "We're already signed." Then he unfollowed Mac on Twitter.

When he got older, he took breaks. He knew himself well. He canceled a tour to go to rehab. I remember him calling me, crying, talking about that. That was one of the only times I heard Mac cry, because he couldn't go on tour. He had to do it—he wasn't burnt out, but going through so many other things. But at this point, with *Best Day Ever*? No, I didn't think he was gonna burn out. With *Macadelic*, it was a lot. At this point, we're still fresh. Doing the legwork then, it was easier. Once you're doing that for three, four years straight, you get something like a *Faces*.

WIZ KHALIFA: Working with him is always organic. We just get a beat, get in the studio, and get an idea going. Mac always did what he wanted to do. He knew which direction he was going in. For me, being a little older than him, he already knew my music, so he was able to point out "I want this type of flow; I want it to sound like this." He was determined, and he knew what he wanted and how he wanted it to sound. Whether it be underground hip-hop beats, or something more jazzy or instrument-driven. He played a lot of instruments. He was talented in a lot of areas, so he would bring all of that together in the studio. He would not hold back at all.

JUST BLAZE: His sense of melody, his sense of timing. He was obviously a young artist, but he had respect for the generations that came before him, which I thought was huge. His thing was, "I love everything that came before me; it's made me who I am. I wanna carry that torch while doing something new." It was a different approach than many young artists take.

QUENTIN CUFF: I admired his work ethic. Mac would be the type to sleep in, but it would be because he was up all night working hard. That was before any drugs were a piece of his life. He was a kid who slept in late, stayed up late, worked hard, and got a lot done. He would be working to try and get studio time, working on his music nonstop. He was a dedicated person.

SAP: It was fun being around him, every time. You never know what you gon' get. He's like one of the people in the business where whether you were a fan of the music or not, if you met him, you became a fan. That's just how he was. It's crazy! He's just one of those guys, man, fuck. The last time I seen him, I was at his house and he had come home, and he had just bought this trumpet. He was just playing it, not really playing it, just these crazy ass fart notes and shit. Just trying to figure it out. That was him! That was him every day: wanting to learn something new, wanting to try something new. That's how he lived life, man. It made you wanna be that way. It made you not wanna put boundaries on yourself.

PHONTE: When I look at his trajectory, I think it's the journey of an artist trying to sound like themself. Most artists, generally, follow a pattern. That pattern is: imitate, emulate, and then innovate. You come out mimicking whoever your favorite MCs were. You just start off as a mimic because you don't even know what your thing is. Then, after a while, you hit an emulating stage. You're still pulling from your influences, but there are traces of [you] that are starting to show through. After that, you hit the innovate stage. That's when you find out what your voice is and who you are as an artist.

QUENTIN CUFF: We were in Silver Spring, Maryland—I think he had sold out a smaller venue. That's where we were when *Best Day Ever* released. I remember him lying on the ground, and he has this cousin that lives in Maryland, and she would always come to every show. I remember she was there. Mac was lying on the floor and he had released the tape: "Dude, I'm just so glad to get this out."

A TOUCHING QUALITY

If we were to define Malcolm's career in a single word, it would be touching. The man affected lives and made tender, effacing, and evocative music from his first creative renaissance to his last. Mac's work warmed us and stirred us to our cores. His soul was effortlessly present in every song. Even on projects where fun was emphasized over introspection—*K.I.D.S.* and *Best Day Ever*—Mac Miller still found time to lay his ever-present heart out for us to have and to hold.

On *Best Day Ever* in particular, Malcolm took up a good chunk of time showcasing his soft side. "Get Up," "I'll Be There," and "Life Ain't Easy" all carried with them a human quality, picking up where Mac Miller's "Poppy" left off, and carrying us into his career on a pillow of affecting work.

There's a weight to such work. It worms its way into our hearts and pulls out all manner of tucked-away emotion. Malcolm understood this weight on *Best Day Ever*, and slipped his poignant moments into pockets of bright sonics and scraggly melodies, but wasn't yet ready to give himself entirely to the wounded side of such music. That said, he was ready to give us shining pieces of himself in his work. He was ready to inspire and delight us as much as he could for the time, and so he did.

With that, the moving quality of "Get Up" comes by way of inspiring us to root for Malcolm. We're already touched by his present success, for we've been cheering him on since he was Easy Mac with the cheesy raps, but now we're enamored by his humility as well. "It's unbelievable these people say I made it," Mac spits amidst a storm of bars populating the first verse. There's something so heartwarming about the way he stands stunned by his success, something so precious and necessary about the way he describes it as truly "unbeliev-able." We pause on the line and get mixed up in its emotional candor, realizing Mac Miller still has those stars in his eyes.

"Life goes on, days get brighter," he continues. "You tune into my station hope you listening / Turn it up and follow on my journey as I live my dream." The emotive quality of "Get Up" evidences itself in the subtle ways Mac shirks confidence and makes himself all the more endearing. Hoping people listen? Rapping about his dreams with a playful air? This is a perfect storm to bring us closer to Malcolm. Was that not the goal of *Best Day Ever*? Was it not produced to give us even more reasons to love Mac Miller after the success of *K.I.D.S.*? All these precious moments shared between us—and we've yet to reach the hook.

The easiest way to identify touching music is to examine the hook. Are we working in the realm of chants and inspiration? Is the song's structure built for us to sink into and feel? In the case of "Get Up," it sure is. "In a world that go round, are you up or you down / You in or you out / You smile or you frown / Just get up, get up," Mac instructs. We feel pumped, invigorated. How could we not, with Malcolm by our side? The song works if only because we realize Mac is on our team, and so the bond between fan and artist grows even stronger.

Here, too, Malcolm plays life coach, as he often will. "Just get up" will one day transform into the mantras that permeate *Swimming* and *Circles*. In the context of his discography, then, "Get Up" is innately special, if only because we know what is to come. The hook is the pinnacle of his music's touching nature, for it speaks to the great ways in which Mac will go on to rouse his fan base and save lives.

For a taste of something more traditionally endearing, Mac includes an ode to his mother. The Phonte-featuring "I'll Be There" is sweeter than sweet, a precious moment between mother and son. Though this song has nothing to do with us or with Mac's relationship with his fans, it still brings us closer to him. It is one of the rare moments during Mac's first creative renaissance where he opens himself up lyrically and goes beyond the punchlines and playful barbs at the game. "I'll Be There" is all Malcolm at a time when the world was still warming up to Mac Miller.

Any sampling of lyrics will summon a collective "Aw" from the listener. Take this moment from the first verse: "Said she'd be there forever / No matter what's the weather / She'd always have my back even when we weren't together." Here, Mac begins to dig into the permanence of love and how it cannot be destroyed. He'll go on to talk about this at length on several songs, namely "Objects in the Mirror" in 2013, but for now, we have Mac's deep appreciation for his mother and her sacrifices. And how brilliant, too—this song is quietly one of Mac's most relatable. We all have a guiding figure in our lives, mothers or otherwise, and "I'll Be There" brings us right to the center of our feelings for them.

Mac evidently understood this relatability factor, for he includes the following bars to close out the second verse: "If you have your moms, you better treat her right / Call her up, say "Wassup" before you sleep tonight / Tell her you love her and thank her for what she did." Once again, Mac goes from Malcolm to life coach, and we immediately take his words to heart. A son honoring his mother and urging his fans to reach out to their own? With the venerable Phonte cooing on the hook? What could, truly, be better?

But Mac isn't done. To help close out the final stretch of *Best Day Ever*, he includes "Life Ain't Easy," a riff on the quality of "Get Up." We fall for the song from the first bars: "When I get old I'mma be real cool / Sittin' on the porch with a fresh pair of shoes / Whole bunch of stories for the neighborhood kids / Tell 'em to believe, they'll be makin' it big." First, we're treated to an image of a wizened and older Malcolm giving game to the next generation. Next, we're touched by his resilience and desire to inspire both us and the future "neighborhood kids." We recall "Get Up" and how we were connected to Malcolm through his humility, which has only matured by "Life Ain't Easy."

"I know / That life is nothing easy (nothing easy) / One day, I'mma change the world / And they'll finally believe me," Mac continues on the opening hook. Here we have the same energy of "Get Up." Malcolm is making himself so endearing by sizing himself up modestly while still looking toward a bright future. We're moved, now and then, because Mac was already changing the world. He'd already broken out with *K.I.D.S.*; we knew his future was bound to be incredible. And yet, he's still looking ahead with a cautious, albeit poppy, eye.

The verses of "Life Ain't Easy," too, contain affecting moments. Mac breaks down his bubbling anxiety over fame and the work of his music career. He expresses anxiety over switching up, losing himself in the mix of the music business. But his woes melt away by the second verse, where he once again rouses humility: "See it's a blessin' that I'm gettin' through the door." "Dear music, you're everything I have now," Mac continues. We believe Malcolm, and we believe in him. By the end of "Life Ain't Easy," by the end of *Best Day Ever*, there's a sense that Mac Miller has done everything he can to give us as much of himself as he had to offer.

Listening back to *Best Day Ever*, we find Mac's aspirations and fears heartwarming. We know Mac goes on to become a star on his own terms. We stumble back, in love with his childlike wonderment. We're touched by the ways in which Malcolm honors himself, his career, his mother, and his future, all while having the time of his life. *Best Day Ever* may well be the first time Mac lets his gentle side out repeatedly on a full-length project. It's special. It's Malcolm preceding Mac Miller. He changed the world, and we finally believe him.

2011

BLUE SLIDE PARK

"No matter what happens in life, no matter where you go, where you're off to, what happens with the park, that slide will always be blue. That will always be Blue Slide Park no matter what. You can go to New York and live for 10 years and become a huge business mogul and then come back to the 'Burgh and no matter how much money you got, that slide is still blue."

—MAC MILLER[4]

4.   Rob Markman, "Mac Miller Talks Inspiration Behind *Blue Slide Park*," *MTV News*, July 26, 2011, http://www.mtv.com/news/1667946/mac-miller-blue-slide-park/.

NOT TAKING HAPPINESS
FOR GRANTED

"You just entered into Blue Slide Park / The place where dreams comin' true, that's where you find heart"

—*"One Last Thing"*

When you spin *Blue Slide Park*, you realize: "Goodness, none of us knew a damn thing." Such is the lore of Mac Miller's studio debut. None of us knew that one young man's joyous, record-breaking romp through Pittsburgh would take him down such dark roads and with such expedience.

When the hazy and playfully forlorn *Macadelic* arrived the following year, fans quickly realized that it wasn't 2011 anymore, and knowing what we know today, it never would be. But what if, just for a moment, it was 2011 again? What if we let ourselves revel in the brightness of misguided youth? Years later, that is the ultimate takeaway from *Blue Slide Park*.

As his career moved forward, the general consensus is that Mac did not want to be traditionally famous. Though his acclaim grew, it became clear that what he wanted most was to be a musician. With a stringy voice leaning into a rasp to sound older and weather-worn, Miller tells us as much on "English Lane," the opening track. "Sometimes I just wanna go / Back to Blue Slide Park, the only place I call home / I hope it's never all gone, don't think it's ever all gone." A wistful wish with ominous implications.

A series of debaucherous, inspiring, and close-but-not-quite introspective moments follow, as *Blue Slide Park* does its fair share of party hopping ("Up All Night") and requisite boasting ("My Team"). The album even tries its hand at getting nasty with "Smile Back"—part hustle anthem, part middling life advice, part come-up tale. Call it frat rap, sure, but don't call it slimy. Beneath the childish and toxic behavior, there is a desire to live forever that has never received its due shine. Miller's pursuit of Always and Forever colors his work down to his final singles. In many ways, *Blue Slide Park* set Mac up to be a tragic figure—someone who would rather live forever than face his fears in order to move on and grow up.

The true story of *Blue Slide Park* is uncovered ground. The album is unexpectedly emotionally spacious, almost to the point of being sparse, but it is not directionless. We witness Mac Miller experiencing a brief loss of identity and increasing paranoia on "PA Nights"; the drug-trap that informs much of his later work is introduced on "Of the Soul"; flashes of depression and burnout charge "Under the Weather"; and heartbreak debuts on "Missed Calls." Each of these tracks chooses the moment over the anxiety, and localized happiness over impending, indiscriminate doom.

Blue Slide Park is emotive; the hot spots are simply fleeting. At barely nineteen, Miller was just accumulating the vocabulary and life experience to break down who he was and what troubled him. Yet, at every evocative turn, there's an immediate reset. The record moves from jaunts on Fifth Avenue to contemplative drives during the classic "PA Nights," where Mac is simultaneously excited and worried about where his music will take him. The pissed off attitude of "Smile Back" is undone by the optimistic nature of "Under the Weather." Even the hard facts of the album make it out to be an in-flux thing. Mac leans into the tropes of youth and dives into his more sophisticated tastes for instrumentation as a diversion tactic.

Mac made a choice to be cheerful and frivolous. The swerves to outsized parties and flashy rapper flexes now sound more like necessities than proof he had nothing to say. In the spaces between "my fam's still the only people that really know me for who I am" and "still sippin' on my 40 when the cops drove by," there is the realization that no one is too good to be happy and that we are all guilty of taking happiness for granted.

For all the joy of *Blue Slide Park*, there is much to critique—unfinished ideas, weak writing, and overwhelming bouts of childishness that dips its toes into abject immaturity are but a few. Yet, the album still manages to whisk us away *somewhere*, to a place where we feel less shame about enjoying the simple things in life. The album is an ode to the fleeting nature of joy and adolescence, while also functioning as a cautionary tale.

Within a year, Mac Miller was sliding into a troubling drug habit. Along the way, he would make some of the most tortured music in contemporary hip-hop. *Swimming*, his final album while he was still with us, ends with a call back to the easier days, but 2009 is not a number set in stone. We would just as soon scamper back to 2011, to those Pennsylvania nights spent plotting his career and planning to take his homies to the castle at the top. This album takes us back even when the past feels inconceivably unreachable. Past becomes home with *Blue Slide Park*. The memory of a simpler existence acts as an anchor for Mac Miller, who is able to retreat into his adolescence as his star rises and adulthood looms. *Blue Slide Park* stands as a place to which we could all escape whenever the world became unmanageable.

Somehow, I'm certain, Mac knew all of this. He knew our future needs and rushed to meet them. This album—and much of his subsequent music—is spent pining for home and peace of mind.

The album ends as it began: with a yearning prayer for eternity. "Blue Slide Park, the only place I call home / I hope it's never gone, forever long" to "when they gonna let me back home / I wanna go back home." The record goes down as a quest for footing in an uncertain industry.

Blue Slide Park is a place, but *Blue Slide Park* was a concept. Mac Miller, too, is far more everlasting and grand than one dot on a map. He was a young man who "got up and took flight," carrying us with him.

QUENTIN CUFF: *Blue Slide Park* is an ode to Pittsburgh. But it's not the gritty side of the younger demographic of Pittsburgh that Mac showed on *K.I.D.S.*; not to say it's super gritty, but there was certain aspects of it that were mischievous.

E. DAN: When we started working on *Blue Slide Park* and he sorta got the first bit of money in his pocket, the first thing we did was go to a local music store, and he started buying everything. We came back with a bunch of keyboards and guitars, and it was funny to us over the years. He spent four grand on this electronic-acoustic drum set. The only time we ever used it on the entire album was a ride cymbal on "Under the Weather."

BIG JERM: He was just excited because it was his first album, so it felt more important to him, I think. When him and E. started working on it, I was on tour with Wiz. I missed the beginning, but we were still sending stuff back and forth when I was able to listen on tour. I remember him being excited, and he bought some equipment for the studio—he was happy to buy some equipment. It was very innocent.

E. DAN: With the *Blue Slide Park* sessions it was very much, "Let's do something like this. Cool?" and we did it, and it was done. Moving forward, it was more like, "Let's do something like this. Now, what if I do *this* to it?" It became this process of, let's turn over every single stone we could find in the search of what could make this song the absolute coolest.

BIG JERM: It was like a fine line of trying to have fun, but I think he was feeling the pressure more than anybody else. We were going with what he wanted to do, sonically. There were a couple [songs] where it was similar to "Best Day Ever," where . . . I would be in the front room of the studio, and he would hear something. Some of it was random like that, but "Party on Fifth Ave" was his idea, the sample and everything. He came up with that idea while I was on that tour.

Clams Casino (producer, "My Team," "One Last Thing"): He shouted me out on Twitter in 2011 or so. He said something like, "I need to work with Clams—somebody that thinks outside the box." I appreciate that. I'm not sure how he heard my music, probably early [A$AP] Rocky or Lil B stuff. [Mac] invited me to come out to Pittsburgh to hang and come to the studio. So, not long after that, I flew out there by myself, and that was the first time I ever traveled to work on music. That was an important trip for me. I went out to Pittsburgh to ID Labs' studio and for one night, we just hung out. I played some beats. We didn't really work on anything there. He was working on his first album [*Blue Slide Park*] at the time. That was the first time we met and hung out.

Quentin Cuff: My memory of the *Blue Slide Park* album is that whole stretch of videos. I was there for the "Under the Weather" session. "Frick Park Market" came out before the album, and it was just... Mac already had "Donald Trump"; he had hits. What's he gonna do? That whole summer was literally a ride, because it was similar to the *K.I.D.S.* summer, but it was a lot more confident. It was a lot more of us shooting videos in Pittsburgh, and people would all be stopping and asking Mac for a picture. A lot of people would be like, "Oh, that's that little rapper, but he's not famous yet." That era, it was still, "Okay, this kid is a budding artist," but not a lot of people thought that's anything crazy.

Big Jerm: It's funny... I have a laptop, and I was using FL Studio at the time, and I backed up everything I ever had. I still have all the original versions of all that stuff. Even from ten years ago. "Diamonds & Gold," that was one like that. I can't even remember when I made that beat. I probably had that sample since 2008. I was just going through samples on my computer and then remade the beat a little bit, and then gave the files to E., and he added some things on there. "Smile Back" was like that too. I was just messing with that sample. A lot of this wasn't planned out—it just kinda happened.

THE BOOK OF MAC

"Up All Night" was one we had done, maybe, the summer prior. That was the first one where Mac played guitar and I did the drums. We totally did that just to do something different, and E. Dan heard it, and that was the one that got E. excited about Mac. "Blue Slide Park" was another one where I was messing with the sample and Mac came in.

Looking back on it, a lot of these were, like, going with the flow. With "Up All Night," we had done it just to have fun, and it ended up making the album a year later. We didn't know [the album] was a thing at the time. I think a lot of these, they just came together. Ritz Reynolds is on here a few times. He would always send Mac stuff; he's from Philly. He's a good musician, so I think that was the start of where Mac got to towards the end. He wanted to be more musical.

BENJY GRINBERG: There was a musicality, but the musicality grew exponentially later. But he could really, really rap, and he could really put full compositions together. He would mess around on the guitar. That was sort of his main instrument at the time, though he could play a little bit of everything. I was just interested to see where this was gonna go.

QUENTIN CUFF: When you look at "Up All Night," Mac was in a very musical bag. "Blue Slide Park" is a precursor to songs like "Here We Go." This is really an ID Labs-Mac album. You got Clams Casino and Young L—he was in the group with Lil B. We loved his work with Lil B. Clams did stuff with Lil B and A$AP Rocky, so we loved his work. Mac was already on some trip-hop kinda shit. "Down the Rabbit Hole" showed he loved that sound and DJ Shadow. He really kept working off what worked on *Best Day Ever*. People loved "In the Air," [and] then you have "Man In The Hat."

CLAMS CASINO: You could tell he just loved to experiment. Something that drew us to each other. He was doing his thing at the time, but I could tell he was more than what people had thought initially. I could tell he wanted to do more. From our music together, it was like, "What can I help bring out? Something different or a bit unexpected." That was something we both enjoyed. From all the stuff we did—it was a wide range of stuff with different sounds—we both appreciate not really knowing where it's gonna go, just having fun and making music.

He's so welcoming and friendly. He introduced me to all his friends he grew up with; they were all hanging out at the studio. It was natural. Felt like I kinda knew him and them already. They showed so much love to me and my music. It was laid back and natural to hang out with him. I didn't know what to expect, but that's how he was. It was like that every time I spent any time with him, right from the beginning.

QUENTIN CUFF: I think Mac was making an album he could relate to, once again. Like all of Mac's albums, he wasn't making it with the intent to relate, but that's what he did. It wasn't, "Oh, people are gonna love this." It was just poetic for him. He was getting shit off his chest, even at a young age. He made what was in his heart. When I really sit back and look at this tracklist, this man is literally a genius!

As far as Pittsburgh stuff goes... The first five tracks! "English Lane," the street before you enter Blue Slide Park. "Blue Slide Park," the actual park. "Party on Fifth Ave," I went to high school on Fifth Avenue. "PA Nights," perfect driving song when you're talking about driving in Pittsburgh at night. "Frick Park Market," the market he went to from when he was such a young kid. When you look at the "Cruisin'" video? The barbershop we're in was right next to Frick Park Market.

"Frick Park Market" was always the plan. When I was going to Mac's house when he was making *Jukebox* and *High Life*, he and his mom had a tab at Frick Park Market. I could call Miss Karen, like, "Hey, I'm at Frick Park Market, can I grab a sandwich?" And she'd be like, "Okay, you can put it on our tab." That's where the whole hook of "Frick Park Market" comes from. It's crazy to me! *Blue Slide Park* shows how much of a benevolent person Malcolm was. He's literally the nicest rapper that there ever was.

E. Dan: With *Blue Slide Park*, it was a little different. There were little glimpses of [his later sound]. Jerm and I both tried to push him a little bit, just thinking a little bit more. I felt like he would phone in some of the punchlines on his verses, and we would give him a hard time about that. There were little glimpses of it. There are actually songs that didn't make the cut, that were more out there, that were maybe starting to point a little bit in that direction.

"MISSED CALLS" IS THE BLUEPRINT FOR MAC MILLER'S UNDERSTANDING OF LOVE

In 2011, Mac Miller made history with *Blue Slide Park*, which debuted at No. 1 on the Billboard 200 chart, making it the first independently released debut album to do so since Tha Dogg Pound's *Dogg Food* in 1995. Though the album was panned, with *Pitchfork* infamously rating it a one-out-of-ten, there are gems to mine. In the context of his discography, *Blue Slide Park* presented many great moments of foreshadowing and is a lesson in not taking life for granted—a lesson in taking the time to appreciate your life.

The song with the most connections to Mac's later music is "Missed Calls," which mixes the pains and pleasures of love into a single track, telegraphing the way Malcolm would write about love and heartbreak as inextricably linked. Each subsequent major release features at least one track indebted to the song: 2012's "Clarity," 2013's "Youforia," 2014's "Wedding," 2015's "ROS," 2016's "Planet God Damn," and 2018's "Dunno." It served as the blueprint for Mac's articulation of the experience of love.

The couple at the heart of the track is entrenched in conflict, going back and forth over each other's priorities, unmet expectations, and broken promises. It's a classic story. One partner is dream-chasing while the other feels left behind. Their fight plays out over two verses, the first being from the male (his) perspective and the second coming from the female (her) perspective. Mac Miller was dutifully attempting to give voice to both sides.

Malcolm is learning that pain and pleasure brush shoulders more often than not, and he's not happy about it. The lyrics and structure, however, only tell part of the story. Ritz Reynolds's plush beat scales back on the tension of the track, which sets the stage for Malcolm to employ juxtaposition. The accompanying Rex Arrow-directed music video brings the world of "Missed Calls" to life with scenes depicting the couple positively in love—before it all falls apart.

"Missed Calls" was the first time Mac presented a complex narrative on the pitfalls of love. Those closest to us have the highest capacity to hurt us, and Mac was coming to understand this as he penned it. There is no love without the risk of getting hurt. Mac carried this sordid knowledge with him from 2011 to 2018, making his love songs potent because of their commitment to the reality of the experience.

In 2012, Mac dropped *Macadelic*, on which love and drugs are presented as a salve. "Clarity," with its exceptional directness, portrays love as a cure-all for his pain. "You take away the pain and I thank you for that / If I ever get the chance, bet I'm paying you back." The leap Mac took from 2011 to 2012 is massive. His lyrics matured, as did his understanding of the depths of certain wounds, which made him an early star in the realm of fan connection. As on "Missed Calls," Mac crafts a scene where love and pain exist in unison.

The painful reality Mac inhabits gives "Clarity" a palpable density. Pain and pleasure are synced, one almost begetting the other. It is *Macadelic*'s sleeper hit, embracing the spirit of "Missed Calls" and expanding upon it with bold lines like, "Misery—you represent love, you the epitome" and, "Everybody who can save me now is not around, chopper down." 2011 was not a fluke—Mac Miller does have the capacity to craft thoughtful love songs.

The trend continues on 2013's "Youforia." Mac takes the pining nature of the "missed calls and emails / All going into detail / About how you just not happy and you think you gotta leave" and turns them into a fully formed track, addressing the flame of desire and how it can drive us mad. We get a touch of "Clarity," in that love is elevated as an all-healing entity ("With you by my side, you are my euphoria"), and get "Missed Calls" in the hint of pain ("I been waiting so long / Been waiting to have you by my side") as we search for something we do not have.

"The pain, it can't stay," Mac declares on the outro. With its rich sonic textures, the song is blanketing, swirling as it washes over us. There's a sense of lovingly being culled into a vat of passion and longing. Mac referencing pain as love's partner, once more, reminds us of "Missed Calls." "It's so hard to pretend that it's like it was way back when," Mac expresses from the girlfriend's point of view on "Missed Calls," a perfect link to the emotive longing on "Youforia." Yearning colors both tracks and will go on to infuse his later love songs.

Faces, regarded by many as Mac Miller's opus, features his best. 2014's "Wedding" is a spectacular display of the ways pleasure and pain interact to develop a nuanced, toxic, and intoxicating love. An irresistible and unstable, inescapable and harrowing love. Much like "Missed Calls," "Wedding" is about a couple on the brink of collapse, shedding light on the difficulties of being in a relationship. The song is an epic tragedy, but the love remains potent. Malcolm cannot get enough of his lover, despite consistently hurting her. And she hurts him back. The back-and-forth structure of "Missed Calls" appears on the hook, morphing from "I'm the worst" to "You the worst" seamlessly.

In "Wedding," "the smile that she faking is tragic, hate looking at it" mirrors "kept breakin' promises you said you'd keep" from "Missed Calls." On both cuts, Malcolm is letting his partner down and feeling the weight of that failure. Back in 2011, this weight drove the hook and resolved in Mac terminating the relationship. On "Wedding," Mac refuses to concede. After three years, Mac has learned that the risk of heartache is a necessity of love. "Wedding" captures the reality of fighting for something that might, at times, make you sick in the same way his earlier work captures the reality of fighting, period. Much like 2012's "Clarity" innovated upon the "Missed Calls" formula, so too does "Wedding."

2015's "ROS," a traditional love song, leans heavily on his canon. Similar to how "Missed Calls" played up tiny details in the midst of unrest ("You could have these shoes back / All of this perfume back, necklaces and jewels back"), Mac opens "ROS" with the minutiae of romance. "You like your vodka with a little touch of lime," he sings, before we get to the meat of the matter: "They say we're no good for each other / And I can't really tell, what is this spell you put me under?" On a subtler note, as with "Missed Calls," the second verse gives voice to the woman, reminding us that Mac is following a keen blueprint.

The hook captures the ethos of all his preceding and forthcoming love songs in just a handful of words: "Your love is not too kind to me." Pair that with the line from "Missed Calls" ("You just don't, don't, don't love me like you used to") and another thread is revealed. This time, Malcolm is expounding upon the back and forth through an alternate lens. Whereas Mac was vexed on "Wedding," on "ROS" we get the sense that Mac enjoys the turmoil. It adds to the reality Mac has established across all these songs. Not once does Malcolm sugarcoat a relationship. Not once do we stop believing him.

Mac Miller's conviction is why 2016's "Planet God Damn" is essential to *The Divine Feminine*. The first three bars are an immediate call back to "Missed Calls": "Yeah, I think I'm stuck inside nostalgia / My mind are in the times when this love was so divine / But now it's feelin' like without ya." Themes of pining, absence, and romanticizing the past permeate both tracks. This is crucial to the success of *The Divine Feminine*, which can be regarded as one long love song. True to his writing, however, he refuses to present a final product at odds with the truth. No love is perfect and, consequently, no love album can be free of friction.

Consider the way Mac ends the first verse with "and I ain't here to break a promise / I'm just tryna keep it honest." These words call directly to the broken promises haunting "Missed Calls." At all times, Malcolm is weaving threads through his writing. From the subtle to the direct, Mac is working within and strengthening his canon. This consistent calling back to previous songs makes Mac's work feel familiar. While he innovates in most respects, by keeping things close to their roots, Mac Miller's music supplies the sensation of coming home.

Finally, 2018's "Dunno" from *Swimming* takes the hook of "Missed Calls" and turns it into a proper song. When Mac sings, "Wouldn't you rather get along," we recall him singing for his lover to just leave him if she's so unhappy on "Missed Calls." In both instances, Mac is desperate for reprieve, presenting himself as a kind of martyr. "Dunno" has the back-and-forth as well, the blending of pleasure and pain. It even opens with the same sentiment as "Missed Calls" with Mac singing, "She do whatever she like / And that just don't seem right." As with all of his love songs, "Dunno" soars where "Missed Calls" merely sprinted.

Malcolm sustained an emotional writing practice for seven years; it's impeccable and speaks to his passion. Even at his most infantile, he was dead set on imbuing his love songs with authenticity. There could be no love without pain, and his music is all the better for it, all the more believable, all the more relatable. His portrayals of love never come across as manufactured or insincere. We ride gleefully with him from first love to final breath because, at all times, Mac understood himself—and he understood us too.

QUENTIN CUFF: I don't think he had something to prove. He went up there and tried to put together the best project he possibly could. He was experimenting with, not necessarily trying to make the *best* music, but to put together what he thought was an *album*. He put some great love songs on there. "Missed Calls" is a fucking tremendous song, probably one of my favorites. "Diamonds & Gold" still holds up in Mac's catalog. That back half of the album, after "Loitering," is slept on and there's some great songwriting on that album. Even with "One Last Thing" with Clams Casino, he tapped into the sound he would make on *Macadelic*.

BENJY GRINBERG: It's nice to be around people that are confident in themselves and are so creative, yet know who they are and what they're trying to do. It's usually not that way. You'll meet an artist who is really talented but doesn't know themselves yet or doesn't have a clear direction. With Mac, he just had a million ideas a second for what he wanted to do, for songs he wanted to make, for videos, for artwork. It all came from him. It was his vision, purely.

QUENTIN CUFF: A song like "Loitering" is a *K.I.D.S.* type of concept. "Of the Soul" is one my favorite songs Mac's ever done. Obviously, "My Team" and my shout out on "My Team" is legendary for me and made me very happy—always makes me happy to listen to it. More than ever, this is the DNA of something like a *Divine Feminine* or a *GO:OD AM*. This is the beginning of "Yo, I'm gonna go in with a very short list of producers, and I'm gonna make what I feel is a great album."

CASEY VEGGIES (rapper): He dropped *Blue Slide Park*, and he called me like, "Yeah, bro, I told you I had a tour for you." This was right when I was graduating high school. I was about to go to college. I was doing my thing with music. I was coming up, but I wasn't at a level where I could just jump on tour. I kinda was on the fence. Should I go to college, or should I do this rap thing? Mac don't really know it, but he was the main reason I chose to pursue rap 100 percent. He brought me on the Blue Slide Park Tour. It was sixty-six shows around the whole United States. That was my first big tour! It was three months long. I graduated high school and then the tour started in September. He gave me the confidence to say, "You know what? College can wait."

BIG JERM: From my perspective, all these things were going well for Mac and Wiz, and also for me and E. Dan. Things are just going up. You can't get too high when things are going well, and you can't get too low when things are going poorly. I was learning that at the time. Everything was going up for everybody, so that's the lesson I learned back then.

BENJY GRINBERG: [*Blue Slide Park* going No. 1] was certainly a highlight of my professional life. It was unreal. We built up this momentum that was really kind of unprecedented, and between releasing mixtapes and touring, his videos were getting tons of views. We felt this thing growing like crazy. So we knew *Blue Slide Park* was gonna be special, but when it actually came out and was the number one album, we were all just amazed, grateful, happy . . . It's hard when you're in the middle of it to sit back and say, "Woah, look what we've done." It's when you look back two years later you can say: "Damn, we had the number one album in the country, and we were fully independent." You only really get that perspective later. Looking back on it, it's fucking incredible.

QUENTIN CUFF: To me, it was surreal. It was a celebration, but I would say one of the only times I saw Mac really sit back and celebrate after working hard for so many years, was when him and Miguel went Platinum for "The Weekend." He never really took a lot of time [to appreciate his success]. During *Blue Slide Park*, we were damn near going Platinum off of mixtape shit. It was just the accumulation of him, Benjy, Artie [Pitt], Miss Karen, E. Dan, Big Jerm's hard work. It was all those people's hard work and their dedication to getting this thing to be as big as it could be.

BIG JERM: There was a big change with him. A lot of critics... the *Pitchfork* review. That affected him a lot. But going into *BSP*, he thought it would be fun. He was serious about it, but it was fun. I appreciated that too. That was the thing. I think he was more hung up on the review than being happy about the number one, honestly. With me, it was surreal, more than anything, to be all over a number one album. It didn't feel real. He made "Loud" pretty soon after. I'm pretty sure it was still 2011 when [I] had made that. "Loud" was a beat I sent to him.

CLAMS CASINO: You could tell he wanted to go somewhere [different]. It wasn't to prove a point or anything. That's why it worked. It was naturally what he loved doing: learning new instruments and teaching himself to play stuff, just [being] inspired by his love for music. Not "I'm gonna do something different just to show critics I can do something different." It was just him being him. That's what I love and respect about him.

E. DAN: I don't think he ever articulated this to me, but I always sensed it... He had some very real fears of being looked at as a corny white rapper, especially after the *Pitchfork* review. He wanted to prove himself to his peers, especially when he moved to LA. He was hanging out with a lot of artists out there. They became his peers, and he wanted to impress those guys. That was the real turning point. It started to get a lot more serious, in terms of just the music. He really had something to prove, aside from "Let me get famous." It really turned into, "Let me do something musically that these dudes and the world will be impressed by."

BENJY GRINBERG: He was sensitive to that sort of thing. I think he wanted to be accepted, he wanted to be liked. Back then, it took a little while for albums to come out because you had to make CDs, unlike today when you can finish an album and two days later, it's up for everyone to hear. It was a three or four-month-long process. I think during those months, he started evolving. I think he was kind of musically past *Blue Slide Park* when it came out, in his own mind and in his studio. He was making these records that would later become *Macadelic* that were very different. I think that messed with him a little bit.

BIG JERM: There was this place called Tamari in Lawrenceville, where the studio used to be in Pittsburgh. We would get takeout every day from there. They had a lobster mac-n-cheese that was good. We had a song called "Insomniak" later, but, you know, he didn't need to sleep as much as everybody else. I just remember his energy at the time; it was different. After the review came out, a lot changed. The reviews weren't that good, but his career was still taking off. That was when he moved to LA. I think it's just kinda like the last bit of innocence, right before *Blue Slide Park* [came out]. It was a nice time . . . We were still outside of the music business, if that makes sense.

QUENTIN CUFF: If he's looking back at that album—and he looked back at it in private a lot more than I did—he was always happy with things. When he looked back at *Blue Slide Park*, he looked at it as: That cemented him as a staple in hip-hop.

E. DAN: The first year after *Blue Slide Park* came out and things were moving and he was getting successful, he came over to my house on Christmas Day and brought my kids a bunch of presents, which then became a tradition. I found out later that he was actually pissing off his whole family because they were waiting for him every Christmas morning to have a meal together and do all this family stuff, but he was over my house showering my kids with gifts for no reason other than the fact that he just loved doing that. That's the type of dude he was. He just loved making people happy. That was his thing.

2012

MACADELIC

"I didn't think about who was gonna like it, or if it was gonna go crazy. I just made a project to get some stuff off my chest... It's some real deep, crazy, trippy stuff."

—MAC MILLER[5]

5.   Mac Miller, "Mac Miller Discusses His New Mixtape, *Macadelic*," interview by Allison Hagendorf, *Fuse*, March 16, 2012, https://www.youtube.com/watch?v=QFqlWpDoHkg.

MAC MILLER'S SECOND CREATIVE RENAISSANCE

"Un amour impossible"

—*"Love Me as I Have Loved You"*

The three acts of Mac Miller's play are marked by *K.I.D.S.*, *Macadelic*, and *The Divine Feminine*. As prolific as Mac was, there are distinct growth points and pivots that denote his evolution as an artist. The speed at which these vast changes took place is remarkable, but unsurprising given his obsessive approach to making music.

Few fans saw *Macadelic* coming. Moments like "Of the Soul" and "Diamonds & Gold" had alluded to his musical ambitions, but not to the budding darkness and introspection he was capable of. Paging further back, we had "Down the Rabbit Hole," which, in hindsight, plays like a skeleton outline of the themes ("Vitamins," "Fight the Feeling") and sounds that color *Macadelic*. Few could have seen that early foray into the haze of tripping and drug culture becoming the project that established Mac Miller *as* Mac Miller.

Where *K.I.D.S.* and *Blue Slide Park* proved Mac could be a commercial success, it was not until *Macadelic* that Mac asserted himself as an artistic force. The risk of releasing this project was significant, but the gamble was worth it. The Mac Miller we cherish today is born directly out of the experimental approach employed on *Macadelic*. In the opening track, "Love Me As I Have Loved You," Mac asks the audience to believe in him as he believes in them. Out of that symbiosis, he hopes they will take to this new music and see it as the artistic direction he was always meant to follow. That ride and that trust are the crux of *Macadelic*'s importance in his discography. Many fans and critics look at Mac's music and declare they grew up with him. Without *Macadelic*, there would have been no growing up. On the heels of *Blue Slide Park*, Malcolm matured, and his desire to share that with the world opened him up to a slew of fans who wanted exactly that: an artist who would expose his inner world and take this knotty journey with them.

Mac proved himself to be an artist willing to create work that reflected every curve and divot in his life, and the fans responded by bonding to him in a way previously unknown. People need music for transitional periods and gray areas. These confounding moments did not scare Mac Miller; they inspired him. As Mac puts it on "Loud," "Ladies and gentlemen, this is Macadelic."

Still sounding fantastic, *Macadelic* was (at the time) his most ambitious project. From the sampling of French women speaking over the subtle clinks of ice on "1 Threw 8" to the vast and sprawling horizon-like production on "Thoughts from a Balcony," you can hear the twinkle of the midnight stars in the keys layered in the back of the mix and the thick clouds mimicked by rich and drifting chords. Mac made sure the contemplative tones were treated to an equally pensive and moving production.

Yet, Mac still knew how to have fun. The twinkle transforms into a mechanical tick on "Aliens Fighting Robots," and "Loud" and "Ignorant" are time-bomb bangers. Then, there's the smoked-up and jazzy feel of "America." Mac always had range, but there's a lucidity to his versatility on *Macadelic* that makes the album his most dynamic to this point. There's a purity to this pivot, and to each sub-pivot. Every new note feels like an honest venture to push Mac Miller's creative limits.

Macadelic is the first time Mac Miller pursued making truly affecting music. "Clarity" remains one of the best love songs he has ever written. His themes are still ever-so-juvenile, but they are maturing, as in the haze of "The Mourning After" dripping into "1 Threw 8" where Mac muses on mortality.

The lyrics are especially potent in the wake of his passing, but it would be disingenuous to appraise his canon solely through the lens of his death. At the time of making "1 Threw 8"—at the time of *Swimming*, even—Mac was roused and excited about life and his future. Though we did not know the gravity of his drug-induced music at the time, his allusions to pills and lean and the avant-garde images that came from his drug experiments were the building blocks to his later growth spurts (*Watching Movies with the Sound Off*, *Faces*, and going sober on *GO:OD AM*).

On *Macadelic*, Mac finds comfort in searching for meaning in his darkness. He chooses to feel everything. That choice leads him to produce his opus just two years later (*Faces*) and brings him still closer to his fans. Mac's obsession with hurt and immediacy, with the ever-rising potential of his death, first took root on this tape, and we took root with him. Perhaps that is why *Macadelic* is so striking: We have gone from blindly loving life to asking the difficult questions life unearths for us all. It's his willingness to ask those questions and his resilience in the face of getting no answers that make Mac Miller so endearing.

Mac Miller's ability to speak for his fans and have his voice touch on topics they did not know they needed to discuss begins with *Macadelic*. This is Mac's maturity in motion. "This is Macadelic."

E. DAN: [Mac was ready to move on to a darker sound] probably the day we finished *Blue Slide Park*. At the very least, the day the fucking *Pitchfork* review came out. Sometimes, I wanna thank that guy, because I don't know that we would've ended up with *Macadelic* if he hadn't gone so hard on *Blue Slide Park*. It might've been more of a gradual progression into something like *Macadelic*, rather than an about-face. I felt like it was more experimental, but a lot of the themes were darker and more real. Some of that was him growing up too. He was very innocent for *Blue Slide Park*. He had seen and done a little more with *Macadelic*. I don't wanna give what's-his-face at *Pitchfork* too much credit. A lot of it was just Mac growing up and experiencing things. He just had more to say.

BENJY GRINBERG: Mac was living in LA at that time, and it was only three months after *Blue Slide Park* came out. I went over to his house, and he played me the songs he had already started for *Macadelic*. Honestly, my reaction was: These songs are dope, but this is such a departure from *Blue Slide Park*, and so quickly! *Blue Slide Park* literally came out a number of months before *Macadelic* came out. I was like, "Man, this is such a change. I don't know if your fans are ready for this yet." That was my music industry advice to him: "Yo! You might throw a bunch of people off who have been riding with you through all the positivity. This is much darker, and I'm concerned about what's gonna happen." That was my honest, initial feedback.

E. DAN: When we were working on *Blue Slide Park*, there were a lot of moments where Jerm and I felt he could have pushed himself more, lyrically, and we told him so. He was just sort of phoning things in. He wasn't pushing himself to make every verse as interesting as he could. We both felt he was lyrically capable of more. The vibe was there! The sound was there! He was so caught up in the process, that to him, maybe, being interesting as a lyricist wasn't the focus yet. He had the undeniable flow and groove to what he did, and that was always there. In terms of what he was saying, I don't think he was that worried about it in the *Blue Slide Park* era. When we got to *Macadelic*, that was the starkest contrast. Now he's pushing himself lyrically, he's trying to take people somewhere. He's trying to make more of a story with words.

BENJY GRINBERG: I never told him no. Ever. I would play devil's advocate, so to speak. I would give him all the possible outcomes I could imagine from making a move, no matter what it was. That's what I did with *Macadelic*. To me, in any of my relationships with any of my artists, the artist always has the final say. I just feel a need to, at least, tell them the positive and negative outcomes I perceive of their decisions ahead of time. It's never to tell them what to do; it's more so to lay it all out for them.

BIG JERM: Before [*Macadelic*], it was happier stuff. *The High Life, K.I.D.S., Blue Slide Park*. I think the reviews for the album changed his perspective. He had all that stuff before, he was thinking about those things, and he felt he wanted to go a little deeper. It was almost like he got called out by the critics. It was surprising to people, but you could see it coming if you were paying attention.

BENJY GRINBERG: His intentions are in his music. I think he wanted to show a deeper side of himself, let people in a little bit to the darker side of the stuff he was experiencing. It was a reaction to the critics of *Blue Slide Park*: "Oh! He's a frat rapper." It was a little bit: "Let me show you who I *really* am." That was part of it.

QUENTIN CUFF: He had relationship issues, and I think it was a perfect blend of that, experimenting with drugs for the first time, and yes, the reviews. Mostly, he got all the review stuff out on songs like "Loud" and "Desperado." He got that out of the way and when you really dive into it, it's him sharpening his lyrical sword and gearing up for big opuses like *Faces*. It's crazy to say, but *Macadelic* was still just the beginning of something. You had such great titles and concepts. The track with Cam'ron ["Ignorant"] was fucking awesome. There's so much of, "Okay, we're out in LA, promoting old music. We've been going for so long." This is Mac [saying], "We killed it after *Blue Slide Park*." People were starting to make fun, so let's go back to making those bangers that Mac got famous for, but with a darker tone.

MAC MILLER ASKS "THE QUESTION," I ANSWER

Dear Mac,

I thought today we could talk to each other. You spend so much of your music talking to us, and we spend so much time as fans talking through you, but rarely do we sit down and have a discourse. Not for any one reason, of course. Your music lends itself to discussion and conversation. You're so comforting; it's easy as ever to sit back and take your word for things. Your lessons are boundless, and every album relisten is another opportunity to learn something about ourselves. I'm reasonably chatty, so let's talk.

I want to go back to 2012, to *Macadelic* and more carefree times. This was the start of your second creative renaissance. Your heart was in a new creative mode. It was a departure. There were nerves, but you were sure. And you were right. It was a beautiful statement piece, and it remains a staple Mac Miller project.

On *Macadelic*, you're mature. Part of that comes from your willingness to ask questions and patiently wait for answers. You grew into a skilled scavenger, ducking into the crawl spaces of anxious thoughts and pulling out whatever you could find as glimmers of hope and truth. It was amazing to witness. It was truly *Macadelic*. But on "The Question," you sound disarmed and concerned, vexed and shaken. The hook ("What am I doing here?") rings throughout my days whenever I am overburdened by life.

I figured we could go over some lines, and I could answer your questions for you. You always made fans feel like you were on their team.

> "Sometimes I wonder who the fuck I am / So I've been lookin' in the mirror and it still don't make no sense / I'm askin' what am I supposed to do? / I've done so much in my short lifetime, but I haven't done shit"
>
> —*"The Question"*

Shit, Mac, me too. I don't think we're ever meant to know who we are, if it makes you feel any better. What I learn from your music is that growth is an endless thing. We are just always approaching a goal, and though we never quite reach it to our satisfaction, there is always the chance to improve. We have agency over our lives. That's something you've been teaching us since *K.I.D.S.*: We have the power to make ourselves into whatever we wish to be.

"I wonder why I sip this devil juice," you ask a few bars in. There's no easy way to say this, but I am in no position to answer that question. I know why *I* drink while I listen to your music. *Faces* was the darkest time of my life. I refused to see the sun or turn on a light. I drank to make myself sick, to feel something, and when I didn't die by "Grand Finale," I walked away from *Faces* another day stronger. Not my proudest moment, but to go back to your question: I think you may have been seeking something else. I know I was. That's another lesson I draw from your work: how to look at myself, even when I don't want to.

The ethos, the moral, of "The Question" is to turn something difficult into something useful. We hear your struggle on the track, but we aren't so depressed. The struggle is portrayed as a necessary facet of life and nothing more, which is another lesson from your catalog. For every overwhelmed album, there is a sunny counterpart. You were always working at balance on the largest of scales. You saw your pain for what it was and turned it into masterworks in healing through love and sobriety. You took responsibility for yourself throughout your career. From "The Question" on, you became ever more capable of generating your own happiness, and even when you stumbled, you were able to look at yourself and become a new man. It's all there in the music.

Now, for the hook, and the real "Question" of the song: "What am I doing here?" Fuck, I wish I knew. I wish I could answer this for myself. But, for the record, it seems obvious to me that you were here to touch lives. Not just to make music, but to impact the lives of everyone who listens, and everyone you've worked with. Every week I get new emails about how touched people are by your work and how much each bar meant. I wonder if you ever knew the impact you were having on people the world over. I hope you did.

That's what you were doing here, rapping and singing your way to official Man of the People status. As for me? I'm just trying my best because I think that's all we can do. The goal for each new day should be doing one small thing to make it better than the last. There's a lot of hope strewn across your work. For as existential and wounded as you sound while fighting through growing pains, we always make it to the next chapter. There is a *GO:OD AM* for every *Faces*.

Mac, your music is that of hope and answered questions. You did the hard work of addressing all of your fears and becoming a man we're all very proud of. The work is a triumph of creativity and knowing the self. It is a lesson in pursuing what hurts you until you are bigger than your pain; until you can gather emotional distance and best your pain. You took risks, shook uncertainty, and it worked, Mac. It always worked. You knew, consciously or not, precisely what you were doing here. And you did it so well. Thank you.

BIG JERM: The beat for "Loud," I probably made it the same month that *Blue Slide Park* came out. Unofficially, he started working on it immediately. I don't know if it was planned out that it was *Macadelic* at that point, but I made it with Sayez on November 22, 2011 at the old ID Labs. That was the first one. I know people say this all the time, but we probably made that beat in ten or fifteen minutes. I might have sent it to Mac that same day, and he sent something back quickly. That's how it goes. It's always those ones you don't think a whole lot about.

"Vitamins" I made on an airplane, coming back from LA. This was when he started traveling more, so a lot of this was stuff I sent to him. "Vitamins" he did in Pittsburgh with me. I feel like most of it was done before 2012. "Vitamins" [is] a Stereolab sample. I pitched it down and chopped it up. The flight from LA to Pittsburgh is five hours, so that's what I did the whole time. Sometimes things feel like they're meant to be. E. added stuff to "Vitamins" too. I was still in that realm with [Mac] where there wasn't a whole lot of thought; we're just gonna do this because it felt right.

QUENTIN CUFF: First, there's Josh Berg, who recorded a lot of songs on *Macadelic*. We came out to record in LA for a long period of time, right before we had started living in LA and filming the show. There's this period of time, Mac rented a house for a month—me, him, and Jimmy. We started going to studios [in LA] for the first time, where they make cookies and they have a runner. We hadn't been recording songs anywhere other than ID Labs and the tour bus. *Macadelic* started there.

E. DAN: A lot of *Macadelic* came together with Josh Berg, most of the important bits. I do remember when Mac was in Pittsburgh, we did the "Desperado" track. That's my earliest memory of working on that project. It was similar to the "Knock Knock" story, except we were searching for samples, and I found this sample. We just [put] that joint together, and all the ones he did with us, he did at the old spot. It wasn't 'til he went to New York that he did all the crazy shit with the skits and everything like that. At the time, I don't remember being aware of what he was working on. I didn't know if he was doing another album, mixtape, [or if] we were just working on songs.

Josh is my fucking hero as far as engineers and people go. A lot of *Macadelic*, to me, was Josh's influence. Not the songs so much, but the layout of things. He just did so much to expand Mac's horizons. Jerm and I, being producers, we had a lot of focus on the tracks we were making for the songs in general, whereas Josh, solely being an engineer, put a lot of focus on doing intricate edits on a part of the beat, or doing this weird arrangement with background vocals no one would've thought of. He was experimental in that way and also in a place in life where he could go deep into things with Mac. Having worked with Josh so much after that, I see what he gave to that whole process. He was key to expanding the arrangement side of things and the experimental vibe and feel to things.

Josh Berg (recording and mix engineer, producer): I went to do a session for [my friend], and we got into the studio, and it was a complete wreck. The guy was like, "Oh, Mac Miller was here!" I was like, "I know who that guy is!" The very next night, I got a call from the studio: "Do you wanna do a session with Mac Miller?" We just really hit it off. It was pretty straightforward—he would record the song, go outside, and I would've styled it out. He walked out the door and was like, "I'm happy with my engineers, but I really like you! I wanna work with you." Then, I promptly never heard from him again, which is fairly typical in the studio environment. Then he hit me back and he explained the concept of *Macadelic* to me. "I'mma be back out in LA, trying to finish this mixtape, you know?" We scheduled these sessions—and I was on sessions all day, so he would come in at night. I would do 10:00 [p.m.] to 10:00 [a.m.] with him and sleep in my car for two hours. It was amazing. That's where I really learned this guy's really awesome.

QUENTIN CUFF: We had the session with Juicy J in LA. Legendary. He came in... He was trying to get a haircut for three or four hours, got it, then cut his verse. That song ["Lucky Ass Bitch"] was a straight smash. It's a cult classic.

People like Iman Omari, who had multiple appearances on *Macadelic*, were people through groups like OverDoz—listening to people like Dom Kennedy—that's where the LA influence comes from. Sir Michael Rocks moved to LA from Chicago. That's how you get an "Aliens Fighting Robots." [Producer] Brandun DeShay, he's a person that [Rocks] worked with. Tyler, The Creator, we reached out to him. The heavy hitters, like "Thoughts from a Balcony," that's Sap. A lot of people don't know that's a part of Mac and Sap's history together. They didn't just do "Donald Trump."

SAP: We started on *Best Day Ever*, and I seen a change when he was working on *Macadelic*. We had did "Thoughts from a Balcony" and I remember him emailing me that and hearing a few things off *Macadelic*... I remember a shift in him. He did songs with Juicy J, even Wayne. He was really on some other shit when he started recording that. He was recording songs for *Watching Movies* as well. He started really incorporating instruments; he started working with Thundercat a lot. On the music level, he started to go crazy. His production started changing. He wanted beats that were a little darker, a little more out there than the super bright beats that you heard on *K.I.D.S.*

QUENTIN CUFF: I was definitely surprised, but I felt like it was due. With *Blue Slide Park*, it was like, "Okay, I really like what you and E. are doing," but the leap he made between *Blue Slide Park* and *Macadelic* was... *Blue Slide Park* was an attempt to give people the eventual music he would make, by trying to make more well-rounded music. It's also the mixtape versus album mentality. When Mac is on his mixtape shit, he gets way looser. He loosened up more when he didn't have any restrictions, and that's what the mixtape game gave him and allowed him to do.

BENJY GRINBERG: If he had kept on the path of *Blue Slide Park*, and whatever the evolution of that would have been without the darker turn, would he have been an even bigger, more-pop artist? I don't think it would've been better. He went where he went, and that's where he was meant to go. He became a bigger, more iconic artist by showing all of his true sides.

E. DAN: He thought every song he was making was the best song he ever made. It's a typical thing for any musician who cares about their craft. Part of that energy is what made him so fun to work with because you'd be working on a song and not think much of it. Then his energy would come across as, "Oh, my god! This is incredible!" That would carry over to you, and you would start to feel the same. It's hard to say whether he thought that particular project was gonna be better than anything he'd done, or more meaningful, because he felt that way with everything he did.

QUENTIN CUFF: I personally made the call to [Jonny] Shipes to put Joey Bada$$ on "America." Casey Veggies, we already went on tour with. When I heard [Mac and Casey] do that song, I was like, "I wanna get Joey on this too." I felt like Joey was bringing that new energy. The video for that, we were in New York and wanted to shoot a video. Who can we get? ILLROOTS literally put together a legendary video. I can't take much credit past the fact that I hit up Mike Waxx and he talked to Mike Carson. Those dudes went on to be legends in their own crafts. Travis Scott makes a cameo in that video really early. The "America" video was an early moment of showing Mac could bring a bunch of people from all around the world together.

E. DAN: At one point, we were all at Paramount in LA. It was the [studio] Tupac used to use a lot. It was me, Josh, and Mac up there in that room, and I started playing the chords for "Clarity." I sorta had most of the beat structured, and then Ritz [Reynolds] came in. Ritz used to walk around with a briefcase full of percussion. So he pulled up to the session and busted open his briefcase full of tambourines, real shit, and just started adding little parts to things. He had his laptop with all these weird synths [and] goofy sounds, which he layered in there. That ended up becoming "Clarity." It was a fun musical moment.

JOSH BERG: That's where I knew there was something important here. That's where he had my heart, when he said *"Love activist."* If this kid is hiding this type of love and these ideas in the rap, his whole generation is gonna grow up with these ideas. If he's saying it and it's resonating, that's this glorious thing for the future. Now I talk to people like you and I bump into people, and it's really amazing to see how true that was. You certainly couldn't ascribe it all to, "Oh, he put that line in a song," but the fact he did put that line in the song and the openness of that . . . I've just been, like, "This is a deeper, spiritual mission." That's when I knew, as simple as it is, he's got something to say. We're saying something here. That's also when I met E. and Jerm and Ritz Reynolds showed up with a suitcase full of tambourines.

QUENTIN CUFF: I always felt like that was a lean-type of simile or metaphor, but . . . I would say that I love that song, because he killed it as a songwriter. And that video, I love. That was his experimenting more and more. That "Clarity" video is similar to the era of shit from *Blue Slide Park* and him diving back into "This is what we do!" Him and Rex Arrow. He always had that good guy feeling to me. He was always that person that was a hero in a lot of aspects. For me, it was just another line. He's a person who moves with optimism and love 100 percent of the time.

E. DAN: It's one of the ones where when we did it, I thought: *That was cool and kinda weird* and didn't think too much of it. Listening back now, it's like, "Man, that was a really fucking cool song." I had such a great time putting it together. It was a good example of the lack of boundaries that there were with Mac, especially being in the rap world I've been in forever. It's always fun to be in a session with *him,* and feel like anything we wanted to do was fair game. "Clarity" is one of those songs. If I made that beat for any other rapper I worked with, they'd be like, "What the fuck is this?" It would've been too weird.

QUENTIN CUFF: "Who am I?" "Why am I here?" It opened up the realm he started to open up. To get a feature from Lil Wayne, who you look at as a legend, to hop on *that* song? For [Wayne] to wanna hop on this song, for an album cut we don't even shoot a video for? That, to me, is deep.

JOSH BERG: When he did "The Question," that was amazing. When he came out of the booth, he was like, "I think this is the best song I ever made." I was like, "Yeah, that's pretty awesome." Then he said, "I think I'm gonna get Lil Wayne on it." At the time, Lil Wayne was on eight of the top ten songs on the radio, and every single person in the studio that did a good song was like, "Let's put Lil Wayne on it." But Mac was just right. I knew he was right, that this would be a vibe Lil Wayne would dig enough to do a deep cut on a younger artist's mixtape. I remember when it came out, it was: "Holy shit, there's the Lil Wayne verse!" At the time, I was smoking Winston cigarettes and Lil Wayne mentioned Winstons in the verse. Crazy!

E. DAN: I remember him being incredibly excited about the Wayne verse. Wally West had already made that beat, but [Mac] had me add some parts to it. I love the last song on there ["Fuck 'Em All"]. He got sued for it. Jerm made the bones of that beat, and we added stuff on it, but there was a sample of some dudes who had some sort of Pittsburgh connection. They weren't well-known, and I'm not sure how Jerm and Mac found the sample. Those dudes ended up suing. It was also after Lord Finesse sued [over "Kool Aid & Frozen Pizza"]. They were real assholes about it too. Great song. I loved that song. I felt like he was starting to come into his own style of layering backgrounds. ["Fuck 'Em All"] was a song where I remember really digging the way he put all the vocal stacks together, and this huge sound he came up with for the chorus. Same thing with "The Question." The way he approached the verses on there, melodically, the way he sung-rapped it and stacked them up. I thought that was such a cool approach. It was just a totally unexpected way of going about the verses on that song.

JOSH BERG: On the song "1 Threw 8," he did this great song, and we didn't really have a chorus. He was like, "Oh, I got it," and went in there and counted to eight. He left and I don't know what inspired me to do so, but I recorded some ice in a glass around that part. I sent it to him, and he loved it. That was [when] I knew I wanted to work with him because he's gonna go and try and do ridiculous stuff.

BENJY GRINBERG: *Macadelic* turned into a whole tour and a whole period for him. To me, I was just making sure it all went well. As much as I would hear the songs and be with him on tour, I don't think I could take a step back and appreciate it for what it was because we were so busy. I was concerned about other things. I was just making sure he was okay. It wasn't until years later, after he left Rostrum in 2014, that I could then take a step back and appreciate some of the albums I hadn't fully appreciated at the time. *Macadelic* quickly went to the top.

MARC-ANDRÉ LAUZON (Mac Miller Memoir Twitter co-founder): I skipped class for the release of *Macadelic*. The anticipation was killing me. Always refreshing DatPiff to see if it had finally been posted. As soon as it did, me and two of my friends sat in silence throughout the project. I absolutely loved it. The first aspect I noticed about this project was how The Beatles had a huge influence on Mac when he put together *Macadelic*. The themes of love, lust, depression, drug abuse made this project extremely personal. I think that's the reason I loved it so much. Through his music, Malcolm was trying to tell us his life story. The songs "Clarity," "Thoughts from a Balcony," and "Angels" are still in my top ten of Mac Miller songs.

E. DAN: It definitely changed the landscape for him. And it made a lot of people sit up and say, "Oh, okay!" Then you think about the people that were on there ... The Kendrick verse. Now, I sort of kick myself [for] not spending more time mixing the Kendrick verse. That shit was so last minute when we got it, I was like, "Okay! Sounds fine, we gotta finish." Now, I listen to it, and I'm like, "Fuck!" That's the nerdy shit that keeps me up at night. It's a real challenge to not pick apart everything in my mind. Albums I've worked on, it takes years to be able to go back and listen to them with any sort of objectivity and to get any sort of enjoyment out of them.

QUENTIN CUFF: It's hard to say which song defines [*Macadelic*], but the one with Kendrick ["Fight the Feeling"] ... A precursor Kendrick, before *good kid, m.A.A.d city*, who goes on to be one of the greatest artists of our time ... I think that time is really special. More than anything, for that time, that "America" video and connecting with people like Wayne and Kendrick, that's the moment. That's his most star-studded project. He became a more insular artist in the long run. His eventual goal wasn't to become this big orchestrator of records to get everybody on. His eventual goal was to be the best artist he could be. It's just him and the mic and his computer, making the beat. Or just him and a guitar, he could do that.

E. DAN: I think [*Macadelic*] stands up as important [as much as] any project if not more, just because of what a break it was from anything he had done before it.

BENJY GRINBERG: Going from some of the more overtly positive, everything's gonna be alright, thumbs up ... There were always little drug references and other things in there that give you a hint of it, but nothing like what came with *Macadelic*. That was the watershed album, which then led to a much deeper and more honest Mac.

JOSH BERG: For him, he's just a driven guy! He had worked so hard to do the rap thing. You're working so hard to put one foot in front of the other, sometimes you don't realize where you get to. Once he got the

No. 1 record—I know later he talked more about it in the *Faces* era—
he was turning into Mac Miller, and he needed to turn Mac Miller
more into him, if that makes any sense. It was like, "Okay, I've got my
respect and my power, I can do that now." To me, it's the start of something beautiful in my life with him. I look back at me doing those
sessions. I went around the world with him because of those sessions.
Everything always points back to that. All the people I encountered,
all the professional and personal growth and all the memories, all the
good times and negatives, all come from that.

QUENTIN CUFF: *Macadelic* is the merger between the *Best Day Ever* and
K.I.D.S. world, and the *Faces* underworld. People were looking at it
like, "This guy's falling off . . . He's doing drugs; his music is shit now."
There were people that were hating on him as he was growing as an
artist. *Macadelic* was him fighting back at the people that couldn't
appreciate his growth. At the same time, it was a stepping stone to
that off-kilter world that him and Josh Berg really built as they were
recording *Faces*.

HOW MAC MADE THE
HOLIDAYS TOLERABLE

Parsing familial love is tricky. Being gay, Russian, and Jewish during the holidays is even trickier. I often describe our holiday season as a grand party everyone has been invited to except me, a party that I am forced to watch through an ornate window out in the cold. Melodramatic, sure, but the winter pulls the drama out of me. Being first generation American, my family did not *do* Thanksgiving. Being Jewish, we did not *do* Christmas. Being gay, I did not get to *do* cute holiday bonding with my partners. Mostly, I listened to music while the entertainment industry I would otherwise escape into shut down for two weeks.

The holidays are a time of confrontation. I am forced to confront how lonely and removed I feel from American culture, from my own culture, and from my family. Our closeness only extends as far as the lies about my sexuality will take me. It's unique torture: being bombarded with images of familial love and warm feelings when you have none of your own. "'Tis the season" becomes an interrogation: What's wrong with you that you do not have this Hallmark thing?

For a long time, I blamed myself for feeling so slighted and empty during the giving season, but there are only so many compromises a person can make before realizing they have nothing left to offer to satisfy the other party. Example: in my family, there is one holiday that we *do*, and that is New Year's Eve. There's a tree and Grandpa Frost, the Ice Wizard. It's a trip; one long black-tie party to toast the upcoming year. I make an appearance alone because it is the thoughtful thing to do. It would spoil our holidays to bring my partner.

These parties start at ten and go until five or six in the morning. They're catered with decadent and heavy Russian foods, and between each rich course, I stow away in another room with a portable speaker to make my own New Year's Eve fun. Anyone gay or otherwise wounded will tell you that the only way to survive the holidays, and the winter in general, is to find your chosen family and hold on tight. The thing about chosen family, though, is that they have their own families to attend to.

Mac Miller was my date to the New Year's Eve bash. You don't know bliss until you're ever-so-intoxicated and dancing to "When in Rome" in ill-fitting high heels while the rest of the party occurs out of earshot. You simply do not know bliss until the feeling of Otherness and isolation becomes insular and comfortable, making that loneliness expansive as opposed to oppressive. Ballistic live renditions of "Watching Movies" and "S.D.S." lifted my silenced spirit and barreled it into a warped cabaret. Mac Miller's magnetism made me believe in fresh starts and new beginnings. If you've never gotten drunk out of self-pity and screamed along to "Insomniak," I highly recommend it.

Before arriving at New Year's Eve, there is the onset of winter to contend with. The lowest of my lows have been well-cataloged, suicidal ideation being chief among the anguish of the season. Somewhere between the darkness and the endless Othering, the weight of mental illness really gets to a girl. It's a unique and sometimes self-imposed misery: lying on the cold floor in the effacing darkness and listening to records while wondering why everyone other than me seems to have somewhere to be.

I found my place within Mac's music. That weight on my shoulders was not so much lifted as it was validated. At the height of one of my many panic attacks, it felt as if someone had poured cement down my lungs, but there was something urging about his music, something within his transparent arrangement on *Macadelic*, that encouraged me to believe in my next breath. Drawing air into my lungs went from unnatural to a labor of love, and *Macadelic* let me love myself to my next breath.

The tape is artful, wintry, and stoic. "Fight the Feeling" has the hollow rattle of Christmas bells heard from a distance, and a somber patter befitting the season. The brightness of otherwise thick synth chords plays like the sun glaring off packed snow. There's a stark and porcelain quality to *Macadelic*, as if the music were somehow bleached before being packaged. "Fight the Feeling" is the most sonically washed-out track—Mac and Kendrick calling in from another planet, with their ties to Earth disintegrating. Really, the track sounds like waking up shivering and disheartened on another winter morning, looking out the window, and having your whole person strain to find beauty in that moment. But you find it; you do.

Where East Coast snow storms erase all notion of time, "The Mourning After" delivers a special type of myopic suffering. Mac lets his mind spool down the tip of a needle. His execution is fine and focused, and the release is just as satisfying. The track is bleak and high-strung, especially on the wiry hook, much like the silent battering of endless snow, through to the release in the final four seconds where a woman's voice takes over: "Don't cry, it's okay, it'll all be over soon." Few artists have deployed women as ushers of reason and stability with as much tact as Miller, who has had a woman's voice lead off damn near every project since 2012.

Perhaps the most underappreciated element comes on "1 Threw 8," where the sound of ice cubes clinking in a glass of dark liquor fills the echo left on the hook. It makes for a contemplative touch, conjuring thoughts of Old New York and the facade of class. Highlighting the impermanence of ice in a warm liquid, emphasizes fragility. That underlying fatality is the brilliant dress for a song pondering the afterlife. An image of scotch on the rocks is so forceful and rooted, yet "1 Threw 8" is about constant displacement, the ice a gentle reminder that security tied to space is a myth. I am left understanding I am exactly where I am meant to be.

The holidays have the uncanny ability to exaggerate the feeling of existing in the margins while somehow making it feel as if the margins are yelling in your face. At every turn, the message seems to be: you are unfit and unqualified for the joy so many others just seem to *get* as if it were nothing. It's enough to make you bitter, but we grow past that in due time. During the most desolate time of the year, finding my place in Mac Miller's music gave me just enough footing and solace to find my own joy and make it to spring. His music functions collectively as a promise that we can *all* make it to spring.

SUPREME FORESHADOWING

It's early 2012, and you're still spinning *Blue Slide Park*. You love the loose flows and the ease with which Mac spits. You love his breezy stories and the way he brings his youth to life on wax. You love his creativity and his accessibility. You're a Mac Miller fan, finding new things to enjoy in each listen. And then, in March, Mac drops *Macadelic*—a total left turn. With the release of the tape, Mac closes the door on his first creative renaissance and begins his second. He takes your hand and escorts you from the streets of Pittsburgh to the corners of his mind.

Macadelic quickly becomes your favorite Mac project. You're arrested by its sudden candor, its drama. In the prolific years following, as Malcolm releases countless new projects, you realize *Macadelic* was not a left turn at all. It was a natural step forward. Looking back, you start to hear *Macadelic* in everything from *Watching Movies with the Sound Off* to *Swimming*. Over time, it becomes more than a beloved mixtape; it becomes a looking glass.

Macadelic is an oracle. It sees and speaks of the future. Each song telegraphs a future song and each project that follows has roots here. There's a symbiosis to the work. The craft choices are reflected and refined across Mac's discography, from opening with a woman speaking (as on *The Divine Feminine*) to closing out the album as an escape artist (as on *Swimming* and *GO:OD AM*). From the tracks loosely referencing drugs like "Vitamins" informing the whole of 2014's *Faces* to romantic cuts like "Clarity" informing everything from 2013's "Objects in the Mirror" to all of *The Divine Feminine*, *Macadelic* is rife with foreshadowing.

One year removed, *Watching Movies with the Sound Off* borrows tones and tropes galore from the mixtape. Their soundscapes are cousins. The broody nature of *Watching Movies* comes directly from the thoughtful content or trippy sonics of "Thoughts from a Balcony," "Fight the Feeling," "The Mourning After"—songs reflected on "I Am Who Am," "I'm Not Real," and "Gees," respectively. Play these tracks in succession, and you'll hear the threads being established. The albums sound like companion projects. *Macadelic* captures Malcolm's playful spirit (as on "Lucky Ass Bitch" and "Ignorant") while *Watching Movies* takes a more tender ("Youforia") and serious ("REMember") approach to Mac's excavating songwriting.

Even so, these minute details almost appear superfluous when we zoom out and think on the major themes of both records. What is *Watching Movies* about if not self-exploration and the pursuit of emotional forms? What is the album about, if not reckoning with the self to the best of a young Mac Miller's ability, all while constructing a sonic world that reflects his psyche? This construction begins on *Macadelic*, where Malcolm got ever more focused with his pen. Up until *Macadelic*, Mac was best known for leading us around his life, just skimming the surface. *Macadelic* was the first time he truly dove into himself. The image of sinking deeper and deeper, then swimming toward the surface, is one sustained across the remainder of his work.

With that in mind, the relationship between the leap of *Macadelic* and the drowning sensation of *Faces* appears obvious. All the curious drug talk—"I'm so high, won't you think about that, babe / On some other shit that tend to make me act crazy" from "Aliens Fighting Robots"—gets graver and more tangible on *Faces*. Every corner of *Faces* is informed by Mac saying, "Cocaine ether creates a strange creature" during "Here We Go." Before tumbling down *Faces*' twenty-four-track rabbit hole of drugs and emotional carnage, though, Mac had to discuss the way drugs impacted his mental state on *Macadelic*.

Before we could get Mac prodding at the notion of mortality on *Faces*, we had to have him ask "The Question" across six minutes, with a Lil Wayne feature for good measure. "Sometimes I wonder who the fuck I am / So I've been lookin' in the mirror and it still don't make no sense," Mac raps to open the first verse. The act of looking in the mirror to discover yourself is the ethos of Mac's career following *Macadelic*. In *Faces*, we get the moment you look in the mirror and do not like what you see. And in the context of *Faces*, we get the moment you decide you're not going to do shit about it. You're going to sink down to your lowest, and that's when you're going to light one up with all your demons. They'll become your companions, as Mac telegraphs on "Fight the Feeling."

Thankfully, 2015 arrives, delivering *GO:OD AM*—the album where Malcolm decides to take action. After the stumbling trip of *Faces*, *GO:OD AM* will go down as Mac's grand revival, one of the many times he saved his own life. The relationship between *GO:OD AM* and *Macadelic* is one of celebration. "Desperado," "Loud," and "Fuck 'Em All" mirror the wanton energy of *GO:OD AM*'s "Break the Law," "Cut the Check," and "When in Rome." While Mac's unique genre of celebration music goes all the way back to *Best Day Ever*, it's on *Macadelic* where Malcolm learns to rage and let off steam. This translates to the hard-nosed raps of *GO:OD AM*, which goes down as Mac's most solid and traditional rap album.

Macadelic and *GO:OD AM* also have craft in common. Both albums have necessary chips on their proverbial shoulders. After the backlash *Blue Slide Park* faced, Mac had to prove he had the rap chops to back up his sales figures and fame. He had to prove he had it in him to make music ranging beyond Big L impressions and a bevy of punchlines. *Macadelic* was his attempt to showcase both his growth and his growth potential. *Macadelic* was his proof of concept and his proof of purpose. In tandem, *GO:OD AM* was Mac's final hurrah in terms of making pure rap records. The album would cap off his second creative renaissance and cement him as one of the most sparkling rappers of his generation. Taken together, the projects complete a perfect circle of Mac Miller's budding artistry.

Then we have 2016 and Mac Miller's third and final creative renaissance. Tipped off by the release of the funky, singing-forward, and love-centric *The Divine Feminine*, this era caught many unsuspecting fans by surprise; however, when we look back on *Macadelic*, we see the writing was not on the wall, but suspended in front of our faces as a neon sign. Though cloudier than the shiny *TDF*, the three-song stretch of "Angel," "Sunlight," and "Clarity" lay the groundwork for Mac's softer side to shine four years later. The thesis of these songs and other choice moments on *Macadelic*—the use of love and drugs interchangeably as salves—mirrors every moment on *TDF*.

"She can get me high when I'm feelin' low" on "Angel" is an infantile version of "yeah, are you my soulmate? / My angel, what do you want with me? / Too high, slow pace / My eyes closed, your body all I see" on "Soulmate." The lyrics "I know I love you I ain't tryna let those words slip / Pure bliss, I knew that we would stay together, we in cursive / Infatuation, when every single move you make is fascinatin'" from "Clarity" sounds eerily similar to "I was a soldier, now I'm coming home / The war is over / Kick down the door, I'll hold ya / Bend ya, never break ya" on "Skin."

Lyrical overlap is nothing new for Malcolm, who masters the art of webbing on *GO:OD AM*. Even so, seeing lines stitch together perfectly several years apart is a treat. For the fans who listen closely, each subsequent Mac Miller project feels like a reward. All of which brings us to Mac's final album. On *Swimming*, we get the most reflective and matured version of Malcolm. We get the most heavenly arrangements and the most introspective and generous writing. All of this stems from *Macadelic* deep cuts, like "1 Threw 8" and "The Mourning After," which taught Malcolm it was okay to open himself up for all to see.

Take the hook of "The Mourning After": "Somethin' 'bout the pain makes me want more / Done a lotta drugs, never felt like this before / I hope one day it all makes sense / It'll all make sense." In 2012, Mac had more questions than answers, but his desire to know himself permeated his music. By 2018's *Swimming*, Mac finally had answers.

He understood the notion of "Self Care," and he'd found his "Wings." He used "Ladders" to showcase the ways in which he was climbing toward better days. If *GO:OD AM* was about survival, *Swimming* was about growing comfortable with yourself. Said comfort, of course, comes from the great discomfort ("The Question") of *Macadelic*.

Each album thoughtfully waterfalls into the next. The connections shown here are but a handful drawn between Mac's work. Everything was everything for Malcolm, but *Macadelic* was the start of a majority of his intra-album conversations. If there's a standout moment for you on any one of Mac's post-2012 releases, there's a good chance *Macadelic* had something to do with it. The mixtape should go down as more than Mac's pivot from pop rap. It should go down as Mac's pivot inward, outward, and upward. The tape allowed Malcom to explore himself, from project to project, with us alongside him, for all time.

2013

WATCHING MOVIES
WITH THE SOUND OFF

"You gotta pretend that no one listens. You gotta pretend that you're just making music for yourself, because when you do something for yourself and only for yourself and it translates to everybody else, that's like what I think true genius takes its form."

—MAC MILLER[6]

6.   Mac Miller, "Mac Miller - Interview!" interview by OFIVE, *OFIVE TV,* June 21, 2013, https://www.youtube.com/watch?v=6dslOfbKl4g.

LEARNING LIFE IS PRECIOUS THROUGH "I AM WHO AM"

*"I waste away in a room spitting these raps / Yahweh
put the world in my hands, I'm giving it back"*

—"I Am Who Am"

I did not ask to be chosen. Neither did Mac Miller. The Jewish condition is one of pressure and high expectations. There is so much
working against me on the worth-scorecard drawn up by tradition.
Somewhere along the way, during my formative years, I arrived at the
conclusion that my life was a fluke. When the surgeons took out my
brain tumor at seventeen, I carried with me the sense that I wasn't
meant to survive. Cheating death, I reasoned, is why I felt so much
like a burden, so displaced and out of frame, abandoned by life itself.

I didn't cheat death. I'm meant to be alive, and I'm happy I lived,
but in the interim, I needed a pathway to finding meaning and to
making my life feel precious and necessary. This is where "I Am Who
Am" comes in. This song means the world to me; it's my favorite. In
five minutes, Mac Miller touches on a niche brand of neurosis, suicide, and growth that makes life worth living. "I Am Who Am" transforms the pressures of the Jewish condition into an imperative to live
for yourself. For that I am grateful.

The song is so effective because it is a conversation. If it feels like
Mac is speaking directly to you, that's because he opens with two lines
from Delusional Thomas, his despairing and anxious alter ego[7]: "I

---

7.   Mac Miller introduced Delusional Thomas as a side project in 2013, a more hor-
     ror-core style rapper who was deeply troubled.

think I'm getting sick / Being in this room like I was hidin' from something." At our lowest, we are Delusional Thomas. There is an immediate wintry air to this song with notes of isolation, denial, and spiritual confrontation mimicking the chilling quality of relentless snow. Mac Miller finds us when we are huddled and alone. "Look, I'm posing a question / How many been empty and holding aggression? / Close to depression / Open your eyes and just focus a second."

Mac hears us, and he has something to say. Thirty seconds in and the stage is set: a dimly lit room, an exposed wood table—just us and Malcolm. He's come to level with us, offering up his own confusion and manic tendencies as a basis of connection. He does not simply hear us; he knows at his core what it means to toil away at suffering and feel slighted by the results. Yet, he knows, too, that the work cannot stop simply because the work appears unappreciated.

> "Praise me I'd rather you not / Cause it's driving me crazy / The fact that you pay to make me into something I love / You come to the club searching for drugs / Drunk, fucking these sluts / God loves me, what if he does, what does it mean? / You're wasting away doing nothing, you're fronting / Why ain't you chasing your dreams?"

Everyone I've spoken to for *The Book of Mac* has stressed that Mac Miller was a regular person. He wasn't exactly suited for fame, but he was suited for music and building relationships with people on a massive scale. Sadly, one could not exist without the other, and the perils of fame prompt much of the first verse. We get shifting perspectives: Mac speaking to us, to Thomas, and to himself all at once. Then we get the invocation of the Jewish condition, worrying over what it means to be chosen and whether or not we are worthy. This is our first tie-in to the Yahweh refrain that gives "I Am Who Am" its spiritual body.

Bars about the dangers of money and a cold and lonely world usher us along to the moment Mac Miller transposes the negative energies of the first verse into a refusal and a pushing forward. "I waste away in a room spitting these raps / Yahweh put the world in my hands, I'm giving it back," he says assuredly. This is the two-piece that reset my thinking. For one, I identify with Mac's consuming creative process. Sublimation is my coping mechanism. My work is my center and the way I measure my self-worth. To be entirely immersed in something until I am rotting away in the name of the creative endeavor, that is the dream, the ultimate value statement.

"Yahweh put the world in my hands, I'm giving it back" is my humanity in a single sentence. The lyric is so multiple and procedural, the arc of my healing in one bar. We start with the Jewish condition, a perpetual state of striving to be enough, followed by refusal. Yahweh put the world in Mac's hands when he was chosen (and by the nature of fame, he is chosen in more ways than one) but he is not having it. He is rejecting being chosen.

For the whole of my struggle with being alive, I thought Yahweh had mistakenly taken a chance on me. I thought of my resignation from the world as a point of order because I had caught onto this grave error. Years went by of feeling incredible guilt every day just for *being*. I could only imagine myself as an obstruction to the lives of the people I cared for, all because my cards had been read wrong by some broader deity. I wrestled with the notion that it was not my fault I had lived, when clearly I should not have lived. How will I repent for this? How will I return the world, this thing that is not rightfully mine?

Instead of returning the world, I crafted my own. This is what "I Am Who Am" urges in the end. Niki Randa's hook plays as a well-timed directive to live: "It's a gift / Our, our time to be alive / No earthly vehicle / Can contain this drive." The drive is the very energy Mac harnesses to shake off the pressure and spin a life free of neurosis in order to create lasting art. We are speaking of life, and Randa's hook keeps the song alive.

After the ghost of her voice lifts, Mac returns to where the Yahweh refrain left us: resignation. Employing symbols of war and death, the writing suggests Mac Miller has given up, when in fact he has simply

123

changed the rules of the game. He steps back before stepping forward, ready to re-engage with the world on his terms. That is how we arrive at the second half of the song's heart.

> "Dealing with death like he work in the morgue, absorbing the souls / Forgotten, he lost his way / Staring down that barrel, thinking not today / Life's so precious, Lord knows that life is so precious / Fight to the death, 'til there's nobody left / You're holding your breath because you might get infected"

The "he" of the second verse is universal, much like the "you" of the first verse. This is a storytelling device, a conversation with Delusional Thomas. Think of the second verse as a Genesis myth, a tale of creation wherein we are all the creators of a life we deserve. Mac is making an example out of the enigmatic "he," to the point of urging us to be better to ourselves. This nameless figure is embroiled in despair but settles on the decision to live—at least for the moment. When Mac remarks on the precious quality of life and fighting to the death, we can understand that to mean that in order to make life precious, we must fight for the rest of our lives. It is not glamorous, but it is the necessity of caring for something sacred.

All of this leads us to the final invocation: "I waste away in this room spitting out raps / Yahweh put the world in my hands, I'm giving it back." Mac returns the world he is expected to be a part of, as he has found his life to be worthy simply because it is. He's ordinary, and the life he can summon suits him just fine. That is the lesson he bestows upon us. Our life is made precious by virtue of it being ours, and what we choose to do with that truth is infinite and empowering. And for those of us looking for more reasons to remain, Mac Miller reminds us that we will always make it to our next joy, however small it may seem, with a pitched-down and comical outro. There will always be one more laugh. Just like that, we've made it. We've lived.

BIG JERM: *Macadelic* opened his eyes to what he could do, and showed people what he could do. With *Watching Movies*, he was trying to follow that direction. He had a decent amount of production on there himself. I had co-production on a couple [songs]: "Matches," that was one I started with a sample. It was our project, we had like twenty-one tracks, and they just kept getting cut as he progressed. "Youforia" was definitely done on the tour bus for the Macadelic Tour. So it was old to me by the time the album came out. Most of these other [songs], he did in LA.

BENJY GRINBERG: *Watching Movies* took the longest to make of the records up to that time. There was a fast string of records between *Best Day Ever* and *Macadelic*. *Watching Movies* didn't come out for another year and some change from when *Macadelic* came out. There's a bunch of reasons for that. One, of course, is that he's touring and other things were taking up his time, [like] the TV show. There was a lot going on. Also, this album went through even more iterations than most Mac albums at that time. I have: "Watching Movies 3," "Watching Movies 4," "Watching Movies 5," "Watching Movies All," "Watching Movies Benjy," "Watching Movies Final," "Watching Movies Live," "Watching Movies Mac Most Recent Version," "Watching Movies Mac Most Recent Version 2," "Watching Movies Mac Most Recent Version 3," "Watching" . . . It just goes on and on.

E. DAN: It was the always-moving target of what songs are gonna be on the final cut. Like everything, there's a whole companion album sitting on a hard drive.

BIG JERM: On the Macadelic Tour, we were talking about doing a project together—just me and him. I even tweeted something, "Listening to *Macadelic* and watching *Robocop* on mute." I tweeted that before *Watching Movies* [on March 24, 2012]. Then we started working on a project together on the Macadelic Tour. He moved to LA right after that tour, in the spring, almost summer of 2012. That's when he got more into producing himself. He started working on a lot of stuff himself, but [the tweet] is kind of where the name came from. Over time, the project me and him had evolved into his project, and he had other producers on there.

E. Dan: They had started on tour, he and Jerm, and a lot of that was Mac picking samples for Jerm to chop up and flip into beats. After they got off tour, Mac got the bug to produce. It was this moving target, more so than it was on a per-song basis. It was the playlist evolving. There [were] a couple songs we went way in on. The one that stands out in my mind the most—we had some crazy number of versions to it—didn't even end up making the album.

Big Jerm: This is when he moved to LA; I was still in Pittsburgh. He just went straight from tour to LA—[he moved into] that first mansion that was on the TV show.

Quentin Cuff: ScHoolboy Q became a real homie. Ab-Soul, Vince Staples became a real-real friend. Him and Mac were doing the *Stolen Youth* project around the same time. Vince was one of the shadowy figures in the "Watching Movies" video. It was a time where we had a TV show going; Mac was a full-on celebrity. People probably look at that studio really fondly. That's how Mac was able to build his rapport with people. Tyler [The Creator] started fucking with Mac because all of Tyler's homies fucked with Mac. He came to grow in respect for Mac's musical acumen, and Mac was a big fan of Tyler. He was a big fan of Earl [Sweatshirt]. We were fans of our peers!

Big Jerm: We went to Guitar Center and got the studio setup started. I don't know when it went from our thing to a concept album. I think it was: I wasn't around and he started working with Josh [Berg] as an engineer, and he started adding songs [to *Watching Movies*] over the course of that year, and it changed from there.

E. Dan: The big thing with *Watching Movies* was the fact that this was the album where Mac decided he wanted to explore producing. That was post-tour. Whatever [he] and Jerm started on tour, sort of got abandoned for, "Wait, I wanna just produce this album." Everything I thought was gonna be the album, got pulled back at that point. Some of that stuff survived, but mostly it ended up going in this entirely different direction.

Chuck Inglish: When he first got really deep into making beats, is when he moved out to LA after we did a tour together. Mac just knew ... I'm not hella domesticated but my house and the things I do are really clean and tranquil. One of the best days I had was when Mac is like, "I'mma get you my credit card, and I want you to go to Bed Bath & Beyond and help me put my studio together." At that time, I'm thinking, "I would never do that shit; I wouldn't give nobody my credit card for nothing," but at that time he trusted me.

I came back with everything that you saw in that studio from that Mac Miller [and] ScHoolboy Q song ["Gees"] that we did. I will never forget helping him set it up. I don't like doing that shit, helping friends move. But it was about being with him while he took a step up. He comes off tour, buys a mansion, got a new car. I was just proud to be with him at that point, knowing that two years prior he was trying to figure out "Was this going to work?" Our early moments, that shit is still here like it was yesterday.

Syd (front woman, The Internet): Being in the studio, being at his house and kicking it with him ... I remember he had a birthday party one year, and his house was full of people, but he was in his pajamas still, from that morning in the studio. That's just what he wanted to do. Not like, "Oh, for my birthday I'mma make music." He was obsessed, and that was inspiring as well. He just wanted to make more, and more, and more. He wanted to work with everybody too. That's something that didn't really inspire me until recently. Since what happened and seeing everyone who reached out and the impact that he had on people when he worked with them was so inspiring. He had a lot of influence.

He had so many hidden talents too. I think a lot of people would've been really impressed watching him in the studio. He can run Pro Tools. He can kinda engineer himself. He's really good at guitar. He's really solid on the keys. Around the time I came around, he was making beats really heavy. I'd walk in and he'd be at the keyboard with loops going. A session with him could've meant anything. He just wanted to try everything, and why not? He was always, at least while I was around, always inspired to write something. I never saw him at a loss for words. He always had something on his mind that he could put out and express.

BENJY GRINBERG: This was during the period where he was holed up in his Studio City pool house. He was locked in that house 24/7. He was experimenting with a lot of different things. He was now working with Josh Berg. All of that coming together ... It made it this fully-realized version of where he had been heading for the last year or two. He was able to put it together, use some of his newfound relationships with Earl and other people, and get it all together in an album. It's an evolution, and he evolved past this and went into the records he did with Warner. The transition was *Faces*, which he made between his time at Rostrum and at Warner. [*Watching Movies*] was a strong stop on the way, where it felt like an artistic expression really coming to life.

It's all part of his evolution. I know I use that word a lot. I compare him to The Beatles a lot, in my own mind. You think of their discography, and how they went from these simple, pop, happy songs to this drug-infused, deeper space. All of that happened in six years for The Beatles. Their whole discography is just a number of years, and they evolved quickly. I think of Mac the same way. He goes from *K.I.D.S.* to *Watching Movies*—I often see them as parallel.

MAC MILLER WAS NO TRADITIONAL SUPERHERO

"Somebody do something / Yeah, yeah, yeah / Somebody move something"

—"S.D.S."

Mac Miller did not want to be a superhero. He became one anyway. First as the hero of big drinkers and partygoers everywhere, then as a hero for the emotionally cut up crowd, and, finally, as a hero to those who worked hard to feel better. Through it all, Mac Miller remained Malcolm. Remained enamored with music, creation, and collaboration. The superhero motif Mac employed throughout his work was subtle, but stood to represent his ultimate desire of "going down as a great one" without all the frills that come with hero status.

Mac tucked nuggets of truth into his music. Due to his increasing vulnerability, sometimes the most honest realizations were breadcrumbed from song to song for us to follow. In tracking the motif, we not only get a more holistic picture of Mac Miller, we also get the sense that no matter how much he changed, his love for the art was always on the upswing.

"Misogynistic with a twisted mind, I'm intertwined / My trigger finger itching, all I kill is time / Initial symptoms of schizophrenic behavior / The mind is like religion, can't agree on who's its savior / The newest flavor of superhero, I'm shooting lasers"

—"I Am Who Am"

There is much to be written about "I Am Who Am," one of Mac Miller's best songs. When we think of celebrity worship and aggrandizement, the things he is attempting to run from in his catalog, flashes of the first verse paint a sordid picture of his take on playing the hero: "Praise me I'd rather you not / Cause it's driving me crazy / The fact that you pay to make me into something I love." These bars signify that the weight of the praise, the avenues it can send a man down, can prove deadly. Celebrity, fame, money, access: all of these worked in concert to fuel Miller's terminal addiction. Recognizing the deadly combination, he is afraid.

Mac Miller was no traditional superhero. Let's call this a defense mechanism. In the final verse, Mac portrays himself as consorting with villains, killing civilians, and shrugging at the binary concept of good and evil. He can be monstrous to himself, he suggests. How, then, can we reasonably expect him to save us? The ask of "I Am Who Am" is to leave Mac Miller to his own devices, to enjoy the music and place the pressure, even when it's well-meaning, on someone else. With that, we are left with a troubling question: could this man really be a superhero? Perhaps more importantly, should he be?

Earlier, on "S.D.S.," Mac is all but invincible, risking his life because he can. His shift from the hero of the night to ordinary guy takes root. Though he's suited up as a superhero in the video, the hook and bridge, the absolution of his own responsibility, reveal something far more important: Mac Miller simply wants to be Mac Miller, make good art, and let the rest happen as it should.

Considering all of the press he did leading up to its release, this internal pivot makes perfect sense. In each[8] and every interview,[9] he

---

8. Mac Miller, "Mac Miller: When I started it was really hard to believe that I was serious," interview by Booska-P, *Booska-P.com*, June 22, 2013, https://www.youtube.com/watch?v=QfGgwevZHlE.

9. Mac Miller, "Mac Miller talks Pharell, Diss on album, Objects In The Mirror, Religion, Jay Electronica, Turtles," interview by Nick Huff Barili, August 12, 2013, https://www.youtube.com/watch?v=kRGgNYUHddA.

promises that *Watching Movies* is his most Malcolm project to date. "It's the most 'me,'" he told *OFIVE TV*.[10] "It's the most true to who I am as a person . . . ." No persona, mask, or cape required.

Yet, Mac is not so much shirking the responsibility of inspiring and saving people as he is opting to step into himself. If Mac Miller does any saving, he will do so as himself. E. Dan said it best: "Dealing with being famous and doing shows, I think that stuff gave him anxiety. I mean, he loved the attention on one hand, but on the other hand, he was such a down-to-earth person."

Corresponding with Mac Miller fans in the wake of his passing, I found that his grounded earthliness is exactly what drew them to Mac and allowed them to project their struggles and triumphs onto his music. The symbiosis of the artist-fan relationship comes from his dedication to humanity.

Lyrically, Mac's shifting relationship to fame began in 2012 and had changed completely by 2015's *GO:OD AM*. By the opening of "Perfect Circle / God Speed," Mac even imagines himself the villain:

> "I came for whoever is in charge / I suggest you go and get yourself a weapon and a guard . . . She say 'I thought you got sober' / And I say 'I wish you'd stop being a bitch / And get to minding your business' / Told me 'Money has changed you.'"

From there, Mac challenges the concept of heroes altogether. "Every devil don't got horns, every hero ain't got capes." Now, he is neither hero nor villain, just a man caught in the undertow.

The prophetic fears of *Watching Movies* come true, in more ways than one. As it stands, Mac Miller is no superhero, not only because he apparently does not feel he deserves to be one, but because he can save no one when he is in dire need of saving himself. Such is the

---

10. Mac Miller, "Mac Miller - Interview!" interview by OFIVE, *OFIVE TV,* June 21, 2013, https://www.youtube.com/watch?v=6dslOfbKl4g&t=501s.

function of love, and *The Divine Feminine*, in this context, is an album about how love saves us from ourselves time and time again. All of which brings us to his final album, *Swimming*, and the underbelly of "Jet Fuel."

> "Used to wanna be a superhero / Flyin' 'round with a cape catching bad guys / Now my head underwater / But I ain't in the shower and I ain't getting baptized"

The imagery is distinct and direct. We harken back to "S.D.S." and images of Mac as a hero, as on "I Am Who Am," but with admissions similar to those that permeate *GO:OD AM*: Mac Miller needs help. We go from admonishing fame to having fame portrayed as a killer. If Mac *were* a superhero, fame and access would be the villainous things. It reads as if succumbing to his vices not only caused him to lose the fight to the bad guys but also stripped him of his hero status.

Now the question of agency arrives. In 2013, Mac Miller made the choice to step away from the hero moniker to simply be himself and allow the music to do the talking, but by 2015 and into 2018, we saw that Mac could not be the hero. It is no longer a question of want, but an insight into recovery.

Mac Miller did not want to be a superhero, and yet his dream of "going down as a great one" is still coming true.

Karen Civil (digital media marketing strategist, friend): It was honestly incredible, because, you know, we all evolve. But him? I remember he bought the big house in LA and it was like "Woah! Really?" That was just the place you went to. His Thanksgiving dinners... That house and him had a way of bringing people together. I met so many people for the first time at that house. Through the years, he added the tattoos. Life changed. His outlook on certain things changed. The way he rapped was different, but change is good. And it was great for him! He just got mature.

E. Dan: A lot of [*Watching Movies*] was getting done at The Sanctuary, just continuing on with Josh, who turned into a supportive role to Mac producing all these tracks. I heard that stuff when I went out to LA for a period of time, just to hang with those guys. We made a lot of music at The Sanctuary. Some of it ended up on *Watching Movies*, and some of it ended up on the live album. The Future song and "Eggs Aisle" all came out of that same few weeks in LA. My biggest involvement overall was mixing the whole project. That was right when I moved into the new [ID Labs] studio. I remember being in the construction phase, but we had just moved all the gear over. I set up the gear in the room—no acoustic treatment. Josh Berg came in to assist me, and he and I just went to fucking town, not only mixing the album, but gathering blankets and whatever fuzzy material we could to stick on the walls, because none of the treatment was up. It was just this echoing room. I had just bought brand new speakers after having used one type for a decade. On a technical end, it was this giant fucking challenge. Not to mention, it being Mac's production... I couldn't just fall back on sounds that I knew worked. [Mac] was using a lot of stock sounds, and he didn't have his sound game together yet. That was a crazy, intense challenge for me and Josh—just on a technical level.

Quentin Cuff: It was the Josh Berg-Mac era, and it wasn't at its peak. Its peak would be *Faces*. You've done "Positive Mac" for so long, and

"Problematic Mac" people came to love. It took a while to get people with the money to be on board, but that was the beginning of the Josh Berg era. Mac and Josh were cooped up in the bottom studio [at Mac's house in LA]. They were cooking up very zany, otherworldly, weird creations. At the time, they really stood out, and people loved it. There's that album, *Balloonerism*, that was probably made before *Faces*. A lot of it was supposed to be *Faces*, and then *Balloonerism*'s its own thing. There's *so many* albums during that time that were in the thought process.

After *Macadelic*, there was this huge response to "Problematic Mac." Despite us starting out from a more kid perspective, he had grown really quickly. That's how you got something like *Macadelic*. With that being a mixtape, and him being like, "This is my *album*." He wanted to come with a refined version of [the *Macadelic* sound]. When you have people like Tyler, [the Creator]; Earl [Sweatshirt]; and The Alchemist, who we went record shopping with in Japan before they made "Red Dot Music" . . . So many things happened that accumulated into *Watching Movies*.

Him and Josh Berg were going into the studio, recording while watching a nature documentary on silent. It just stuck. For us, even in the moment, it became iconic.

BENJY GRINBERG: When I listened to some of the first ones, old versions of songs he eventually redid, and songs that didn't make it on there, [there] were still dope songs. One or two of which we added to *Live from Space*. "In the Morning," with Syd and Thundercat, was a contender for *Watching Movies* that didn't quite make it; [it] just didn't end up fitting.

SYD: Honestly, I don't remember the first time we worked together because we worked together so many times. I remember we got together because he came to the first concert we ever had. After, he was like, "Yo, you guys, come hang out at my house." We're like, "Oh, for sure!"

We started going to his house and hanging in the studio. A lot of the time, we would just watch him work. At the time, we were recording a lot of live instrumentation, and he was really interested in it, and he had the space and the money to accomplish some of the things that we kinda couldn't. He took us with him to Guitar Center in a twelve-passenger van. He was like, "What should I get?" He wanted to set up a live jam room. We helped him pick out a keyboard. He bought a new guitar. I think he already had a drum set. I think they might've got some microphones for it. He saw Matt [Martians] and I kinda fanning out over this plug-in called Omnisphere. It's a synth plug-in, and [Mac] saw me and Matt kinda staring at it. We couldn't really afford it, so we were just staring at it like, "When we get this, it's gon' be a wrap!" And he saw us talking about it, and when we got back to his house, he pulled it out of a bag like, "Here, I got this for you guys."

CHUCK INGLISH: He was just a selfless person. He cared about the people. Not just cared about them, but would be there for you and help you out. And not just give you something that could get you from point A to point B, but give you something that could get you around the whole alphabet. I think he had a producer's mentality, but not just musically. He liked to see things come together and get created. That's another thing that makes him so well-missed. There aren't too many people like that. He'll make sure that if you're around him and it ain't a family thing going down for you, he'll create that for you. If he could get you there, he'll get you there. There's a lot of camaraderie in rap. Everybody, when they're in LA, hanging around Alchemist for a bit, and then when Mac came out here, it was like two different versions of rap camp. You go over Mac's house and anybody could be there. I could pull up. It be ScHoolboy, it be Vince, it be Earl. There be people there by themselves. Everyone wanted to go to Mac's house because it was a safe place to create. It was the spot! He created those moments.

A lot of people found their sounds being around Mac. It was a real steel-sharpens-steel situation.

SYD: Without that tour, I don't know what we would've been doing at the time. We had nothing better to do, except stay at home and make some more music. That was one of the biggest learning experiences in our career, just being on that tour, learning how a well-oiled machine is supposed to run.

As an artist, I think a lot of us get pre-labeled as prima donnas, and he was just not! It showed us that you can do this and, especially for me, I had done a couple tours already, but as a DJ. Those tours made me think I hated touring. I've been on the other side of it. I've been on a tour that was not fun, for me at least, and the energy was not good. Touring with him kinda showed me that touring can be fun. You can create a family out here.

BONUS TRACKS, BONUS LESSONS

The beauty of Mac's discography was the immense growth from record to record and how it enabled us to grow alongside him. While *Watching Movies* proper was a beautiful look into the depth of Mac's mind as he understood it at the time, the bonus tracks gave us an even deeper appreciation of his endless Mac-ness. With three songs, Mac proves the importance of blowing off steam, of wrestling with mortality and legacy, of worldbuilding, and of the importance of using lightness to contrast the intensity of being alive.

From "Goosebumpz" and "O.K." to "Claymation," Mac creates an auxiliary world to the warped *Watching Movies* universe. In the space of the bonus tracks, he is unencumbered, trouncing his depressive episodes. The tracks feel weightless and impressive. Key lines give us the impression that Malcolm was as self-aware as ever, understanding his position as rap's vulnerable brother, but also that he knew his capacity was greater still. The brusque quality of these additional songs reminds us Mac Miller was more than his pain, and his art always extended beyond what hurt him to include the thrilling and the enchanting.

"Goosebumpz," is pouncing and boundless. He begins the track with violence, stunting, and discordance. It's a jarring swerve from the calm ecstasy of "Youforia." The close of *Watching Movies* is so grave and emotional; Mac uses the first bonus track to show us he does not need to live in this space. As the great poet Ocean Vuong once told me, there is no reason to live in the dark place once you've gotten all you needed out of its void.

There's an aggression to "Goosebumpz," which Mac appears to be using to blow off the steam collected across the meticulously crafted and emotionally direct *Watching Movies*. "'Bout to party with drugs though, turn it up, bitch, feel the bass," he spits with a playful ferocity. Mac sounds breathless and enthusiastic, relieved to simply be partying, not working at a higher concept or trying to open himself up further, further, further. He goes so far as to break his own character ("Throwin' money in your face, feelin' good, livin' great"), giving in to the materialism of hip-hop life. The shift in tone is Mac's way of escaping himself. As he does on the close of all his albums, Mac Miller transforms into a notable escape artist.

It's the hook where we find our first big lesson: "When I die, bet she fuck my hologram, though." Mac uses "Goosebumpz" to explore his anxieties in a safe environment. In this case, we are dealing with his fear of death and the encroaching conversation of legacy. By 2013, Mac had more projects to his name—and Easy Mac's name—than most rappers releasing their sophomore albums. It's possible Mac had been considering his legacy since 2009's *The High Life*. That said, *Watching Movies* was already so packed with tension, any more woes would break the album's back.

Mac is sly in his admissions, using sex to mask his concerns. If we glance quickly, we might consider the hook a breezy flex, but, upon further consideration, we understand Mac has real apprehension on his hands. Who will remember him, he wonders, beneath a veil of stunting. Though we know Mac Miller will live forever in our hearts, to hear him ask these questions so subtly is moving. Even at his lightest, Mac was angsty. This dichotomy is one of many reasons we felt so connected to him. His complexity humanized him. He was Mac Miller, but he sounded like us.

Complexity is at the core of "O.K." To understand this one, we can look at the end of the first verse where Mac astutely declares: "Album filled with all sad songs / But this the one that I can laugh on." Mac Miller's happiness was at the forefront of his friendships. Laughter was essential to his operation. Mac left everyone with the impression that smiling was an imperative part of living. After the emotional daggers of "I Am Who Am" and "REMember," it's important for Mac to take a moment to chuckle to himself.

The juxtaposition of this line against the pangs of the original album ensures Mac does not lose his mind. He is self-aware enough to know he's a wounded soul, but also that there is so much more to him than that. The fun and absurdity of "O.K." ("No respect, 'cause you wear a V-neck / I mean stress, pressure that could even make Keith sweat / I wish Narnia was on a GPS / I wish Rihanna was DTF") provides relief from the serious moments of *Watching Movies*. Tyler, The Creator's chanting for Mac to "get 'em," too, lightens the mood. "O.K." is all about beating 'em up with clever punchlines and his killer grinning nature. It's a wink to listeners who have made it this far: don't worry about Malcolm. He'll always come out jeering.

Things slow down and get pensive on "Claymation," which takes its time to reveal itself. Every step is crucial, though, much like every shot of a claymation production is critical to the final picture. Syrupy and sonically different from the other bonus cuts, "Claymation" feels like a companion to "Youforia." Its swirling and enveloping quality gives us the sense Mac Miller has come to construct his own reality. Equal parts gorgeous and tar-trapping, "Claymation" has a languid feel, and, in the context of what will soon be released (*Faces*), feels like an ode to Malcolm's future.

That said, "Claymation" is about savoring the present. The urging to "take a Polaroid picture" on the hook is a reminder to make tangible memories while you can. While Mac spends most of the hook escaping himself as a ghost who cannot stand the haters, this line gives us a clear picture of his final anxiety on *Watching Movies*—the same anxiety beginning the bonus cuts. It's all about legacy. Will he be remembered? What will those memories look like? What happens when or if they fade?

"Claymation" and the bonus tracks are about building a life after survival. They are about the practice of actually living with yourself. Though we know Mac will test his survival once more in 2014 and live again in 2015 on *GO:OD AM*, he ends this chapter in 2013 by showing us a slice of his humanity. *Watching Movies* was the most Mac Miller album to be released at the time, and it was in the bonus tracks where we found the most thriving version of him. We learned how Malcolm lived with himself, and by extension, we learned a little something about living for ourselves.

BIG JERM: "Matches" was a sample from Black Moth Super Rainbow. They're actually from the Pittsburgh area, which is random because I didn't know that when I found the sample. We did "Matches" in that mansion, but the studio was upstairs next to his bedroom. It wasn't in the pool house. It was a beat I made in Pittsburgh, and [when] I was in LA with him, I played it for him. That was one of the first things we did in that mansion. Ab-Soul did his verse a little later, I believe.

"Someone Like You" was pretty much done, and then we did some additional production at the end of it. "Claymation" was another one I did. I just played that stuff on Nexus—it's a plug-in. That was another one I did on an airplane—I don't know why he picks all those ones. I took it back to Pittsburgh, and then E. and Sayez added some stuff. Then Vinny Radio, who's my good friend, Mac got him on there too. The other ones we have credit on are pretty small, additional things.

I'm looking at this hard drive I have of his, and it's stuff back to 2010. He has so much unreleased music, it's kind of crazy. There's this one called "Distress Call," which was [made] probably on [the Macadelic] tour. I like that one. There's one called "I Come in Peace," that's after [the Macadelic Tour].

Before *Blue Slide Park*, we had been working on stuff together. He would play keys or guitar. So, "Distress Call," this is one where he played . . . I had another plug-in (Omnisphere) on my laptop, and I think he played some of this [instrumentation] and I did the drums. The beat is pretty much half-and-half, then he does the vocals on it. There's another one, "The Difference," that was good too. There's a lot of stuff I totally forgot about.

QUENTIN CUFF: I really love the original "Star Room." That album . . . It was just intended to have that fucking intro. It was intended to have the original "Star Room." Mac had Earl make that intro with Josh. That beginning spooky part, that's a Josh Berg creation. Then, when the guitar comes in, that's all Earl. I would just say, I love the original intro, and I wish we could have cleared that [original sample]. Some of the most interesting things about this album is the Earl and Mac beats, and The Alchemist!

We got Sap on there. A Flying Lotus-produced single. And one song by Pharrell Williams and one by Chuck Inglish. Mac produced "Aquarium," bro! He produced "REMember," "Aquarium," and a song with Jay Electronica ["Suplexes Inside of Complexes and Duplexes"]. That's just high-level artistry in one album. I'm super blessed to have been a part of this album.

SAP: "Watching Movies," actually, he produced the end part of that. When it gets real slow and crazy at the end. Mac is just out there, man. I can't explain it. It's nothing you can pinpoint about him. It's so many records that I have, I don't even know the projects they're from.

QUENTIN CUFF: The most interesting story for this album is Mac having to email Kate Rothschild . . . We couldn't get a hold of Jay Electronica for a little bit, and Mac had to go back and forth via email with Kate Rothschild in order to get Jay Electronica's verse. Mac was such an email genius! He would be mad when I would miss emails. He was just a businessman, so on top of his emails. I remember him showing me, "I'm emailing Kate Rothschild right now." Come to find out they dated.

Then, "Objects in the Mirror" with Pharrell . . . People always talking about "Pink Slime," but I was in the sessions in Miami, and we were playing Pharrell "Loud" right before *Macadelic* was supposed to come out, and we wanted this huge project with Pharrell, *Pink Slime*. They just didn't come back to making shit after having a couple good days in Miami, where they did some incredible shit. Pharrell sent Mac a bunch of beats, and that's where "Objects" comes from. When he got that, [Mac] immediately knew, "I'm saving that for myself." I think "Objects in the Mirror" is a precursor to a lot of Mac's music. It's a refined version of things like "Mourning After." It was just a proud moment.

BENJY GRINBERG: While I was aware of there being songs like ["Objects in the Mirror"], for me, he had always sung. A lot of his hooks were melodic previous to this album. It didn't surprise me at all. Also, it's different for someone like me, who was privy to other versions of the songs before they came out. It was a year before this album came out, so we had been listening to this music and to where he was going for a while before the album actually dropped. I was used to him heading in that direction.

QUENTIN CUFF: I remember, at the "Gees" video... ILLROOTS helped us make the video, staying in line with our success off the "America" video. ScHoolboy Q was eating El Pollo Loco chicken. That was a great video and a precursor of a whole era of videos. You hear people like Cole Bennett... He talks about the "America" video influencing him. It was just a great time. First album, we didn't *fall* on our face. Monetarily and success-wise, we were on TV, living in a fucking mansion. Everything's good! To come back with *Watching Movies*, take the craft more seriously... We took as much constructive criticism as possible. Mac was growing as a person and as an artist. He was starting to feel the respect around him, as an artist, and he showed up to the task.

BENJY GRINBERG: I love "Red Dot Music," "Bird Call," "Avian," "Gees," just some of the more head nod-y songs. I listen to "Claymation" *a lot*. I actually have a Spotify playlist I made for myself, which is my personal favorite Mac songs [for when] I just wanna not feel too emotional, if possible, but jam with him. Feel good, the sun's out, I wanna listen to some records that make me feel good, and for him to just be with me in those moments—celebrating him and the more upbeat records he made. ["Claymation"] is one of my go-tos. Same thing with "Gees," but "Gees" is so disrespectful. When I listen to that record, I just kinda shake my head, like a parent might do when their kid says something ridiculous, because it's so over the top disrespectful. Obviously, "Objects in the Mirror" is a beautiful song.

QUENTIN CUFF: "Avian . . . ." Mac said the theme of the album was birds. "Avian," the name is fucking incredible. That song is him and Josh Berg in the studio, going crazy. "I'm Not Real" was always a favorite of ours, because it was Mac and Earl; it was like hearing Raekwon and Ghostface [Killah], bro. Such a sharp duo of lyricists. "S.D.S.," in retrospect, is not my favorite song. Mac and FlyLo have other music in the tank that's really crazy.

Mac was in every lane. He had serious videos like "I Am Who Am" and then he had that "S.D.S." video that took you back to that "Smile Back" [era]. "Bird Call" was one of the hardest songs. Mac performed that song on the last show I did with him. Shout out Clams Casino. "Matches" is almost like a *K.I.D.S.* part two. It's about reminiscing over that happy era. I love reminiscing about his childhood, because he was a young-ass dude talking about times when he was fourteen as if it was forty years ago. Such an old soul. "I Am Who Am" . . . The Big L flow, I was always so impressed with what Malcolm did on that song.

SAP: *Watching Movies* is actually my favorite album. I think that album should have gotten a GRAMMY nod back in 2013, especially with him dropping around the same time as a lot of heavy hitters, which people would have avoided, probably. He stood with them, he dropped the same day as Cole and Kanye. People still was listening to his shit. A lot of other people would be like, "Nah, let's wait a couple weeks." But he was like, "Let's do it." I fuck with that courage. He was just fearless. That's why he gave us so much of himself. It still, to me, feels like he's still here.

BENJY GRINBERG: When we first decided on the release date [for] it, we didn't know it was gonna turn into this big day in hip-hop, in terms of releases. Kanye West and J. Cole had the same date. We were thinking: *Do we change our date?* We had come off a No. 1 album, and we wanted to continue to prove ourselves, and with Kanye and J. Cole coming out, it was unlikely we were going to be No. 1. We talked about it and decided it's cooler to stick to our guns and stick with the day we chose and be a part of this moment.

It was the first commercial album that he was very, very proud of and that he stuck with. Even doing a live album showed his commitment. He would've never made a *Blue Slide Park* live album. [But now] he was touring Europe with a lot of his friends that were very, very musical. In that sense, there was definitely a freedom. He felt like there was a lot of room in these new songs and in his own musicality that he could make different versions of the same song and express himself in many ways.

E. Dan: I think that's what he was asking himself at the time. Who is he, as an artist? Is he a rapper? Is he capable of more? He's watching guys like Tyler produce their own shit. I think he was an artist in transition from—I don't wanna say one-dimensional, but in his mind, he had one job as a rapper and occasional singer. Then he started looking at it more holistically as a musician and producer and general conductor. I feel like *Watching Movies* was the beginning of Malcolm exploring his own musicality beyond being a lyricist or vocal performer. It was a process he was just starting and was something he continued to just get better at over time.

LIVE FROM SPACE AND BEYOND

"It ain't no party like aristocratic parties / Yeah, yo, yo, yo, oh / Said, ain't no party like aristocratic parties"

—"S.D.S."

Sometimes, we just have to scream until we feel better. We're all just a mess of lightning bugs in mason jars vying for freedom, everyone all mixed up all the time. The ultimate function of the live album is to be a communal shouting match against ourselves (one we always win). Mac Miller's *Live From Space* brings us not only closer to Mac through a string of live performances and B-sides, but closer to a personal freedom of expression.

Mac Miller's studio albums capture potent emotional arcs, but *Live From Space* is freewheeling catharsis. The album, released December 17, 2013, is a ballistic offering, presented as two-thirds live recordings made during the Space Migration Tour with The Internet and one-third bonus tracks from *Watching Movies with the Sound Off. Live From Space* is the deluxe album of our dreams.

"I love performing and we have a show that's different and it is good live and there's maybe a couple songs where you can't understand what I'm saying, like watching Lil B, because there's too much screaming, but other than that, it breathes new life into the record," he told *Noisey* in 2013.[11]

Sure, Mac's delivery becomes indecipherable at best. Sure, he probably invented mumble rap while on stage. But allow me to call a

---

11. Jeremy Gordon, "Mac Miller Had the Best Year Ever: 'Live From Space' is a mix of live recordings and unreleased songs," *Noisey Music by Vice*, December 17, 2013, https://noisey.vice.com/en_us/article/6eqqn6/mac-miller-live-from-space-interview.

spade a spade: *Live From Space* is not meant to be deciphered. You're meant to rage alone in your living room and pull a muscle to this record. The live version of "Watching Movies" with Mac snarling into the microphone is the ultimate decompression. You can feel the steam rising off Mac's body, bursting through the vents, and blasting through your speakers.

What better way to free the lightning bugs and revel in our pent-up eccentricities than to the eddy-like drumming on "S.D.S."? How else to lose ourselves in the flushed emotions of "REMember" and "Youforia" than with the glowing, live ambiance? There's a husky magic to Mac Miller becoming all red-faced with spittle performing "I Am Who Am" at five-times speed. The smoked-out ease of "Bird Call" becomes wonderfully beveled and sly with the addition of humor and a live bass.

Live From Space is a cleansing vortex. Every call back to Tay Walker is a moment of precious camaraderie. The continual transformation of "Best Day Ever" into a shimmering and enchanting performance reminds us that Mac Miller is always innovating. Even the incessant "God damn!"s at the end of an eight-minute version of "The Question" feel compelling and consequential. Mac brings us deep inside the venue, gives us the space to catch our breath, and offers up some necessary perspective: look at all of these people right there with you. Outer space is cold and desolate, but this Space is predicated upon warmth and community. God damn.

Hearing the various cities shouted out across the album gives it a tangibility that I find myself craving more and more as I continuously come to terms with Mac's death. Something as simple as Mac announcing, "San Diego, California, we gon' start this one like this"— before launching into a frenzied performance of "I Am Who Am"— gives his legacy one of many waypoints, a "Mac Miller wuz here" sign, if you will.

Then we have the unsung heroes: the five bonus cuts. Like much of Mac's music post-tragedy, these five songs are exceptionally gutting. Take the hook of "Eggs Aisle," where a distant Mac Miller calls out: "Be safe homie / In this life or the next life / I'mma see ya." The pain here is self-explanatory and thick, the layers difficult to wade through. Mac is the speaker and the subject, as are we.

We also have some legacy-building. "Black Bush" exists in a special pantheon of songs that sound like nothing else he released. We can liken it to the basic motif of *Faces*, but even so, we would be missing the mark. The alien quality of the track, the haunting understatement, is singular, as if the "product of a witch's spell." Mac brings a brooding gravitas to the track, sounding like a man apart from the world.

"Life" is a clear *Faces* prelude, sounding like the mood board for the "Happy Birthday," "Wedding," "Funeral" three-piece. The groaning delivery of "we can talk about all the things we should have done / All the arguments that you probably would have won / But I'm stubborn, baby, you knew that when you told me you loved me" will be matched only by the dragging first verse of "Wedding": "The smile that she faking is tragic, hate looking at it / That magic I tried to grasp it, she's had it with the dramatics / Fantasizing love so classic, attracted to what she got up in her attic / Can we mind fuck?"

Mac had an innate ability to write from the position of someone in a perpetual state of longing, surrounded both by beauty and degradation. He could parse the rot from the fruit like few writers could. We love him for it.

"In the Morning" is a snapshot of the Mac Miller connective tissue magic. Working with Syd and Thundercat, the trio produced a hidden gem of multi-genre music. "Ideas never stop flying through him," Syd said in a 2013 interview with *Complex*.[12] "Me and Thundercat wrote the hook . . . and we just did right there. We recorded some more live bass over it. It's really one of those songs that just happened in the night. We left his house at seven the next morning and continued about our

---

12. The Internet, "Interview: The Internet Talks About Touring With Mac Miller, Chance the Rapper, & interview by Dharmic X, *Complex*, December 20, 2013, https://www.complex.com/music/2013/12/the-internet-live-from-space-mac-miller-interview.

lives. Until then, we were literally in the dark just slaving over this one song. The whole song happened in four to five hours." That's the sum of Mac Miller's creative ethos.

"Earth" is a love song, and I'll still be damned if there isn't a better catch-all for Mac Miller's music than the smooth declaration, "Your beauty handed me my mind back." If not an apt label for the function of his discography, then at the least, this lyric breaks down the excellence of *Live From Space*.

Mac Miller found his shelter on the stage, and across these songs we are treated to the undoing and rebirth of a man night after night. The beauty is the music, and by proxy, the mind is beautiful. One nurtures the other, and we nurture ourselves. That's the Most Dope Family in motion.

2014

FACES

"Faces actually started forming in my blanket; got some demons in there."

—*Mac Miller*[13]

---

13. Mac Miller, "Mac Miller: Confessions," interview by FACT's Confessions, *FACTmagazine*, August 24, 2016, https://www.youtube.com/watch?v=fIP4-jX2K7I.

FIGHTING FOR HIS LIFE

"So many things that I've created, but this right here might be my favorite."

—*"Here We Go"*

I write through my trauma. This is a lesson I learned from Mac time and again, especially from his 2014 opus, *Faces*. My favorite Mac Miller project, it was the soundtrack to my self-harm, the darkest period of my life, and the consequential soundtrack to my recovery. It may well have taught me that the purpose of great writing is to elevate the person receiving it.

The mixtape is a paranoid stumbling through the cocaine ether, the perceived fragility of mortality, and the anxiety of only knowing how to create, not necessarily how to live. Across the twenty-four tracks, Mac covers damn near everything within the scope of the human condition, resulting in his most expansive, challenging, esoteric, flawed, and affecting offering to this point in his career.

Mac Miller found freedom on *Faces*, and so many of us used *Faces* to find our own solace. After years of listening to the tape, I've come to understand it as a battle for peace, a purging of the fear of death to get to the pursuit of life. Even after his "Funeral," music provides a life after death.

In a swirl of jazz, Mac begins by proclaiming that he should have died already, establishing *Faces* as a confession. He's getting higher than we've previously heard about, celebrating his success with a variety of drugs while documenting the difficult descents from riding so high. Mac vacillates between being at his highest and lowest, but his rapping is at its best. In the storm of this mixtape, he never lets us forget that he is just a twenty-two-year-old guy trying to get his mind right. As listeners, we have a natural concern for Malcolm, but we also find ourselves attracted to this brink-of-life music.

Miller often referred to music as a religion, especially on his press run for *Watching Movies with the Sound Off*. Consider *Faces* the inside of a church, with the heat of the devil filling the air. We hear ourselves fighting our battles as best as we can, putting on our personas so no one worries. On "Diablo," we hear the humor and hysteria of a depressive episode ("I been poppin' like a kernel, readin' Justin Bieber's journal / Treat you like a urinal") and the nervous jitter of unraveling ("Look at what you did to me, look at what you did to me"). The song is ripe with angst. ("I ain't a star, I'm way farther with the constellations / Contemplatin' suicide like it's a DVD").

> "And kill me now if I did it all for hip-hop (K-ch, blaow) / I might die before I detox"
>
> —*"Malibu"*

From Mac shouting, "You piece of shit" at himself, to flirting with death in the service of his art, to the animalistic declarations of, "Well I'll be damned if this ain't some shit" and "I'm the only suicidal motherfucker with a smile on," "Malibu" is packed with lines that communicate the ethos of the mixtape. The fallacy of a smile is the core essence of *Faces*. The tape is an exposé on the lies we tell ourselves in our fight to get better as well as an expulsion of those lies from Mac Miller's fragile system.

Faces is not meant to be agreeable; it's meant to be honest. Paging through lines admitting to suicidal tendencies might make our skin crawl, but there's an authenticity to each word that keeps us coming back. Mac flourishes in confounding spaces; about to die, he sprouts and blooms. The precipice is a sexy place, everything extreme and laden with meaning. There is so much intensity, it's impossible to be bored. Why not set up camp on the edge of mortality, just to see what fun can be had? Mac says as much about his drug use in his 2016 *FADER* documentary.[14]

With anxiety permeating the tape, "It Just Doesn't Matter" stands as one of the most human moments. The track is its own personal undoing, with non sequiturs funneling into honest depictions of drug use overtaking his life, and how as much as this saddens him, he just can't stop ("Buggin' out, had it all, I'm nothing now . . . I bust your speakers with some bullshit rap / I'm on drugs, all my new shit wack"). His woes are plentiful and bone-deep, with a bar like "Everyone I know ain't nothing to God" capturing the desolation he feels inside The Sanctuary, trying to create his way back into the realm of the living.

> "Cause I smoke dust, overdosed on the sofa, dead /
> Woke up from a coma / Poured up with a soda, smoked,
> went back to bed / Never thought I'd be such a loner"
>
> —*"Polo Jeans"*

Faces is not prophetic, and reducing Mac's legacy to one of predicting death obfuscates the point that this was music made to survive. Mac presents his death and then resurrects himself through his music. That should be his legacy.

Considering that this tape is followed by Mac's awakening on *GO:OD AM*, we can remember him and *Faces* as experiments in seeing how close to death he could fly, even symbolically placing his own death at the center of the track listing. "Funeral" does not, however, represent the end for Miller. Rather, the song leads us further down the rabbit hole of his manic self, after which he emerges as the "rap Diablo," reborn as an immortal obsessed with spitting some motherfucking raps.

Mac Miller imagines and confronts his death in an effort to achieve freedom and power. Ending a verse with "Finally, I don't even

14. *Mac Miller - Stopped Making Excuses*, directed by Rob Semmer (2016; New York, NY: FADER), https://www.youtube.com/watch?v=UQ3w99trVUk&t=514s.

need my fucking eyes to see / Come and die with me," we get the sense he has ascended and wants to bring the whole team up with him. When he raps "And I inherited the thirst for self-destruction and I'm scared of it / I wanna be buried with a novel and a chariot," he repurposes death as salvation.

Mac comes up for air once more on "New Faces v2," where he once again affirms a fear of taking his last breaths in the booth and making each one count. He recalls a time where drugs and fame terrified him before the powder consumed him. "Where did all that go?" he asks of his fears, reminding us that *Faces* was made to be a journey back to Malcolm. This desire to return resurfaces later in Mac's career. *Swimming* concludes with: "Like a circle, I go back where I'm from."

All of this brings us to "Grand Finale," a song conceived under the premise that he might die if he ever left his studio. As he once said, "Part of the mentality was like if I die when I leave this room—cause that was my fear . . . Like I won't survive in the world. I will survive in this little room called The Sanctuary that I'm okay in." The closer showcases his rebirth. Mac emerges fearless ("I fear nothin' on this odyssey of dark roads") and spiritually renewed ("We are the prophets . . . I'm a bit surprised that I'm even still alive"). "Grand Finale" perfectly intersects with the first words of *Faces*, making the project a complete circle, a fortification of Malcolm's legacy and endurance. The fireworks are a celebration of the achievement. Still being alive is a testament to his unshakeable will to make it through. Mac gave us *Faces* to help us survive.

Josh Berg: With *Macadelic*, we were client and vendor. I was studio staff. I came with the room, although we enjoyed each other. By the time *Faces* came about, I had spent nearly every day at his house or on a tour with him for a year and a half. We were family. The work was brilliant. We were at the height of our flow. We knew each other's languages and shared so much creative experience and references. We didn't need to speak. He would walk in the booth without mention. I would hit record. I knew when to punch and edit, every effect and treatment. As I became aware of this, I made it a point to stretch it as far as possible. We could nearly do a whole song without discussion.

Big Jerm: This was when he was recording *so much*, I didn't know if there was any purpose. I never knew what the plan was, but "Therapy" might've been the first one I sent him. E. added the bass. I don't remember the beginning of the whole [*Faces*] process. To me, it was random.

E. Dan: With most Mac projects, that one included, I never knew what the fuck we were working on—other than *Blue Slide Park* and *GO:OD AM*. When we were working on those, I knew definitely that's what we were doing. With mixtapes, they were more like . . . we never stopped working. When we were in the room together, we were gonna make music—that's what we did. I don't know that I ever knew what he was working on until he was like, "Here's this whole project." I'm sure that's the case with *Faces* because it was in between labels. I had no idea what he was doing. I knew he was courting some labels, had left Rostrum. I thought he was gonna wait 'til he got with a new label to work on a project. It was a surprise to me, but we had worked on several of the songs together in the months prior. I just didn't know they were gonna be on *Faces*.

Big Jerm: Just from talking to Josh, I knew he was living in the studio. Even though his bedroom was upstairs, I don't think he was going there very much. There was a constant stream of people coming over to work, so it's almost like he wasn't even able to get out of the studio, even if he wanted to.

JOSH BERG: It was during the run up to the project. We were heavily recording and [Mac] was not sleeping very much. He reported vivid hallucinations, seeing faces in his blanket. This was profound to him. He knew he was far from shore, but he also heard the siren song of revelation. He explored this philosophically. There were songs composed about people with imaginary friends that only they could see. He seemed fascinated by these ideas: the imaginary and imagination. Who is really there anyways? Where are we? Is that so static?

During the *Faces* era, which actually extended a bit beyond the project itself, there was an extraordinary amount of raw musical experimentation. It all started with Thundercat, but often Taylor Graves would be there as well, or one of the other Bruner brothers.

THUNDERCAT (bassist, producer, "Inside Outside"): My first time hearing Mac's music was on the account of us working together, I believe. When I started to dig into his music, I started to understand the type of person he was. He put his musicianship first. It wasn't necessarily about where we had been, it was about what the possibilities were of what we could create and what we could do. I knew who he was; I heard his name mentioned many times. The funny thing we always talked about is: Neither of us could remember how we met. It was weird. "Did I just show up at your house one day?" "Did you pick me up somewhere?" I don't know how we met. But I remember . . . it definitely started with our working relationship, and we immediately took to each other.

JOSH BERG: In 2014, Mac Miller was free. For the last few years, he had ridden this incredible wave of success, but that success came at a cost. He had been doing 200-plus shows a year and in this last year alone (2013) he had completed his bravest and most creative experimental album to date for which he did a summer tour across the U.S., two side projects, *Delusional Thomas* and Larry Lovestein [*You*], an EU festival tour, an arena tour in Europe as support for Lil Wayne, along with all his own shows, and he filmed two seasons of a reality show. Towards the end of the year, you had to literally pry him out of The Sanctuary with a crowbar. That was the only place he really wanted to be. He was intending to lock himself inside the studio and make music every day, and that's exactly what he did. I remember recording "Inside Outside" when [Mac] said, "Everybody wanna be God besides God, he wanna be like us." He freestyled that . . . That type of profound statement was just coming out of him constantly.

THUNDERCAT: That song is a special song to me. There was a little bit of everything. There was a different part of the spectrum showing between both of us at that point in our lives. We were really in it. We were in it for the creative energy. We were in it for where the feeling meets the technicality, meets the ability to process. And so many other elements. On [*Faces*], he had a bit of a breakthrough personally. He felt freed up and open enough to let everybody in and not be scared or lose who he was. Even when he's saying, "On the inside, I'm outside, all the time," it felt prophetic. It was almost as if everything had been turned inside out: That introvert that was maybe hiding, he was walking into who he was becoming or who he was. And you felt it.

JOSH BERG: They would just be hanging out in the room and burst into jams spontaneously. This was the whole point: to see what would intuitively come from the conversation. We had albums of this stuff. So many moments, from meeting Ronald Bruner who was quite a bit more boisterous than we imagined. We gave [Ronald] a kick drum festooned with pots and pans and a silverware caddy from the dishwasher.

THUNDERCAT: Creating with him . . . I'm a person that likes to play too. The ability to play together, sometimes it represents more than the part you jam with somebody. There's a level of communication that gets masked in the ability. Different things hide themselves away sometimes. It's almost like speaking in code. Me and him, we would always be trying to speak a different language to each other. We always had something to say; we always had something to play. We would go full-on with ideas. We would never stop playing. He would be playing piano; I had my bass plugged up. We were always trying to be in each other's heads.

E. DAN: I've only gained the perspective of how fucking incredible it is over the last few years . . . When he first sent it to me to start putting it together from a mix standpoint, I was mostly overwhelmed with the amount of tracks. As it goes for me, when I'm in the middle of a project on that level, it can be hard to fully appreciate it from the perspective of a listener. There's songs on there that were, immediately upon hearing it and to this day, some of my favorite songs he's done. "Inside Outside" I love, and I love that Josh is screaming all over it in the background. The Rick Ross track ["Insomniak"], I loved that.

BIG JERM: Actually, my friend Shod Beatz had that sample. We both use FL Studio, so he sent me the project file. He had the sample in there, and I just remember that drumroll on it, that's kind of offbeat—I added that. We had the 808s. Mac hit me up wanting more of a banger, and sometimes it just works out where that was the one I had made right when he asked. I sent that over and didn't really hear much. I assume he recorded it, and then he sent the Rick Ross part. That was pretty cool, just to hear Rick Ross on one of our beats.

JOSH BERG: Another session titled "Rick Rubin's Piano" [came] from a field recording of [Mac] playing piano on a field trip to Rick's house, which led to a side-splittingly ridiculous exchange. Another time I literally rolled on the floor laughing when [Mac] burst into an operatic pass on a song. So much music was done. There were at least half a dozen albums in progress at the time. No exaggeration.

One day we had been up all night to where people started answering the phone again and we somehow got Om'Mas [Keith] to come over at like 8:00 a.m. and Larry, he and Thundercat and myself all went to Stein on Vine where he bought [Thundercat] an upright bass, bought a cello, violin, bass clarinet, and a ridiculous assortment of percussion bits and some silly squeeze pump horns that looked like they came off of clown cars. We went back to the house and started jamming. Om'Mas played the flute.

[There] was the intro to one of the lost albums featuring SZA and it's one of my favorites. [Mac] absolutely killed that organ. And, of course, SZA did an amazing verse. Still gets stuck in my head all the time.

I remember doing "Thumbalina." It was a night where it was just him and me in the studio and he was remarking how the neighbors had formed a committee to evict him. It's not hard to see how that one got started.

Big Jerm: You could hear the trajectory from *Macadelic*. They have a similar vibe to me. When he put *Faces* out, I was like, "Wow, twenty-four songs." But it works! I always tell people, for an album, I think ten to fourteen songs is good. You never want it to feel too long, but *Faces*, I think is ... eighty-five minutes long.

E. Dan: There [were] songs on there—"It Just Doesn't Matter"—that when I heard them, "Fucking wow! I love this shit." There are twenty-four songs on there, so I was completely overwhelmed from a mixing perspective of popping open all these sessions and trying to make sense of things. I didn't have much time to get it done, so I spent more time being overwhelmed than I did thinking about how amazing it is. It took me a good couple of years, if not longer, to forget about how intense the process was and listen to it, hate all of my mixes, get over that, and appreciate what an awesome project it was.

Big Jerm: He picked the right beats to all fit together. He definitely is getting deeper on it too. I get lost in the beat part of it. I'm listening to the snare when everybody else is listening to the lyrics.

E. Dan: There was a looseness to it. I don't think he did a lot of second-guessing. I think he was going through some dark times making that record. Mac was pretty good at keeping that side of him away from me because I'm older . . . We had a deep friendship and the dude was a part of my family, and *is* a part of my family. He really, really went out of his way to keep the heavy substance use away from me and Jerm in particular. I haven't quite nailed down why that is. Whatever the case . . . When he was going through a lot of difficult times . . . If I was around him, he'd do a good job of not letting me know that. It's hard for me to say exactly what space he was in, you know?

By all accounts, just talking to Josh and [Quentin Cuff], it seems like there were some pretty rough times around that. Maybe not the roughest times. Maybe some of those were still yet to come. But it maybe was the beginning of some dark days. Whenever you hit an intense level of feeling, emotion, whatever in life, that shit comes through in your art. For better or for worse. And it resonates with people. It just comes through on those tracks, and that's one of the reasons why people feel that way about it.

THE FREE FORM MAGIC OF "COLORS AND SHAPES"

Produced by Mac Miller himself, "Colors and Shapes" has a fragile and silky essence, a swerve from the anxious, obsessive, feverish energies comprising *Faces*. Mostly sung, it precedes the berserk "Insomniak" and the rap-heavy "San Francisco" and leaps out immediately. Early listens left me wondering what the song was doing on the mixtape. I couldn't quite understand Mac's rationale for breaking his momentum with this flowing cut. Now, over two years into my mental health recovery, and understanding that recovery is nonlinear, "Colors and Shapes" makes perfect sense to me.

The track is a slow and steady exhale of all the pent-up mania Mac has been carrying for the past hour of *Faces*. As the seventeenth song, it is tucked far enough into *Faces* where the listener has come to expect a certain mode from the mixtape. Thwarting that expectation immediately catches our attention and causes us to lean in to discover all that Malcolm is attempting to teach us. The song is delicate and gorgeous with a cascading energy, lulling us with its tender lines and putting Mac in the position of being our Ferryman on this dark odyssey.

"If it was colors and shapes, the imaginary / Instead of all of this weight that we have to carry / Would you be able to breathe?" he sings, giving back to the listener, attempting to replace the jagged lines of the preceding songs with a lightness meant to ease our souls. He's right there with us. Employing "we" puts Mac on our level where he thrives as rap's empathetic brother. Simultaneously, he is inventing a new setting for the world of *Faces* because it's getting too heavy, even for him. On this song, we're meant to escape reality, its free-form magic creating something of a wormhole. We sink in and float away, as if in a dream.

The first verse is a search for comfort, not giving up or giving in to depression, but seeking something we cannot see. On the hook, Mac sings: "Oh, it feels good to fall." We could read this as an indication Mac has quit on himself, choosing to tumble down the rabbit hole of his emotions rather than stand his ground, yet the song demystifies pain, causing it to lose its hold over us. At the close of the second verse, Mac notes: "While floating through galaxies they said I couldn't / I noticed how sad one can get." He details the ways in which we can escape our heads and expunge our pain.

"Colors and Shapes" is so airy, it's easy to imagine ourselves falling as Mac falls, only to realize we haven't been falling at all. We're drifting. We're floating. This song is a sanctuary, a safe space for us to interrogate our emotions and gain the upper hand. Let the feeling wash over us, Mac posits, and feel *through* it. Eventually, it will pass.

Escaping into the magic of "Colors and Shapes," those few minutes spent floating through depression are not a moment of weakness. Rather, they mark a new battle plan. Oh, yes, it feels good to fall, but what Malcolm also means to remind us is that it feels good to rise. And we will. We always do.

JOSH BERG: I feel conflicted about it. Some things defined the period as an ultimate immersion in philosophy and other things represent his struggles with drugs. Cocaine references in particular did not fit the braggadocio of rap. You can rap about how much weed you smoke or pills or lean, but it doesn't make sense to rap about cocaine the same way. It's much more of a secret drug. It just felt so vulgar and wrong.

THUNDERCAT: He started blending the worlds together. There's instrumental pieces on there; there's parts where he's playing the different instruments. He's going into some vicious rapping. He stopped separating the creative energies. He saw it and said, "This is one [and] the same. This is the same person." It came out almost like vomit; that's how it happens sometimes. He took the barriers off and let it be what it was and stopped worrying about if people are gonna be able to say, "Oh, yeah, he's a rapper!" He let everybody see what it all was.

JOSH BERG: To me, in retrospect, it seems like *Faces* touches on the intangible spirit of things the way you could see faces in the moon or clouds or other things, a spiritual identity more representative of our pre-modern understanding of things. If it has a face, it is a being type of idea. The different faces we wear, the faces of our friends and family.

E. DAN: Also, it's his least overthought project. He didn't let himself get in the way. He didn't have a label to answer to, so it didn't feel like he had some sort of authority figure involved with the creative process. With *Faces*, there was this sense of freedom in so many ways. He was firmly established in Los Angeles, on his own, mostly away from family, and he had all these new friends and that was coming together as his new life. He just left Rostrum. There was just this *freedom* to him. And! He had already gone through *Watching Movies with the Sound Off*, which is the project where he steps up and says, "I wanna produce myself." It was a combination of those things.

Josh Berg: Perhaps it felt like a rebirth or the start of a new era, which it certainly was.

E. Dan: I think he was simultaneously—with every project—incredibly proud and, at the same time . . . He probably secretly hated half of it and wanted to redo everything ten times over. That's a typical thing for an artist. You're always growing, so the last thing you did is your favorite thing. He was probably right on to the next thing. I got the impression from him that *Faces* was like, "I need to get some of these songs out. If I don't get some of them out, I'm gonna reach a point where I'm so confused with what I have and what to do with it." That's part of where its beauty lies: He didn't overthink it.

"THE HARDEST WORKING PERSON IN THE UNIVERSE"

Mac Miller declared himself "the hardest working person in the universe," and he had a special way of detailing his obsession with making music. His work ethic was a marvel, and, among other themes, he used *Faces* to showcase his lust for the art of hip-hop.

Mac brings an unparalleled conviction to each bar on *Faces*. We get the double-whammy of believing him and believing *in* him. His bragging about working relentlessly inspires the listener to follow a similar path. He gives obsession an attractive feel, which summons our own passions; we should all be so lucky as to find the thing that makes our heads spin and puts us in a creative daze.

"Angel Dust," "Malibu," "Therapy," "Insomniak," and "Uber" all speak to Mac Miller's obsessive nature. "Writin' on writer's block, haven't slept in days / They wanna put me in the psycho watch, everyone's afraid / Of what I do inside my studio, worried I'mma lose control." These three bars from "Angel Dust" illustrate the lengths Mac will go to to make his art. Hard work is how he *maintains* control. Obsession is his anchor.

"Kill me now if I did it all for hip-hop," he declares on "Malibu," contemplating his legacy. He is working toward something greater. In death, as we've seen, his impact on people cannot be overstated.

Then we have the most relatable of Mac's hard work proofs: "Insomniak," which begins on a characteristically humble note: "I'm the mothafuckin' greatest," a direct mirror to "Here We Go," and a shift from the somber energy of "Malibu." "Insomniak" is peak obsession. Mac is blue-faced and teetering on derangement. Every lost second of sleep compounds into a series of roaring moments ("I'm a maniac, crazy, act insane / Think I might need a cage in fact;" "God damnit, this ain't a drill, do not panic / Let me see how loud you scream"). At the apex of the song, we have Mac with his chest out, beaming with pride.

In America, pouring your whole self into the pursuit of success is your moral imperative. On "Insomniak," Mac is a knight in shining hustle armor. He doesn't need a reward—he's rewarding himself by creating. It's the perfect dopamine loop. Mac Miller's work ethic makes him feel everlasting, as if he really could live to 102, sitting on the stoop, tapping out beats on his MPC to amuse neighborhood kids.

Faces is a fearful and guilt-ridden outing, but Mac keeps us sane on this psychedelic trip through the fringes of his mind. Bars about hard work humanize him on the one project he claimed he made on another plane of existence. Hard work is how Mac Miller returned to earth.

MAKING PEACE WITH THE END

"And if by chance this is my grand finale / Bury me in Allegheny County"

—"Grand Finale"

"Grand Finale" was a test. Malcolm conceived of it being driven by the haunting idea that it could be the final thing he left behind: What comes once the fireworks of the track fizzle away?

The irony is that Mac Miller opens "Grand Finale" with his closing thoughts. "Bury me in Allegheny County" is a powerful directive, revealing yet another layer of his identity. A Pittsburgh legend through and through, should Malcolm not survive this song, not survive *Faces*, we must lay him to rest at his roots and remember him for who he was as man and musician. This sobering note reminds us of Malcolm's loyalty as well as his humility and humanity, for as much as Mac had achieved by 2014, he never strayed far from his beginnings or who he was prior to his success. We'll see this blossom the following year on *GO:OD AM*, where the Pittsburgh references are plentiful and being an everyman is the bedrock of the writing.

In "Grand Finale," Mac is pouring out every last ounce of himself. We get a sense Malcolm desperately wants to be surrounded by people he can trust ("And no famous friends for me, just old faces") and is struggling to reconcile his ever-shifting self-image: "Not a king, I'm no David." The sum of these worrisome bars reveals the Mac Miller of "Grand Finale" is conflicted, wounded by his addictions but continuously drawn to drugs, resentful of his success while enjoying its spoils, and serious about escaping his pain while simultaneously reveling in it. The dichotomies Mac draws up reveal him to be deeply unsure of his place in the world, especially given his earlier material, which portrayed him as one of Generation Z's go-lucky leaders.

> "Let us have a grand finale / The world will be just fine without me / The clown got a smile on his face / Slow it down, we goin' out with a bang / Are you ready for the fireworks? / It was a silent night 'til the fireworks"

Malcolm's "old Jewish mind" has been through enough. There's a peacefulness to the send-off, contrasting the ominous notes of the open and the dire straits of the tape itself. Mac Miller uses "Grand Finale" to make peace with his mortality. There is no spite or malice to the declaration the world will be just fine without him. The hook is born from a place of acceptance. Understanding Mac's consistent use of self-deprecation across *Faces*, it's easy to assign him the role of "the clown," but even that comes with a tinge of peace. As the hook turns and Mac addresses his audience, the air of the bars does not shift. He is not pleading. Asking us if we're ready is merely a courtesy from an artist keenly aware of the breadth of his relationship to the listener. Then the fireworks arrive, and Mac Miller's legacy, for the time being, is sealed.

Until the second verse. Until the next album. Until... The strategy of packing the ending of the song into its hook, making the conclusion of *Faces* incremental through repetition, is an age-old trick: repeat something to yourself enough and you'll believe it. The record cannot end after the first hook because we've yet to buy Malcolm's meaning, and, perhaps, he's still working on believing it himself.

We move in steps over time. Everyone's first brush with mortality is different, arriving at different pivotal moments, but once we are cognizant of it, it remains with us. People spend the better part of their lives either running from or running to their death. Malcolm spends the better part of "Grand Finale" on the latter, doing the work to welcome the end. The conclusion is not a thing to be feared. It is simply a fact of life Malcolm wrestles with to the point of pinning it down. We know as much because the second verse opens with: "I fear nothin' on this odyssey of dark roads / God lives in my dog's soul." Later, Mac adds: "Even God will one day be forgotten" and "My old Jewish mind, REMember Music, you'll be fine." Where on the first verse Malcolm was wrestling with himself, on the second, he's come to find comfort in the way things end. Where people generally fear being left behind, forgotten, or fading into oblivion, Mac Miller has transcended these concerns.

The note about God is telling too. The second verse begins with God and Malcolm on the same level and quickly becomes a commentary on how no one and nothing is exempt from disappearing—why concern yourself with the inevitable? Contrast this idea with Mac's mention of David in the first verse, and how he does not wish to see himself as a deity. He only sees himself as blessed. That comfort in self comes from a comfort with the end. By the second verse, peace becomes the operative mode.

"Who am I?" Mac asks in his final line. It's an incredulous moment, as if to say: "Who am I to live forever?" The vocal effects create the illusion of Malcolm leaving his body. As we enter the closing hook, we have a fresh sense of calm. The fireworks take us out. *Faces* ends. We've made it out alive, and Mac Miller has elevated to another plane. It was always meant to end like this.

2015

GO:OD AM

"I was like, 'I'm going to just focus on living. And going outside. And just getting my life right.'"

—*Mac Miller*[15]

15. Rembert Brown, "Mac Miller Finds the Way," *Grantland*, August 20, 2015, https://grantland.com/features/mac-miller-good-am-album/.

"WHEN IN ROME":
A BERSERK WAKE-UP CALL

In 2015, Mac Miller was at the height of his second creative renaissance. The brute raps he seeded on *Macadelic* sprung into the gorgeous and well-woven bars of *GO:OD AM*. Malcolm took everything he knew about hip-hop—and himself—and crafted a foundational text of a hip-hop album. Combined with the notion of introspection being king, taken from *Watching Movies with the Sound Off*, everything coalesced into the perfect storm of an album, which shines most when Malcolm wakes up and tackles life head-on.

GO:OD AM swells into a berserk wake-up call on "When in Rome," which boasts a feverish and chaotic energy that takes Mac from rapping to barking and yelling. He pants, spits, and gnaws through the beat. To call the song high-octane is disrespectful to the aura of Mac's true pinnacle on *GO:OD AM*. This song marks the moment Malcolm's spirit awakens.

Drawn in by the summoning arpeggios and jumping production, we tumble into disorder. Mac begins with a narrative non-sequitur, talking about freaks and girls—his punchline pocket—which *feels* like a dramatic transition from the hyper-serious close of "Perfect Circle / God Speed"; however, when we take into account the life path Mac has drawn across the album, it becomes clear that there was no other way to start this song. He understands he must take life by the reins and enjoy it. Bring on the women, the disarray, the party. It's time to *live*. It's time to enjoy this world for all it offers.

Mac's picking fights and losing his technical footing. The song feels like a war cry, which is what makes it so successful. "Feeling great, I'm the man here / If you got a problem don't stand here," he

175

announces. This is the only moment of personal reflection in the first verse. As such, it's the most telling. For all of the song's overt debauchery, there is the overriding sense he's just having fun, man. Great fun had become Mac's modus operandi, and his lust for life was channeled fervently into every aspect of the production.

The repetition of the simple, animalistic hook is disorienting. When you sing along, it warps your voice—vowels sink and consonants crumble. You lose yourself, literally, in the soup of repetition. This effect serves a potent purpose. "When in Rome," and by extension, living life to the fullest, is about action. It's about doing as much as you can for yourself before you expire. That's why the words stumble over each other, why Malcolm absconds the airtight raps decorating the surrounding songs on GO:OD AM. Perfection is boring; imperfection is a sign of humanity thriving.

Mac's lust for life continues in the second verse, in which he details his desire to see the world and live uninterrupted. In this context, Mac yelling, "I don't got time, bitch I'm high, ain't a secret" reads like him staking his claim on his life. The line also pairs well with the third verse "I'm going ape shit on all of my verses," which implies Mac will not waste a breath. While much of GO:OD AM does battle with Mac's mortality, here we see finality as fuel. We scream these words alongside Mac Miller because we, too, understand life is short and precious and must be an endeavor, not a series of random circumstances.

Mac is not simply waking up on "When in Rome." He's leaping out of bed and running out the door, sprinting down the street in his PJs. There's no time to waste. From the opening to the aggressive outro ("Shut your motherfucking mouth bitch... I'mma keep killing shit, let them all hate") we are confronted by a radically passionate and dedicated Malcolm reminding us that he's devoted to being as alive as possible.

QUENTIN CUFF: He was in a good place! He really was sober, man. This [was] a sober Mac. He was getting through [relationship problems]. At the end of the day, that album was him in a very good place. He was happy to be doing things on his own. He was out of the shadow of Wiz and different people. We had our own wave. We did the label [deal] and with *GO:OD AM*, he really was happier! It's more so showing people, "I wanna make *real* songs."

BIG JERM: He came to Pittsburgh for the whole summer. He was planning on that album before [coming to Pittsburgh]. Then he came to get some tracks from us, but to also pull it all together. [ID Labs has] a good amount of stuff on there. "Brand Name" was one that was just us in the studio. I found that record. It's a J. J. Barnes sample, which is an old soul record, one of those where we were just going through records and came across that one, and I chopped up [the sample]. Before he came to Pittsburgh, he had "Weekend," "Clubhouse," maybe "Perfect Circle / God Speed," and "Cut the Check." He had a good portion of *GO:OD AM* done. With "Jump," Sap made the beat originally, and then we got it and added some details. DJ Dahi did the same thing. It was a lot of back and forth on that one.

QUENTIN CUFF: His first album on Warner. This was a tester—he'd gotten some good reviews with *Faces*, and this was a time where Mac is working with different video directors. He's working with the Clancys as his management full-time. During this period, he became more of a celebrity. Mac had a lot of star-studded projects, but I look at this as, "Okay, he got his shit going as far as all his homies." The song with Chief Keef . . . I don't know how that got set up, but it's dope. If you look [at the credits], it's Frank Dukes, Vinylz, ID Labs, Miguel on "Weekend." There's so many good moments! The "100 Grandkids" video was interesting. "Rush Hour" was the shit. "Brand Name" video!

BIG JERM: I remember the day I did ["Brand Name"], I did the sample and drums, and when Mac's ready to go, he's ready to go, as far as recording. I'm pretty sure he just jumped in and did it. "Rush Hour" was an E. Dan one, and Sayez probably added to that.

QUENTIN CUFF: What really spoke to me, was the fact that Mac was very aware of where he was during *Faces* and the other albums, and he wanted to make something that was still exciting, but it came from a more sober mind. I just love "The Festival." This is another album, similar to *Watching Movies*, where the original version to "Jump" is one of my favorite Mac songs of all time. We had to remake "Jump." It would've been a bigger hit, and it would've hit like a "Donald Trump," but the great thing about this is "Weekend" went Platinum. I always loved that. That was a real surprise, because it's not a typical 808 banger. People love this album, and it was a different wave for Mac. Mac put together a sound that wasn't built off one artist or one producer.

BIG JERM: "100 Grandkids" was already a song. The Sha Money XL beat was already there. Then we had the second half. On that one, Mac gave me that loop, and I added the drums and either me or E. did the 808. That was another one where they were working on it, and Mac wanted it to go in a different direction at the end. He and E. were in E.'s room, and they just sent it over to me in my room at the studio. I did the drums and played it for him. It was pretty easy. [Mac] just wanted it to turn up a little more. That was the first video that came out. "Weekend," I'm credited on there, but FKi started that beat, and ID Labs ended up with credit because E. added stuff at the mix stage.

"When in Rome," I made that beat... It was probably a year or two old by that time. It's a Bo Hansson sample. Our beat is first on that one, and then, Sledgren (he's also from Pittsburgh) did the second half. He's a really good producer too. He's close with Wiz and Taylor Gang. I think Mac just wanted a hype one, and I had that beat already. I sent him that beat, and then he added on the Sledgren part when he was in Pittsburgh.

Vic Wainstein (friend and engineer): I was brought [in] for *GO:OD AM*. We holed up in a studio in Santa Monica for five days straight. I didn't leave the studio. I got brought in because his other engineer, Josh Berg, would call me to fill in whenever he wasn't available. Because Mac's work ethic was quite voracious, and me and Josh being older, we don't have that young man energy. We had to ration what we had left. [Josh] was doing a long streak with Mac prior to the five days I did with him, and those five days, we got a lot done, including elements of "Cut the Check." The whole song "The Weekend," with Miguel. That was the first time Mac met Miguel. It was almost like [Mac] floated in the room when he came in. The rest is history.

Justin Boyd (friend and photographer): The "Weekend" video shoot was cool. That was a really late night. We started at nine and wrapped at four in the morning. Mac was a big Miguel fan, so I know that whole experience was cool for him, and me as well. We did that one in LA. "Brand Name" was in Pittsburgh.

He always closed that tour with "When in Rome." What's funny about that song is there's the part where it switches up towards the end. It's actually two different songs he put together in the studio. That was how that song came about. Live, when that part drops— "Shut your motherfucking mouth, bitch"—the crowd would go absolutely insane. I will always remember that; how crazy that set ended every night.

Big Jerm: "Ascension" was one of those ones that was meant to be. I even ordered that Curtis Mayfield record from Dusty Groove, a record store in Chicago. They have a pretty good online store for used records. We were just going through samples, and I found that little piano part, then the "Between heaven and hell" vocal sample. They're all from different parts of a song, and I pieced it together. I'm proud of that one. E. added some stuff on it a little later. That was that.

Justin Boyd: *GO:OD AM* still felt like he wanted to just have some good raps and hit people with it.

Big Jerm: On "Jump," that was more E . . . That was Sap first. There's a guy, Harrison [Wargo], he's a musician from Pittsburgh. Sap made the beat, it probably was a sample, and then [Wargo] added stuff and E. added stuff. DJ Dahi came on at the end of that one.

Quentin Cuff: The first three songs are a perfect encompassing of where Mac was: He's still with the home team. ID Labs produced ["Brand Name" and "Rush Hour"] and then Tyler, [The Creator], produced "Doors." Mac's working with Tyler's management, the people that birthed Tyler and Frank. This album showed Mac could work with big names, small names, and everyone in between, and craft his own sound. This is really him going back into his bag. This was Mac being like, "I got a new team; I'm not with Rostrum, but I'm still sticking to that ID Labs sound." I think he spent a lot of time in Pittsburgh, finishing this shit. I think he [also] did a lot of shit with Josh Berg. This is where The Sanctuary, ID Labs, they kind of collide. And they made *GO:OD AM*.

FACING DEATH AGAIN ON
"PERFECT CIRCLE / GOD SPEED"

"Admit it's a problem, I needa wake up /
Before one morning I don't wake up"

—*"Perfect Circle / God Speed"*

Forever alchemical, even in death, Mac Miller has altered our relationship to his music. Some listeners can parse the writing from the circumstances while others get lost in the themes of death that always colored his work. *Faces* is infused with a fresh terror in the face of Mac's overdose, but no song forces us to experience his death over and over again like "Perfect Circle / God Speed."

Clocking in at nearly eight minutes, everything from the chilling opening choir to its raw autobiographical nature make the song one of the most gutting in Miller's catalog. But before coming to one of the soberest and most plain-stated moments of Miller's career, we have the thump and dank creep of the music filling us with the sensation that we are arriving somewhere, pivoting away from something sinister. At the time of writing, Mac Miller certainly was.

"I wash these pills down with liquor and fall / Leave it to me, I do enough for us all (I do)," Mac slurs on the hook. Here we have the crux of the track: he's hurt himself so we do not have to. "Perfect Circle," then, becomes an offering of wisdom. Our trust in Mac is twofold. As we absorb the themes of sobriety and recovery, we trust him to get better while also trusting him to shoulder burdens on our behalf. We learn from his mistakes. "Perfect Circle" presents Mac as a wizened spirit, matured and all-knowing. If this places Malcolm in some ivory tower for the time being, then so be it because what follows is a gruesome revelation: he is going to die. For now, he is fighting to live.

> "Everybody saying I need rehab / 'Cause I'm speedin' with a blindfold on and won't be long / Until they watching me crash / And they don't wanna see that / They don't want me to OD and have to talk to my mother / Tell her they could have done more to help me / And she'd be crying saying that she'd do anything to have me back"

"God Speed" examines dichotomies. Mac Miller appraises his life and death through the same critical lens. He muses on death to keep himself alive. In the wake of his passing, the song becomes a barbed jab to the heart.

The startling, autobiographical aspects of "God Speed" are almost too much to bear, but, as the centerpiece of GO:OD AM, the song is a reminder that Mac Miller was a fighter through and through, no matter how willingly he seemed to toe such a dangerous line. The emotion here appears impossible to reconcile. How can a verse so entrenched in a very real death speak so much to Malcolm's desire to live? That was his dutiful dance, it seems.

Ever self-aware, Mac Miller knew he was playing a perilous game with himself. Above all else, this is what makes "God Speed" a challenging listen, both before and after his passing. The harrowing realism of the writing coupled with the accidental nature of Malcolm's death make the song all the more heartbreaking.

Facing Mac's death in this way leaves us with an important task: preservation of memory. This is why we have The Book of Mac and why it is imperative his music continues to be played. For as tragic as his passing was, speaking to his collaborators and listening to his work, we know him to have been full of life.

Though death was prevalent throughout his work, we cannot allow it to overwhelm his legacy. Mac Miller wakes up at the end of

"God Speed" because the plan was to live and prosper. The humorous skit at the end is evidence that, nose to nose with his death, Mac still loved to laugh. That remains the most essential element of his legacy.

> "I said that I thought it was a disservice to Mac's memory to turn his life into speculative 3 a.m. bar gossip and to second-guess the fond recollections of the people lucky enough to have met him in the interest of playing caring sleuth and insider to an audience of strangers. Dying young doesn't retroactively make an artist's entire life a meditation on death, even if death is present in the margins of their work. They were trying to escape it, using art to locate and share a moment's respite, and even though they didn't beat what was bugging them, they should be honored as people who fought to live, not people who sat around waiting to die."
>
> —*Craig Jenkins*[16]

Mac Miller was never trying to die. He was vying for life with every bar about the cocaine ether, though it may not have been obvious. He was creating to purge himself of his darkness.

In sweeping waves, his approach worked. Mac saved lives. That was only made possible because, beneath every mention of his death, was an overwhelming desire to press on. That is what compelled listeners.

He does not want us to sit in his death or our sorrow. There was always the next step. That is the triumph and tragedy of "God Speed." Even after his death, Mac is urging us to press on.

---

16. Craig Jenkins, "Lil Peep's *Come Over When You're Sober Pt. 2* Encases His Triumph and Tragedy in Amber," *Vulture*, November 13, 2018, https://www.vulture.com/2018/11/lil-peep-come-over-when-youre-sober-pt-2-album-review.html.

BIG JERM: I had been hoping he would do that for a while, just come back and work on something. We pretty much shut the studio down when he's there. I'm not sure if it was a getting clean kind of thing, just being away from The Sanctuary, or if he just wanted a change of scenery. It might've just been that he wanted to get back to *Blue Slide Park* and our vibe of working together. Me and him had our little moments of not getting along, but 2015, we got closer again. When he was in Pittsburgh, it felt like the old times. Over time, he got more comfortable with live instrumentation.

QUENTIN CUFF: One of my favorite things about *GO:OD AM* is the Clancys and this guy named Brad Scoffern who used to work for 4 Strikes [Management]. 4 Strikes threw this great event for us. We threw a three-day festival when *GO:OD AM* came out, in Pittsburgh. That was my favorite part because I got to work with 4 Strikes, and Warner, and Mac. We got to do a dinner with the mayor. That was Mac clean[ing] up where Mac was during *Macadelic* and *Faces*. He got better. As sad as it is right now, how Mac always looked at [the title] was an epiphany for him to get clean. It was "Go OD" and then "AM" was the wake-up call. It was a wake-up call so he *wouldn't* OD, essentially.

BIG JERM: It seemed like he was in a good place. From what I saw, he wasn't doing drugs or anything. It was nice. We would be in the studio all day, then go to the bar, and there would be a lot of his friends from high school. It was nice for everybody. It was almost like he wanted to simplify his life at the time. Pittsburgh is a lot more of a simple place than LA. It's slower-paced. It's more Midwest than people think. He wanted to get back to that more simplified lifestyle. I remember he was staying at his mom's house the whole time.

QUENTIN CUFF: Man ... If I played back "Perfect Circle / God Speed" after him passing away, I would definitely cry. I love that song ... As I'm reading the lyrics, it's crazy. It's him telling us that he hopes we can always respect him. I feel like this is a message from him, spiritually. Him not being here . . . A lot of the time, his music was like little letters and messages to his friends, family, and people he loved, to remind them of who he really was. Yeah, bro, that's who Mac really was—I really think that this is a perfect thing. "Perfect Circle / God Speed," they hit it right on the nail.

That song always meant a lot to me. There's a Bob Marley sample I think they couldn't clear. Mac says on the song something about "Buffalo soldier," and they had to switch it because the original was a direct salute to Bob Marley. That's why Mac said it in the verse, because there was a bridge or pre-chorus where Ab-Soul was talking all this "Buffalo Soldier" shit, but they had to take it out. You can get a sense for what Mac and Miller's relationship was in that moment. Miller just wanted to know his little brother was okay. "We don't talk a lot, but I hope that you're doing good."

BIG JERM: "Ascension," that was a pretty pure Mac Miller record. There was no overthinking is the best way to put it. I liked that. I hadn't thought about it like that, like [GO:OD AM] was the last real hip-hop [album], but that's true. *The Divine Feminine* is definitely not just a rap album. Maybe that was his plan: Go back to Pittsburgh, do it like he used to, and then move on from there. He always had a plan, even if nobody else knew it.

JUSTIN BOYD: He loved performing. He just loved seeing all the people that came out to see him. He always recognized he wouldn't be anywhere without his fans. *GO:OD AM* was a good tour. The Europe run of that was a lot of fun. That was my first time in Europe. It was crazy to me to see all these people in all these other countries that are so excited to see this kid. Just being from Pittsburgh, that shit's wild to me. From Pittsburgh to Australia, people everywhere knew this kid. That was awesome.

He loved to tour. That was one of his favorite things to do. He got to be with his friends every day. We got to be in a new city every day. We got to do cool shit, whether it [was to] go to a mall, or ride some go-karts, or watch a movie. It was fun to be with your friends in a different place every day, to see the world. And the fact that music brought him to do all that? How could he not love that?

QUENTIN CUFF: [*GO:OD AM* is] underrated, kinda gets lost in the shuffle, sometimes. When you stand it up next to any other album in his catalog, it's pretty fucking crazy. I think it'll always be underrated. He was being himself on this. "100 Grandkids," he gives a great update of where he's at, and that's one of his daring singles. He got Sha Money XL to produce that shit. At a time where everyone was going to Metro Boomin and the "hit makers" to capture their hits, Mac stuck with his guns, worked with ID Labs, Sap, and this cool lane like Frank Dukes, DJ Dahi, and Sevn Thomas. And him working with Miguel was huge. Him having his first major-label single with a big artist, and it being this organic thing, not like [Mac] getting the label to make him a single ... In his legacy, Mac went up against the major-label machine, and he came out with a really good product.

JUSTIN BOYD: There was a moment on the GO:OD AM Tour where it was just him and a light shining on him. He knew everybody wanted the high-paced raps and the shit that just goes hard, but he loved those moments. I think, as his fans matured with him, they loved those moments as well.

"FROM THE GRAVEL TO THE MOTHERFUCKING CASTLE"

"Through rain, sleet, snow / I'mma keep gettin' dough /
You can find me on my grind / So put your muthafuckin'
hands in the sky"

—*"Castle Made of Sand"*

Mac Miller loved motifs. He operated within his own psychedelic creative unconscious. Across his albums, the threads are plentiful and provocative. Mac was always sowing seeds, and, for ten years, he cultivated the image of his career and passion for growth through various lenses of castles. These structures stand for the beauty and fragility of the music business, and how Mac's career could at once feel towering and grand while simultaneously unstable and difficult to maintain. This dichotomy speaks to Mac Miller's work ethic. He was an always-striving musician—striving because he never doubted the fragility of the industry and his place in it. The tension made for an incredibly prolific career.

"Cuz I'm on the rise and I reside / In this castle
made of sand"

—*"Castle Made of Sand"*

We begin with *The High Life*, one of the final remnants of the smooth, easy-going Malcolm McCormick. He's confident, and the reference comes off almost incidental, but something tells me that Mac could sense he was on the brink of fame; still, I cannot imagine he was plotting a discography-long motif in his bedroom when he wrote this song. Nevertheless, this is the bedrock of what will become a sobering commentary on how fame consumed and wounded him. At his most wide-eyed and green, Mac still knew how fickle the industry would be, that what felt like stable ground would eventually shake and move.

Yet his hunger does not wane. Instability does not thwart his drive and his yearning for success, perhaps because he still does not fully know what is to come. Bars about Mac remaining king pepper the track, too, signaling an understanding and anxiety that this could all be washed away by an unforgiving tide. Packed sand could very well stand up to proverbial concrete, but a strong tidal wave does not care about metaphors. Sometimes fame robs artists of all they're worth. In the case of Mac Miller, this leads us to *Faces*.

Faces begins with one of his best songs and his most subtle castle allusions. Tucked into the psychedelic layers of "Inside Outside," at the twelve-second mark, is a sample of the soundbite that plays upon the completion of a level in *New Super Mario Bros. 2*. Mario leaps to the top of the flagpole, the flag slides down, and Mario celebrates and emotes. At the same time as the sample rings off, Mac raps, "I should've died already / Came in I was high already."

The allusion to Mario fits right into the overarching fragility painted by the castle motif. By nature, video games are based on temporary highs, repetition, and a sliding scale of difficulty. You complete one level, liberate one castle, and then—as if your progress means nothing—start another. It is an addictive feedback loop, mimicking the rat race of fame.

Coupling this repetition and the temporary feeling of victory with the opening lines of "Inside Outside," we stumble on an altogether shocked and disillusioned Mac Miller. In terms of his drug addiction, the lyrics are self-explanatory. In relation to success and fame, the message is clear: his career should have wilted by now. The castle should have come down, and yet it is still standing. Is this a beautiful thing, or perhaps something far more ominous? That answer lives on the eighth track, "Therapy."

"Since before I was a goddamn mastermind / In that castle of mine, I came up"

Perhaps the brightest song on *Faces*, "Therapy" is a sonically hopeful moment with underlying energy that's nothing if not sinister. In the context of the project, we are not feeling better so much as we are experiencing a manic, drug-fueled high. We can gather this mindset from the frenzy and self-aggrandizing on the hook ("How it feel to come and hang around a motherfucker like me?"). Elated, for certain, that invincible sensation presents a dangerous and destructive state of mind, which we see across the rancor of the verses.

The castle thread comes in on the second verse, after a moment of lucidity: "I'm back on these rap songs / Feeling that's never gonna last long." Still, in a manic state, Mac remarks on the expediency of his come-up. Success on "Therapy" reads like something obvious and naturally deserved. Yet, whenever there is a manic high, there is a subsequent crash and burn—the reckoning after our inhibitions all but evaporate. Thus, we get the same fragility through the lens of a mental break, and so, too, we get our answer: beneath every beautiful feat lies some measure of terror. Suspicion is not callous; it is welcome.

The paranoia of *Faces* takes on additional meaning—drugs propel the work, but *Faces* also interfaces with fame, which not only drove Mac to drugs but also wore on his mental state—as evidenced in his writing. The paranoia of the album expresses fresh concern over fame and its fickle nature. At any moment, this could all come down. Mac Miller is both living in his castle and figuratively waiting in the wings for its collapse. Little is said about doomsday preparations on any of his work, either because in his heart he did not imagine his castle crumbling, or because he was ready to go down with his beloved structure. Regardless of the "Why not?" we're treated to an even more ferociously delivered guiding image on *GO:OD AM*'s splitting banger "When in Rome."

"Look, mom, I fucking made it" could be the subtitle of *GO:OD AM*, an album about Malcolm coming into his own as sober, lucid, and ready to embrace fear for what it is and not the beast it stands to become. The glimmering cloud of static and chuckle that opens the song says it all. Mac Miller made it to the other side of *Faces*—to the summit of this chapter of his career. There is no concern over the structural integrity of this castle, no circling set of anxieties to detract from this riotous moment of celebration. What we have here is a success story. Full stop. Even when he spits, "How it is when you young, blowing up too much," there's no admission of struggle. Struggle is demystified, treated as matter-of-fact, not something cutting. We fucking made it.

In this moment of Mac Miller's career, stable footing was the wave, not a feature of his imagination. During the Celebration of Life concert in October of 2018, a clip played of Miller speaking about dark lyricism with Rick Rubin at Shangri-La. "I don't think that that's the only aspect of life." He said it best: we can let the joy be enough.

> "I turn the hotel to a castle / Livin' like a king for a grand
> / I don't do nothin', that's a hassle / Besides, even that
> castle's made of sand"

Too much can change in three years, as evidenced by Mac's sound, career, and tragic passing. He entered a creative renaissance with *The Divine Feminine*, the arc of which was followed by his final album, *Swimming*. Where Mac was once marking down his sobriety, his disease once again had the better of him. By not releasing an album in 2017—the only time in his career he took a gap year—all of the above compounded into the bare-faced nature of *Swimming*. The castle motif returns on "Ladders," and this time it seems to catalog all motifs and career highs before it, concluding with a fresh and resolved outlook on fame and its transience.

The castle bar on "Ladders" begins rather alchemically, as much of *Swimming* is transformative. From hotels to castles, the notion here is that Mac Miller had his career grow in phases, and his spheres of success may have robbed him partly of a home base, but what it did give him was an undeniable sense of accomplishment. Subsequent lines about living like a king, for as cheap as can be, begin to hint at the rickety quality of fame. We're not in a stone structure, but one made of tense wood, one that creaks to make its weatherworn status known.

And so, we return to our original image: the castle made of sand. His placid delivery, not unlike his approach on *The High Life*, reveals that this fragility does not scare Mac. Thinking of "So It Goes," the album's closer, that same mantra applies to Mac's view of fame and status on "Ladders." Even the castles made from hotel rooms, from tours, from seeming unshakeable career highs, erode away. Everything, it seems, can be undone.

THE ART OF WEBBING

GO:OD AM was a mature triumph for Malcolm, who spent the years leading up to it battling his demons on wax with such candor that we fell into a deep love with his work. Through the art of webbing—songs alluding to other songs on the album and other albums—Mac put *GO:OD AM* in conversation with itself. Through a series of inter-album allusions, the record evolves from a piece of music to a living, breathing setting of its own.

GO:OD AM gave us a sense of *place*. We strolled through the album as it interacted with itself. The experience of catching all the notes of webbing gave us the feeling of Mac as a superior craftsman. The buildings of his *GO:OD AM* city not only stood tall but also bent to his every whim. Through the art of webbing, *GO:OD AM* grew ever-dynamic as you dug deeper into the album. The allusions began thoughtfully on "100 Grandkids," and ran until "When in Rome" signaled back to "100 Grandkids." There is even a moment ("Time Flies") where Malcolm verbatim signals a bonus track off *Watching Movies with the Sound Off.*

Mac begins his webbing phenomenon on the outro of "100 Grandkids." As Elle Varner sounds off with some spoken word, Mac interjects with "time flies," the title of the next song. Not a giant leap across the tracklisting, this first allusion simply sets us up to catch further allusions. Here, Mac was letting us in on the trick of the album, showcasing the bonds between songs and hoping we were apt to play along as the record progressed.

There's a satisfying element to this first note as well. We go from Mac's "time flies" chant to Lil B on the intro of "Time Flies" itself. Once we make the connection and catch on to Malcolm's game, we can't help but smirk. At first, the webbing feels fun, and gives *GO:OD AM* a small modicum of body. The songs are not yet in full conversation, they're whispering to each other. For the first arc of the album, this effective pillow talk is enough to keep us listening. Our interest is piqued enough to see where Mac, mayor of the city he's constructing on the album, will lead us next.

"Time Flies" takes the game several steps further, borrowing a line directly from 2013's "Goosebumpz": "So when I die, these bitches still can fuck my hologram, goddamn." Where moments earlier Mac established the relationship between *GO:OD AM* and the album itself, on "Time Flies," he goes on to establish the relationship between *GO:OD AM* and his discography. With this one line, we understand *GO:OD AM* to be a continuation of Malcolm's studio album story. As his major label debut on Warner Records, *GO:OD AM* would go down as a major outing for Malcolm—his first release without independent backing.

By calling back to *Watching Movies with the Sound Off*, he reminds us he's the same old Mac Miller, regardless of the major label support. It's a promise not to change and also a means of suggesting that he's been creating with his future in mind the entire time. Something of a time warp, this allusion is just as satisfying as the first. Mac's discography becomes its own setting too. We come to appreciate it as a solar system. Consequently, *GO:OD AM* elevates from city to planet. It feels as if many conversations are happening at once within Mac's work, but they never feel overwhelming. Everything is tightly woven—the fabric of his work soft to the touch.

This weaving brings us to the ninth track, "In the Bag," which houses several allusions. All of these notes live on the second verse and come in rapid succession, giving us the sense that we are playing in a shooting gallery. "In the Bag" heightens Mac's game on *GO:OD AM*, making it more fun for the speed at which we have to play. The three allusions of the track give the album a vibrancy and set an admirable tone. We've spent the time prior to "In the Bag" warming up, and now we're headed into the main event.

First, we have the line "They just want to break the law and find someone to fuck," which refers to "Break the Law," the following song, A ways away from the song itself, you only realize Mac has made this connection minutes later. It's a delayed pay-off, but a satisfying one. The distance creates something of a loop between "In the Bag" and "Break the Law," as it does to a smaller degree on "100 Grandkids" and "Time Flies." We bounce between songs in our minds, thinking *Wait, what did he just say*? The distance between allusion and subject only increases our respect for Malcolm's writing.

Next, we get an allusion to the album itself with Mac saying: "That's what I call a good morning" just a few bars after the "Break the Law" tidbit. Signaling the whole of the album is a wise move because it reminds us Mac is working with large concepts. He's not merely drawing a roadmap of his own album but letting the album properly work its way into the songs. There's a thoughtfulness to "In the Bag." The conversation truly begins here, and with such a mighty connection drawn to the whole of the record, we're encouraged to pay more attention to Mac's every word.

We're also inclined to take the themes of "In the Bag" more to heart. Here, Mac satirically bemoans materialism and his relationship to fame—one of the major themes of *GO:OD AM*. The second verse delivers a good dose of irony as Mac has a one-sided conversation about importance and money, all to the point of showcasing how material goods can strip you of your humanity. None of these ideas are particularly difficult to grasp because Mac has already told us, in his own way, to pay close attention to his language. So, we do. And, again, we are rewarded.

"In the Bag" is also the first song to take a few leaps forward with its signaling. We jump to track fourteen, "Cut the Check," with the line "They just cut the check." Again, we won't know Mac is planting seeds for future songs until we arrive at track fourteen but the set-up to the pay-off stands to be huge. At the least, such a gap between allusion and subject gives us the desire to run "In the Bag" back and gives "Cut the Check" a sense of familiarity, with its title already festering in our minds. The world of the album becomes part of our world. *GO:OD AM* becomes a reaching album, one full of literal internality.

We close out our allusion-spree on "When in Rome." The blustery track houses two notes, one of which nicely takes us back to where we began—a closed loop to lay the foundation for Malcolm's obsession with perfect circles, of course. Firstly, "Tell 'em cut a check for a young'un', and I'mma cash out" loosely references "Cut the Check," which is still two songs away. Loading up on allusions for "Cut the Check" makes us do three things. One, we think back on "In the Bag" and hopefully realize what Mac was getting at so slyly. Two, once "Cut the Check" comes on, as with "In the Bag," we pay close attention to Mac's writing and his motifs as they relate to the rest of the album. Three, we are prepared for "Cut the Check," meaning it no longer feels brand new. Rather, "Cut the Check" feels like an "of course" moment. We're left feeling Mac Miller will always deliver on his musical promises.

Finally, "When in Rome" brings us back to "100 Grandkids" with "Got another hundred grand, but who's counting?" We catch this line instantly, for we have been trained to be on the lookout. By this point, we realize Mac effectively turned *GO:OD AM* into a game. The album comes to life from thread to thread. *GO:OD AM* thrives within itself, speaks to itself, and consequently, speaks louder and louder to the listener. We feel the life of the album flowing out of our speakers. By the end of "When in Rome," we realize *GO:OD AM* was meant to be traversed, quested through. The whole runtime, we were meant to be collecting allusions and connecting dots.

These tiny details keep our attention as the album spins, making the case for *GO:OD AM* to be one of Mac's most satisfying offerings. Between it being his major-label debut, his comeback from the cocaine ether of *Faces*, and his foray into life music, we could walk away from *GO:OD AM* with the impression of it as Mac's tightest creation yet, his most playful. That's what we call a good morning.

2016

THE DIVINE FEMININE

"I've made a lot of love songs in the past, and they always end up being my favorites. I think it also opened the door for me to become a bit more vulnerable with how I speak and what I say and how I use my voice."

—Mac Miller[17]

17. Patricia Garcia, "Mac Miller on Love, Ariana Grande, and the Last Thing That Made Him Cry," *Vogue*, September 27, 2016, https://www.vogue.com/article/mac-miller-the-divine-feminine-album.

A DELICATE NATURE

Delicate love is huddling under a weighted blanket in the wintertime and weaving your legs together for warmth. It is brewing a cup of wildberry tea and dabbing away tears. This is not the pawing passion of tenderness. There is a lightness to this genre of love, a baked-in understanding between partners. It is hushed and all-baring. You give yourself over entirely and spin a sugar tower of precious emotions. This mix of fear and fearlessness, of synchronicity, is the heart of Mac Miller's understanding of love in 2016.

The Divine Feminine is a propulsive display of romance at its peak, a perfect blend of Mac's playful nature and the hyper-serious high of falling in love. We're a long way from the tawdry qualities of 2009's "Crushin' Round the Clock" or "Fly in Her Nikes"—both early sophomoric attempts at parsing love off his beloved tape *The High Life.* In 2009, sex was an achievement, not a union. It was about putting up numbers and netting the baddest bitch—to boast and assert his masculinity—not about finding fulfilling love.

By 2016, the way Miller appraises his lover's body has been slowed down. He does not miss an inch or fail to savor each second as he pores over her skin, as on "Skin" itself. Delicate love is about achieving a oneness with your partner without imposing yourself on them. It's about mutual respect and not letting desire rule you, while also giving in to every affectionate whim. It is the ultimate form of cherishing someone.

"Skin" runs deeper than pleasure. Mac elevates the track as a moment of pure surrender and fusion. Here, we have the type of sex where ego is absent. "I opened up your legs and go straight for your heart," Mac explains on the hook. It's the kind of sex where you can't tell if you're panting from the rush of activity or emotion, or trying to catch your partner's breath on your tongue—anything to get closer. It's a fine line between affection and obsession. This sliver of space fosters delicateness by design.

Earlier, we have the pleading "Stay," which is secure in its vulnerability. Here, Mac is practically begging his lover to remain by his side. The song is funky and expansive, with blooming trumpets and an infectious cadence. The timbre of the track is light, but the emotions are serious. How often have we felt desperate for togetherness? How often would we do anything to be touched?

Mac is demanding. He cannot help himself. He needs to be with his lover. Mac is uneasy. And yet, when speaking directly to his partner, he returns to form. "I don't wanna be polite no more," he raps on the bridge. Though most of the song is spent yearning, by the bridge, we have a loving reunion.

There's more to *The Divine Feminine* than sex. "Congratulations" basks in a delicate glory with images of kale for breakfast and a shared hamper. Making momentous occasions out of the motions of ordinary life is as thoughtful as it gets. There's an overriding tenderness—not animalistic—baked into the song's easy touches.

These tiny bumps of love come up again on "We," where Mac is so absorbed by his lover, he seems at a loss for words. "You can be my . . . " he trails off, unable to conclude his thought. Love is not about ownership. Instead, love is flowing and overcoming. Just like "Congratulations," the feeling is born of the smallest details: "I'm in love with the way that you say my name / Every time it sound brand new."

This spellbound energy gives us "My Favorite Part" and "God Is Fair, Sexy Nasty." On both, Mac sounds positively enchanted. The Ariana Grande-featuring "My Favorite Part" is, as its name suggests, an ode to the best part of loving someone. "God Is Fair, Sexy Nasty" is the most Mac-like rendition of sex on the album, fully giving in to his freaky side but with a gentle touch. Mac breaks from the physicality to deliver: "You're the only thing for me in this fucked up world."

The Divine Feminine achieves a gentleness in the sonic space as well, with the climbing and plucking second half of "Cinderella" standing as the perfect example of lightness. Here, Mac is beyond obsessed with his lover, and he's more than comfortable being consumed by her. She's in his thoughts and in his dreams. It's a perfect storm of affection that could stand to break our senses, but hangs on the precipice to our immense delight. Mac appears ready for a lifetime of love and cherishing someone, ready to follow them to the ends of the earth.

There is love, and there is delicate love, and here we are treated to the sweetest emotions. *The Divine Feminine* succeeds because it tempers our carnal instincts. With this album, Mac matures his understanding of love, delivering living, breathing love songs built to last a lifetime of romances.

Vic Wainstein: The first time I linked up with Malcolm, it was through Tyler, The Creator. They were slated to do a song together to wrap up his series of songs he did for *Watching Movies*, and it's possibly the worst song I've ever heard either of them record. But they were so excited about working together. That night, I was not too familiar [with Mac]. I knew who he was and his phenomenon, somewhat. My full idea of him was built that night. I remember calling Josh Berg. I was like, "Damn, man, your boy can *rap*." He laughed at me because I had no idea what I was walking into.

There was something else that happened later that was indicative of how genuine of a person he was. My car broke down in the studio parking lot. I had the studio working on getting me a cab so I could get home. Malcolm pulled around the corner in his Benz, saw me standing outside, and rolled down the window. "Yo, bro you need a ride?" I'm like, "Awh, man, don't worry about it. I live on the Westside, which is a significant amount away." He's like, "I'm not doing shit, get in!" He gave me a ride home to a place he had no reason to go, besides to drop me off. When we get there, he asks to use my restroom. I'm like, "Dude, that's the least I could do! You drove me across LA, 'cause you're a nice dude. You need a hot towel or something to drink?" He used the restroom. I was just sitting on my couch. He proceeded to sit down and watch *SportsCenter* with me for three hours. Then we just talked. After that day of finding out how immensely talented he was, then finding out how much of a real human he was shortly after, that set the precedent for how I revered him moving forward. He was a class act, on and off the field.

Aja Grant (pianist, Phony Ppl): I can't remember the first time I heard his music—I remember the first time I heard about him. He was on TV and it was when *Blue Slide Park* made history. I found out he's my age and that's the first time I heard about him, but my sister is a big fan of his. She's also a DJ and listens to a lot of great music. She always raved about him. I remember, she went to one of his concerts when he did *GO:OD AM* here in New York. [She] loved it so much, she bought the hoodie with his face on it, yawning. She used to wear that every single day. I didn't really listen to his music like that, but I used to see him every single day because of my sister. My dad knew about him, my mom.

Before we even met, he had tweeted my band. We were so geeked off of that tweet. We thought it was dope he reached out. A couple years down the line, he tweeted: "Can somebody send me some beautifully played piano?" A couple people tagged me in that tweet—I didn't know, I was at the movie theater watching *Star Wars*. I was in the theater with my sister and my dad, and my phone was going *off*. I saw Mac Miller's name, and I thought it was for Phony Ppl. During the movie, I was like, "Lemme see what's going on here." I looked at my phone and saw Mac Miller [replying] to Aja Grant. I'm like, "What is going on right now?"

I went to the bathroom during the movie, and people were just congratulating me. It was hundreds of people, and my Twitter was super quiet. I scroll up, and he tweeted me: "I trust you." That was his first tweet to me. Then he DM'd me. It was so cool. I was so grateful. It was December 26, 2015. He said: "What's good man? I'm making a love project, and I need some piano to sing on." I was like, "For sure, I'll send you a couple ideas." He sent me his email and I was like, "Word, I'm gonna send you some in a few." He was on a flight to India with Nomi [his girlfriend] at the time. He was geeked he had WiFi on the flight.

I gave him my number and I *ran* home. Got home—I was still living at my parents' house at the time—and I have this upright piano my dad found in New Jersey when I was in high school. I set my voice memo up and I just started playing; I sent him probably five different voicemails of stuff. I was insecure about it—I'm gonna play my heart out, but I don't think he's gonna like it. But everything I sent, he's like, "Yo! This is exactly what I was looking for, I'm in tears right now." He was like, "I'm 'bout to move to Brooklyn so I can record. I wanna really get into this project." So, the song he liked, he wanted to record it for real.

Two to three weeks later, into 2016, we went into the studio—I thought it was gonna be a typical rapper session. But it was just him and the engineer there in Blast Off Studios. It was very intimate, personal. We spoke for a while. I was starstruck, a little bit. This is *Mac Miller* and he wants to work with *me*? I'm gonna do the best I can do. There was this beautiful piano in Blast Off, this baby grand piano. My heart is pounding, my palms sweating on the piano. But he was so comforting. He made me feel [relaxed] like, "Hey, we're just hanging out. Just do what you do, 'cause I love what you do." He asked me what color I wanted the room; we made the lights blue.

He explained to me he was working on that love project and said he was gonna call it *The Divine Feminine*. I played the piano part [I had sent him], and it sounded so beautiful. He rapped on it, and he already had everything written out from the voice memo. We pieced it together, together. "Let's put this part here, this part here. Let's add a little bridge section." That song became "Congratulations," which is the first song on *The Divine Feminine*.

He texted me, "Yo! I have string players in the studio *right now*, when can you get here?" I was like, "I'm not even halfway done." So, I finished it, printed out all the sheet music, and I ran . . . I remember I had no money in my pockets. I think my dad gave me train fare. I got lost. Got there mad late, but I got there. Here I am, mad sweaty. The string players are recording ["Planet God Damn"], and he also had a trumpet player who did the horns on "Dang!" and I guess he put together that string quartet of Julliard kids. It was super intimidating because I didn't even go to college. I just remember putting the sheet music, and when they played it . . . I was in tears. I can't believe what I did just came to life.

VIC WAINSTEIN: [A studio session] usually consisted of a lot of listening to music that he had plans for and music he just liked. Once we were lost in that, sparks started to fly. The next part would be trying to figure out his role with the music, and his pocket with sounds he was excited to use. He would try to write to stuff. Sometimes he would write by himself. Sometimes he would get in the booth and spitball whatever came to mind, melodically or lyrically. He would try a bunch of different things until things started to stick. He had a way of getting into his bag and building it out. We would go through everything we could to spark a creative fire. He'll sit down at a drum kit. He'll sit down at a piano. He'll write something that was just going through his mind or something he thought prior. There were a number of ways he would get in the mood. We would just keep switching until we struck gold.

That was an interesting time, too, because the album started and stopped. I saw Malcolm go through a full range of emotions. We were at a studio in Hollywood, and we started a song I produced on *TDF*, called "Skin." The night we did that, we were up until five in the morning, throwing shit against the wall, trying to get it to stick. We ended up making some leaps and bounds creatively. We were probably at our limits creatively for the day. I sat on the couch in the control room, my eyes starting to close. I'm about to go to sleep. Then I hear: "Dog!" I jolt up! I think he broke something or he erased the file. He's like, "Prince died!" That was the first news we got of Prince dying, and Prince is his absolute favorite. He proceeded to cry so many tears for about three hours. I'll never forget where I was when Prince died because of that. I'll never forget anyway, but it was such a significant thing because I shared it with Mac.

AJA GRANT: He was playing it so cool, trying to play the super-producer role. I remember him sitting on the couch, with his hand on his chin, thinking, or dreaming about what his project was gonna be. He appreciated those strings so much. He was like, "Yo, I need *you* on this project. If I'm in the studio, just come through. Just think with me." After that, every other song, he'd be like, "Just try something on the keys."

I was in the studio with him every other session. It was really, really, really dope to be around him and see the way he would work. He was very focused; he was always thinking of ideas. It was amazing when they did happen because it would be the way he was thinking about it, you know? I always envied that and thought that was something I wanted to have in my toolbox. Every day, if I'm in the studio, I'm thinking, *What would Mac do in this situation?* Even when he was alive, I would think that. That was after the first session.

VIC WAINSTEIN: He was more hell-bent on being diligent on his artistic efforts. What happened closer to the *Swimming* and *Circles* era, he worked smarter not harder. Before, he was working a lot harder to find out his creative ceiling. Once he figured out it was a lot higher than what he had thought, he started being a little more concise about his efforts. Everything started hitting the first time. He became more sure about what he liked and what he didn't like. He had a healthy fear of shit not working and not being good enough. It drove him further and it served him. It forced him to think out of the box and figure out how to make it work rather than not acknowledge it at all. He was so passionate about it. The fear drove him. The vulnerability drove him. I don't know if it was ever as dire as he could lose all his fans, but the fact that his world could change publicly based on his artistic decisions probably scared the shit out of him. Only real innovators know that [and] still decide to take that risk.

AJA GRANT: After the "Congratulations" session, I thought he wouldn't call me, like it was a one-and-done thing. I remember the second time he called me; I was at a bar and he hit me up. I was raving to my friends, like, "Yo, man! I was in the studio with Mac Miller." He called me as I'm telling them this. I went outside, answered the phone: "What's good, man?" "Yo! Where you at?" "I'm at a bar; you in the studio? Should I come through the studio?" "Nah! Today's my birthday. Come to my crib; I'm celebrating my birthday." That's when he was living in Dumbo, Brooklyn. With the quickness, I called the Uber over, went over to his house. He had a few people in there—I was intimidated by his apartment.

We did some music in there because he can't stop doing music. He was playing me what he had of the album so far. He had "Dang!" without horns. He had a couple other things on there. The whole project is different. The way you hear it now and the way he had it before, it felt like one long MP3. It felt like a vinyl where you don't even hear the stop of the next song. I think *The Divine Feminine* was, in my opinion, his album for Nomi. They really loved each other—a lot. [The released album] is a completely different project, but the soul is still in there. But what it was initially for, he had to chip away at it. It was a lot of love stuff on there. There was this one section with a ton of sex noises—the concept was so dope. It was really psychedelic; it went in waves. It was dope.

VIC WAINSTEIN: I wasn't surprised because I had learned about his [musical] abilities before. I was actually enthralled [when] he decided to share that side with his fans. Before that, it was very rap intensive. Although he was doing more musical stuff when he was touring, a lot of people didn't know if that would be a mainstay for him. What they didn't know was, it was always there. He just had a fanbase championing the rap stuff a lot more. Part of his development was figuring out how to balance that, which we ultimately got to with *Circles* and *Swimming*.

AJA GRANT: *The Divine Feminine* was a great project. It was *different*. He went in. I wish people could hear the original version, 'cause that is special.

THE IMPORTANCE OF
"PLANET GOD DAMN"

A seasoned writer, Mac understood the importance of including such a hard turn as "Planet God Damn" to add texture and vary the tone of his otherwise pastel pink record.

As *The Divine Feminine* marks the start of Mac Miller's third creative renaissance—the era of softer musicianship that pivots away from pure hip-hop displays—there is a new burden of proof placed on Malcolm. *TDF* was such a thematic departure from the tumult of *GO:OD AM*. Mac had to show us how, exactly, he could exist in a new sonic space with the same conviction that guided his previous material.

"Planet God Damn" stakes his claim on this new era by drawing lines between the past and present. With its well-measured raps and darker images, the song harkens back to albums of old, reminding us *TDF* still houses the same believable Mac Miller. Simultaneously, with a silky Njomza feature, choral chops, and nicely hollowed chords battling over rattling drums, "Planet God Damn" squarely belongs on the glimmering *TDF*. It is a thoughtful and crisp moment tying together all the dynamic elements of Malcolm's artistry on an otherwise insular album.

This song plays right into the canon of Mac Miller love songs established back on *Blue Slide Park*'s "Missed Calls." That is, we understand the mix of pleasure and pain as a function of romance: "Yeah, I think I'm stuck inside nostalgia / My mind are in the times when this love was so divine / But now it's feelin' like without ya." While a majority of this album is spent floating through a luxurious love, here Mac is scampering about, trying to deduce where things went wrong:

"How the fuck did / We get into a place we ain't accustomed to lovin' inside of?"

This does not simply function as a tonal pivot, but as a volt of energy in the epic poem that is *The Divine Feminine*. Consider the song's placement, following the long and soaring "Cinderella" and preceding the poppy and direct "Soulmate." From the tracklisting alone, we understand "Planet God Damn" to be a critical palette cleanser.

We listen and recall the Mac Miller of 2014's "Wedding," the one who cannot stand to see his lover hurt but cannot help hurting her. We recall the Mac Miller of 2013's "Objects in The Mirror," who makes fabled minutiae into "love's currency." From Njomza's hook on "Planet God Damn" begging Mac to tell the truth, we recall 2015's "ROS," where love is not too kind to Malcolm, but he presses on anyway.

Following the life music of *GO:OD AM*, it would be natural to shy away from *The Divine Feminine* and label it too sweet for Mac Miller's canon. "Planet God Damn" rebukes that notion. The song feels like a promise from Malcolm to his fans—a promise that nothing will keep him from seeing life in his splendid and honest way. Even at the height of love, when every moment feels like a microdose, Mac Miller still has it in him to see the world for what it truly is. This unhindered sight was his superpower, and the reason we still love him.

2018

SWIMMING

"I've had a life that was completely carefree. The very beginning of my career was completely carefree. I felt invincible, I felt . . . just, zero sadness. You know? For a moment. And then I've had all sadness, just all darkness. But I think being in a place where you can spend time in both and gain perspective on that other side, makes you appreciate what each brings to the table."

—MAC MILLER[18]

18.   Mac Miller, "An Interview with Mac Miller," interview by Craig Jenkins, *Vulture*, September 13, 2018, https://www.vulture.com/2018/09/mac-miller-interview.html.

REBIRTH

"Inertia"—the freestyle Mac Miller dropped two days before the release of *Swimming*, with its themes of constant movement, time-bending, and rebirth—is the prologue. "Inertia" is our past darkness and our foray into the resurrection of Mac Miller.

The video opens with Mac poking around and setting up the beat. Once he's settled and ready, the freestyle begins in The Before: "I've been a God way before a synagogue." These details suggest Mac Miller is the master of his own timeline, much like *Swimming* sets out to prove that Mac is the master of his own destiny.

"Inertia" does not romanticize The Before. Mac quickly makes it a point to draw lines between desire and reality ("This is not what you wanted, but this is what you got / You live with what you got") amidst images of liquor and magic brews. The gentle surrealist bent suggests Mac is aware of the knots of his past, and while there is an attractive element to escaping in the present, he does not want to simply run to his vices as he had in the past. We are getting redemption as well as growth.

> "And you ain't nothing to the planet but a little dot / Suddenly hit the water like the line that's on a fishing rod / Simple thoughts got me itching like the chicken pox / Knitted socks, with fingers tryna scratch a lotto ticket off / When I made it, I was getting all the bitches off / See I was faded, now I'm counting up the minutes lost"

Mac is in his writer's bag, taking stock of his minute place in the world and battling back against the aggrandizement of the celebrity that he has feared and resented for most of his career. Of course, we get the direct allusion to *Swimming* when we "hit the water" and a secondary nod to producer alter-ego Larry Fisherman.

Swimming's "Come Back to Earth" opens with: "And I was drowning, but now I'm swimming." "Inertia" is the drowning, but as we only grow from anguish, we only learn to swim by flailing in a dire situation. So, the freestyle is not an admonishment of struggle, but rather a verified thank you. Taken in concert with the album, "Inertia" is a celebration of pain—not a glorification—and a note to how important it is to cherish where the hurt can take you.

Eventually, Mac incites a conversation with himself. "I overdid it like the way the roller coaster spinning / Homie, that's inertia / I'm the moon to the sun how I birthed ya," he declares. Mac is careful with how he speaks to and about himself and his addiction, which is critical, too, to his growth.

Mac speaks in tongues to his fears and acts as one with his rebirth. He becomes a new man by his own hand, not by a stroke of luck. In the journey of his growth, Mac Miller is the agent of his own ascension.

All of this is why the final couplet of "Inertia" is a relentless punch to the stomach: "You ain't nothing till you die and come back to life iller / They haven't made a motherfucker realer, Mr. Miller, yeah." He comes back to life quite literally on "Come Back to Earth." Still, "Inertia" ends in motion, and *Swimming* maintains that forward movement, but freshly reborn, he course-corrects. Instead of barreling toward his demise, on *Swimming*, Mac Miller advances forward to heal.

VIC WAINSTEIN: We were working on a lot of the songs that became *Swimming* without actually [having] the full concept. The concepts came from two places: Certain things we started to achieve musically helped [with] driving the concept home. And he started thinking, thematically, of the idea of what he wanted to go with. It just so happened part of it came from the stuff we were currently working on. A lot of the efforts we were in at the moment fed into his concept. The timeline is really interesting. [The concept came together] probably a little over a year before we released it.

QUENTIN CUFF: This was when Mac was going back and forth about "Should I do a rap mixtape?" With *Swimming*, looking at the track-list, at one point he just had "Jet Fuel," mad long ago. He had a few other songs, maybe "Wings." "Jet Fuel" is the oldest song I remember on here. From "Jet Fuel" he was like, "Maybe I'll just drop" this mixtape that was just a picture of him outside his house with the G Wagon. A quick mixtape, like another *Faces*. "Jet Fuel" was gonna be on that with a few other songs, and "Conversation Pt. 1" was in that batch too.

VIC WAINSTEIN: He is one of the hardest working music guys I've ever been around. The fact that [*Swimming*] was easier than anything he'd ever done worried him. He knows firsthand how hard he had to work to get the shit before that. Since it didn't add up on the mechanical side, he couldn't turn it off at first. There were times I had to talk him out of ruining records because he wanted to try everything under the sun. Some of our ideas probably wouldn't have made it out alive if he spent more time with them. Shit's only finished when you have to hand it over. It worked against us in a way, but once he grasped the idea he was hitting the mark, that work ethic . . . It made it easier for us to get the results we were looking for the first time. We got good at the editing process and making the right decisions rather than trying a bunch of stuff and hoping. He got smarter, and so the harder-working Malcolm didn't have to exist as much during the *Swimming* process.

QUENTIN CUFF: Josh Berg came over one day, and in that one day, me, him, Mac, and Jimmy started the skeleton for *Swimming*. I was sitting in the studio for three hours before Mac woke up, and I re-found the song "Come Back to Earth." It was on the cutting room floor from a long time ago. I was like, "Bro, this sounds incredible!" We brought that song back and it was the intro. Then, Jimmy and I had found "2009" and we were like, "Bro? What about this song?" Once we found those two songs it was [clear] this was gonna be more of a heartfelt album. Every moment had to be a poignant moment.

ERIC G (producer, "2009"): We have a couple other songs that never came out, but "2009" was the first one that I actually got to be there to record with him. It was in Seattle when he was on tour [in 2016]. We had dinner at the Space Needle one night with him and Ariana [Grande] and all the people on tour. Went to the studio for two nights in a row. The way he did the song, he did it so quickly. He works really fast and does a lot of stuff at all times.

It was a sample chop that I had. I did all the drums, the bass, the piano. The chords. I did the whole thing. It was just a beat on my computer that I had. He was sober for a while at this point. He was looking all healthy and stuff. It was just me and him there, and I was kinda going through my own thing at the time, and I was asking him for advice. We just talked about that for hours, going in and outside, smoking cigarettes.

He was like, "Play me some beats." And the first or second beat I played was that one. He just paced around the room for a little bit, with the beat playing. Then he put it in Pro Tools and then he paced around for a little bit and did the first half of the song in a pitch-black booth with no phone or anything. I don't even know how he did it, and for it to be so meaningful. It's crazy that it just came off the top of his head like that. He does the whole first half, and he goes, "Oh, that was tight." Then he did the rest a little later, but he didn't write anything down. It was really crazy to watch.

When we recorded, it felt like something super meaningful to me. It was relevant to my life, in a way. It's relevant to a lot of people. It's real emotional. It means the same thing to me now as it did then, but a lot more. It holds a lot of relevancy considering the situation. It's one of those songs that brings you back to a time that you can smell how it smelled when you first heard it type thing. You can feel how you felt. You know, those things that make you time travel? I saw him the next day and he was showing me—played it for everyone who was on the tour, and all his close friends. Everyone said they cried.

NICK DIERL (friend and publicist): The degree to which he felt comfortable with expressing honesty in the emotion he was feeling was the single best part. I say that because there were a lot of great qualities he had, but that was the quality that changed the way I lived my life. It's self-evident on his records. He was comfortable being honest with people and taught me that it's okay not to be good all the time. It's much more important to be real with yourself about where you're at. You can't address where you are if you're in denial.

QUENTIN CUFF: "2009." That's the song that's hardest to listen to, as far as songs that sum up the era. "What's the Use?" too, 'cause I know Mac really wanted to perform that one. He was really into that one and wanted to perform that one really bad. For me, "2009" and them putting a string section on the beginning... I think Mac knew how much he bared. Sober Mac just wasn't a person that put hella shit into his [music]. And *Macadelic/Faces* era, as much as it seems like he's revealing... You're getting a bunch of *bars*. The real bars came on certain songs in certain eras, and *Swimming* was one of those eras. Everything said on there was a pure fact. No fantasy world or character. It was all just diary-like songwriting.

WE DON'T CRY NO MORE

"2009" makes the temporary less scary. By way of blooming keys and enveloping strings, life feels less random and unfulfilling and more fluid. When Mac says we must jump in to swim, he's telling us the only way out is through, and it will be okay once we get to the other side. Mac Miller is not sullen when he admits it's no longer 2009; he sounds grateful. His tone is matured, and he projects fresh wisdom unto the track.

Wisdom feeds the hook. His gentle and declarative, "Yeah, I know what's behind that door" leaves us with the sense Mac is no longer scared of the future. He's lived through enough, and perhaps he now knows there is always good to be had. The anxieties of a young man about to stumble into fame are multiple, but having lived through the highs and lows, he's come away with more highs than he'd realized. The humanity of the track, then, is how Mac embraces the lows. Singing of demons filling his mansion and materialism failing to fill his heart, we do not receive resolve without conflict. "2009" paints the necessity of conflict not as a boogeyman, but as a pit stop. Not once during the song do we feel as though happiness is out of reach; we're already there.

This song is about accepting that the good times have to end, but only so that better times can occupy their spaces. The song is bittersweet in the purest sense of the word. The magic of "2009" derives from how assured Mac sounds that things truly are better now. The nostalgia factor almost melts away, because he is no longer lusting after his past despite how carefree it felt. He is content in his present, a fighter who has come home to bask in the glory of appreciating the day. It's a becoming moment for Mac Miller, who spends most of *Swimming* telling us about his battle to stay alive and live in earnest.

"2009" is the crux of *Swimming*; it teaches us the lesson of forward motion and hope. We can love it or leave it, as on "What's the Use?"—but we have to live through life nonetheless. Mac's propensity to chase after life—his natural-born joy that he spread to his fans and everyone he worked with—sums itself up on the song. Darkness comes into play but does not cloud the track, just like Malcolm refused to let darkness cloud his life. The song exists as if to say: there is always going to be something better, even when it's good. Even when it's bad. There is always going to be a better chapter. We are one in our humanness by the end of the cut, and he's got us, as always. Mac Miller's grand overcoming is our overcoming; we don't have to cry no more.

"An angel's supposed to fly," Mac sings. He is, and he does.

VIC WAINSTEIN: *Swimming* happened completely on its own. We didn't have to super-navigate the efforts. A lot of stuff just happened organically. There was a point towards the end of wrapping up what we were doing before *Swimming* where he would constantly put himself through the ringer. He lived that "pressure makes diamonds" stuff. To see *Swimming* come a lot easier, he was surprised at that and couldn't really believe it at first. Part of that is how good he got musically and how good he got at editing himself.

CRAIG JENKINS (Music Critic, *New York Magazine*): He was serious about the craft. You could tell because every time you heard from him, he'd figured out something different. He got a little better at it. That's kinda rare. Often, you'll hear an artist come out, and five years after the beginning, it'll be comparable or worse. Mac was someone who when you thought it was a complete picture, he'd figure out a new room or a new angle every time.

NICK DIERL: Malcolm was an open book, both about the highs and the lows. The irony is, I think *Swimming*, retroactively, has been read as a dark record when, in fact, I don't think I ever knew a happier, healthier, more beaming Malcolm than the one that existed in the year leading up to the release of *Swimming*. In some ways, he felt empowered, because he was in such a great place personally, to let some of the lows come out in the music.

VIC WAINSTEIN: He was always confident. He was always ready to take risks. But he hit a new bar with confidence and his choices musically. That was the most noticeable shift. He became a better piano player. He became a better guitar player. Also, he was finding himself in a space where he relied on himself more. Previously, he had this world he built via his own brain and a collective of artists he trusted and admired. With *Swimming*, he kind of implored himself to do more, rather than relying on someone else ... A lot of the stuff he did, we kept! It was great. It came out exactly how he wanted it. We were stoked to reach that landmark. Once you saw the world he built, it was an amazing place. We couldn't wait to put [Swimming] out, that's how awesome it was to us.

KEHLANI (singer): I went over [to Mac's house] expecting to make a song, and we always joke that we didn't end up doing the song. We sat there, and we watched the Mary J. Blige commercial, the Burger King commercial. The whole day we were crying over him re-enacting this commercial. I did his birth chart! We were supposed to get lunch the day that everything happened. That's the beginning to the end. It was very deep for it to be very short. We were talking every day. We were talking about relationships and getting very close and talking about my baby.

CRAIG JENKINS: You would hit him up like, "Yo, there's this thing going on," and he would pop up at it. He was at the studio, and he was like, "Come by." He was accessible, and he made time, even when he was working on an album. I figured there are a million other people ahead of me with more pressing things to offer the guy. Just the fact there was still enough time for me, a guy who's not necessarily in the picture, was amazing.

As far as white rappers go, this is someone who understood his place and utility in the hierarchy of all that. A lot of people don't. This is the era where Macklemore starts getting serious about privilege, so we had a lot of interesting conversations about how that works and people who aren't doing the thing right. One of my favorite stories is when he had his birthday at a spot downtown, and I brought a friend who got super drunk and was like, "Kendrick Lamar is trash." [Mac] tolerates it and at a later date is like, "Your white homie needs to figure his shit out."

KEHLANI: Even when it came down to talking about things that could potentially upset him with other people, it still came from the angle of, "You know what? God bless him." That always ended up being the verbiage when it came to speaking on other people. It's really rare to find people like that.

NICK DIERL: Malcolm had an uncanny ability and sense for making people that were in the room with him feel good. There's a lot of people who feel like they need to put on an air of being cool or being kind of aloof, but he had a knack for reading a room and making sure that everyone was in a good spirit. Having the ability to do that in times where he wasn't in very good spirits . . . He would take it upon himself to make sure everyone in the room was feeling good and prioritized that ahead of his feelings. There's something to be said for the self-lessness that he showed in being attentive to other people's emotions, whether he had known them for five minutes or fifteen years.

QUENTIN CUFF: He was on the cusp of truly becoming the man, the older version of himself. He was learning to grow . . . With the overdose, he wasn't doing amounts like he was trying to kill himself. At the end of the day, he was working out. He was making some of the best music he's ever made, and I think there were certain mistakes he made. He made human mistakes like anyone else . . . For him to go through the break up [with Ariana Grande] and almost come out on the other side unscathed, after a lot of public scrutiny and eyes on him . . . *Swimming* was a shrine for him. All he wanted to do was tour that album with a live band and really turn the tide on his place in his career.

We called in J. Cole [to produce] "Hurt Feelings." The "What's the Use?" video was planned with a bunch of people—actors, friends. The night before he passed away, we were trying to put together that video. "What's the Use?" was gonna be huge. "Perfecto," he finished at this studio in Chile. "Ladders," incredible. Mac wanted to get more songs like that, more like a single, like a "Dang!" type of single. Every song is so strong on here. It's not cookie cutter. That's why I really like this album. At the end of the day, this was the album where he perfected making songs.

VIC WAINSTEIN: I did like when we came up with "Perfecto." I redid it in Chile. We went to this recording studio that was out in the middle of a vineyard. We were isolated and we had to dig deep, and ["Perfecto"] came together so quickly. We had the notion to [add] hand-drums, and we were in the mecca of hand-drum players, being in South America. The way it lined up for us to go there, musically, was so perfect. That's why we called it "Perfecto." The concept was built around how effortlessly it came together. That was a really specific and cool energy we had when we were in Chile. If you saw the video for "Good News," the first scene where it's me and him in the studio, is in that Chile studio.

I argued against "Self Care" at first. Obviously, there are different versions of stuff, and when it started, I didn't think it was as strong as it needed to be to be a part of everything else we had. I fought him 'til almost the end. He changed a few lyrics and changed the arrangement, and then I made amends with it. There was a long time where I was like, *That has no business around the rest of these awesome songs.* Obviously, I'm just one filter in all this, but he had the vision very certain in his head. He had moments like that often, where he saw the bigger picture and the rest of us were like, "Nah." Then it's like he pulls a rabbit out of the hat, and we're like, "Holy shit! He's right."

NICK DIERL: I remember being in the studio with Vic and Malcolm while he was working on ["Self Care"] and he finally landed on "I'm switching time zones." We must have gone through five iterations of that little phrase and how best to say that. I give that small example as an example of, on a larger level, no matter how confident someone is, it doesn't absolve you of the smaller challenges.

VIC WAINSTEIN: "Wings" was a part of another song I liked, which came out on the deluxe edition of *Circles*, a song called "Floating." "Floating" and "Wings" were in tandem, and they were supposed to go on *Swimming* together, but in the fourth quarter, we split them up. We decided "Floating" was more in the world of where we were going with *Circles*, so we just decided to save it. "Wings" was a special one for me because it was such a beautiful thing we put together. It was a piece of what we loved about where *Circles* was going. It was a good drop-in point, and [we] thought it was a perfect example of where he was starting to go.

NICK DIERL: One of the biggest changes I saw in Malcolm was post–*GO:OD AM*. Maybe this was happening through the process of making the album. With *GO:OD AM*, there was some pressure felt to deliver a rap album, but post–*GO:OD AM*, you see a very clear pivot. He always was highly musical, but you see him on *The Divine Feminine* say, "I wanna make albums that aren't necessarily great rap albums." That level of aspiration and seeing him put his talents to use in a new way... You can feel that he was working toward what would have been the opus.

VIC WAINSTEIN: *Swimming* was the most perfect go-between the worlds that we could've ever achieved to prep his audience for what was coming. I thought that *Swimming* was perfect, because knowing where we were going, they needed that context. They needed the breadcrumbs to digest what they were gonna find with *Circles*.

Swimming meant a lot to me, as a person, as a fan, as a counterpart, as a colleague. As far as what it's gonna say about him, he definitely reached a creative pinnacle and was able to see it live in a way that excited him for his future. *Swimming* was a cornerstone in having him develop a sense of self. There's nothing about *Swimming* that is like his other work. There might be elements that were available previously, but what happened on *Swimming* was its own thing.

SOARING OVER STRUGGLE

As with the majority of Mac Miller's catalog, the supreme message of "Jet Fuel" is to save yourself, a theme also telegraphed across the essential *Swimming* cuts "Self Care," "Wings," and "Ladders." With each of these three songs, the main visual mode is one of scaling up, and, consequently, growing into who we have always known ourselves to be. By the time we reach "Jet Fuel," we realize Mac has spent each key song on *Swimming* climbing higher and higher, to reach the mountaintop of wholeness. On "Jet Fuel," though, we're no longer ascending. There is no need. The song is all about sustaining height—growth—and realizing we can be our own engine.

As the eleventh song, "Jet Fuel" elevates the necessity of struggle without glamorizing it. Mac toasts the "bad times," sure, but the song presents difficulty merely as a fact of life. "I was out of town, gettin' lost 'til I was rescued," he sings on the hook. We can take this line and the use of the present progressive to mean that in spite of his pain, Mac finds respite. "Now I'm in the clouds, come down when I run out of jet fuel / But I never run out of jet fuel," Mac immediately continues. The implication of "Jet Fuel," then, is that once you overcome, you reach your pinnacle—and if you play your cards right, you get to stay there.

The image of the "Jet Fuel" itself contrasts sharply with images of "Wings" and "Ladders." "Wings" tire from flapping. "Ladders" can only reach so high. There's a reliance on the external, which is why these songs come first. We are climbing on *Swimming* while learning to be self-sufficient. He has survived enough to grow and keep himself flying high.

"I don't need nobody!" Mac declares on the second verse, and we believe him. Mac can keep himself high all on his own. As the eleventh song, too, we get the sense there is no way to begin in the clouds. You must make it there, and once you do, your entire attitude to pain changes.

In truth, this song toasts the "bad times" because by the time we reach the song, we've come to understand hurt as a simple thing, not a looming entity. We've made it small and easily cradled. We've made it part of our lives but not a ruler over our emotions. Mac toasts his woes because they've made him into the man he is today, floating high above strife and enjoying life. The height, then, can also be read as a note on perspective. All of this goodness, of course, comes at the cost of going through hardships. At least Mac makes them sound worthwhile. May we never run out of "Jet Fuel."

2020

CIRCLES

"I would just tell myself to worry a little less and not hold onto—don't create all of this weight for things. Everything has so much weight, but it's all just chapters. It's all just pieces of the story. There's gonna be a next part. It's not a big deal. It's not."

—MAC MILLER[19]

19. Mac Miller, "Interview with Mac Miller," interview by Craig Jenkins, *Vulture*, September 13, 2018, https://www.vulture.com/2018/09/mac-miller-interview.html.

AN ALBUM TO BE THANKFUL FOR

The first time I heard *Circles* was October 7, 2019, during a private listening session in New York. I was nervous, afraid of the emotions the album would pull out of me. Of course, I cried. I cried my eyes out from the first hint of Mac's voice to the final note. I was smiling too. Mac sounded so in tune with himself, so alive, as if he had finally stepped into the man he was always aiming to become. He sounded like he had fully harnessed his magic.

There was an unseasonable chill moving through the air as we processed the weight of each song, and while the album played, I felt Malcolm's energy enveloping the room. His whole heart blanketed the space. Stealing glances at the few others invited, I saw nothing but downturned heads and closed eyes. Each listener was nestled in their own world, embracing Mac's final musical offering, taking in the importance of the moment. If *Circles* teaches us anything, it's that Mac Miller will never die. His spirit cannot be extinguished. Everything about him and his life's work is forever.

Warbling over twinkling instrumentation, Malcolm's gentle voice opens the album—nothing but beauty dripping from his every word. Lines of whiskey and wine, delivered with unprecedented tenderness and fullness, in a weary voice heavy with resignation, make "Circles" the first of many arresting moments. Malcolm is raw and frayed, summoning all his strength to say, "Well . . . This is what it look like, right before you fall."

This is followed by the more traditionally hip-hop-sounding "Blue World," which, even still, features Malcolm's soft singing. The song works to remind us of Malcolm's roots as he evolves hand over hand. Lines about being a God and absconding the devil on his doorstep fit right into his canon. As self-effacing as the music now sounds, Mac's raps still have their signature swagger and ease: "Mmm, don't trip."

Mac replicates this swagger on "I Can See" between moments of saying, "I need somebody to save me," and slipping into syrupy singing. The dreamy hook feels like a salve on our hearts. It's exorcising the darkness out of our collective chests. And just like that, we're back to a quietly breathless verse. Finally, "Hands" features some potent spoken word skating along the same surface of swagger and signature slurring. The song reminds us of *GO:OD AM*, of simpler times, and how much we love Mac's spitting.

"Complicated" twists and evolves sounds as if it's going through a wormhole of emotion and synths, melting right into the sample and stutter of "Blue World." It is just one of many moments where the songs on *Circles* take on their own isolated and stunning life. On "Everybody," Mac reminds us how he spoke so thoughtfully through the piano. The unveiling of its chorus and strutting melody is utterly captivating.

And the writing, my goodness, the writing! Take this early line off "Woods": "Things like this ain't built to last / I might just fade like those before me." Every bar is a personal quotable, a lyric to keep pressed to the chest for a rainy or sunny day. If he stripped himself bare on *Swimming*, then on this album, Mac drills into his bone marrow and digs out every last bit of himself, serving it up to us on a circular platter.

Mac spends much of this album wrestling with the futility of life, as he did on *Faces*. Think: "I don't have a name, I don't have a name, no / Who am I to blame, who am I to blame?" and "I just end up right at the start of the line, drawing circles" off "Circles." Or "some people say they want to live forever / That's way too long, I'll just get through today" off "Complicated." Then there's "all I ever needed was somebody with some reason, who could keep me sane / Ever since I can remember, I've been keeping it together, but I'm feeling strange" on

"Hand Me Downs" and "they love to see me lonely / Hate to see me happy" off "Hands."

This time, though, instead of rushing through the cocaine ether and damaging his health, as was the energy of *Faces*, Mac contends with life by extracting meaning out of everything—and by keeping us in his heart. "I can keep you safe, I can keep you safe," he sings. Across *Circles*, every chord is a door to a better place. Every dancy progression and swipe of synth a portal to a galaxy only Malcolm could access. Every note sung a chance to rediscover himself and invent a life worth living. Make no mistake, Mac saw life as all-the-way worth living.

We come away from this record realizing Mac Miller was a musician's musician, destined for a long life of strumming away and writing out his whole soul. *Circles* is the moment Mac comes into himself as a man, as Malcolm. "Everybody mean something / When they're stuck on your mind," Malcolm sings on "Once A Day" to remind us of his eternal nature. There's no guessing left; there are no questions unanswered. *Circles* is everything Mac Miller was meant for in his cut-short life, and then some. We were so lucky to have been able to witness Mac Miller.

VIC WAINSTEIN: We were just working! We created playlists the whole time through, figuring out what was gonna be where. *Swimming* had like five playlists we would rotate songs in and out of, just to see what groups of songs worked better with each other. A lot of those songs ended up being on *Circles*. *Circles* came of a second energy—it was almost like having twins. You got pregnant once, but we had two babies. It's the best way I can explain it. We had all these songs that could be their own album, and only at that crossroads did we understand we should make a second thing. At the beginning of *Swimming*, there was no running concept for *Circles*.

Circles came as a byproduct of the [number] of songs we had that existed in an alternate world we were working on. [Mac] made the hard decision late in the *Swimming* cycle, to [create *Circles*], because so many of our favorite songs . . . If it were to all be on *Swimming*, we would have twenty-something tracks. We had to figure out a plan B so that some of the stuff we were equally excited about could live somewhere and be championed in the same way as everything we ended up putting on *Swimming*. Who knows? He might've had this planned since he was a kid.

JUSTIN BOYD: When we did the Blue Slide Park Tour, he used to come out with his white guitar and do covers. He'd play "Another Night" and a cover, and he always loved that part of the show. He always wanted to have those moments in the set where it's just him and the piano. He would have those small moments, but as it went on, he realized, "Maybe, I *can* do this." That led to *The Divine Feminine*, and you can see it more on *Swimming* and obviously *Circles*. That was his whole goal. He was like, "*Circles* is gonna be my singer-songwriter album." He talked about that for years. He always wanted to do that.

I think it just shows you how diverse he was. He could do regular boom bap hip-hop. He could do love songs. He showed his versatility as an artist. Even though *Circles* was the last body of work, you'll remember how much of a hard-ass rapper the dude was, the skill he had in every genre of music. Anything he wanted to do, he could absolutely do it.

NICK DIERL: When we spoke [in 2019] I was aware of the existence of *Circles* and the intent to have it come out. I do feel like that *is* him realizing what he had been working up to. I also feel like, on a broader level, had we been able to see him continue, it would have been reasonable to expect the work to be at this level. Looking at his career, it would be fair to expect that [future releases] would be beyond even what *Circles* is, given the way he consistently grew release after release.

VIC WAINSTEIN: Obviously you've heard it explained, how swimming in a circle meant rediscovering yourself and finding your way back from where you came, how a lot of the singer-songwriter stuff was also part of where he came from. Before he decided to rap, he was in bands. He loved to sing; he loved to play piano. He also felt that contributed to the idea of a circle because that's where he came from. Now he's gone through everything else and made his way back to it in a way that was warm and innovative and just as important as everything else he's done.

Also, it meant part of his humanity. Being able to get back to himself. There were, emotionally, some tough times for him throughout his process of releasing albums. Him finally coming to peace was the idea of a circle. The idea of a circle became so relevant in so many different ways to him. That's why it became a no-brainer that it needed to be titled such. It was one of those things he didn't have to look for. He loved it.

It was a beautiful accident. With *Swimming*, we had this thing in mind of being innovative and progressive with his sound. We wanted to do everything we could to honor that and put ourselves in a position to grow musically. He had taken to being around new creatives that brought different things out of him he had never experienced before. It got him excited to push that envelope and put himself in a more uncomfortable environment to figure out new ways of thinking about his songs and how to make them better. He always had this taste, but [*Circles*] was a graduation of it, of the singer-songwriter stuff. He never had a platform for it to live and be looked at through the lens of a serious effort.

Nick Dierl: I think he felt like he had something to prove to the world. Some of this is really well-documented on a personal and physical level. I've never seen him in a better exercise regimen and clear headspace. Getting up early in the morning, going to the gym. There are some incredible videos from that era. If I'm not mistaken, [there was a time] he was at the gym and Pusha-T is roasting him. He's sort of in a push-up position but he has weights in each hand. Of course, in typical Malcolm fashion, he's still flexing while he's doing that. He's wearing hella chains, and Pusha's there, roasting him. I would get videos from him, selfie videos, and he's being goofy as hell while out on his morning run. Really good lightness of spirit, while also focusing on getting his mind and body right.

I think it needs to be said, he wasn't just working on these songs. He was doing press [for *Swimming*], working on finishing *Circles*, also preparing to tour. As someone who's notorious for giving an incredible live show, he was definitely looking to turn that up a level when touring *Swimming*. He was very hands-on in terms of [how] *Swimming* was gonna be promoted and in conceptualizing music videos. One of the last times we hung out, we were in the car driving across LA for the better part of an hour. I think he was in touch with Guy Fieri, Mac DeMarco, and a couple of other people all over the course of the drive, just getting ready for a video shoot.

Vic Wainstein: As far as the timeline, I want to say it was right before we went to Hawaii that a lot of the singer-songwriter stuff started rising. We realized this stuff is building its own world. How do we incorporate it into the other stuff we're doing? Or do we? We're scratching our heads about it for a while. The decision for [*Circles*] to be a separate album didn't come until later, but the decision to pursue this set of songs started right before Hawaii.

We went to Hawaii in December 2017. I remember it because my father had just passed away, and I was in Hawaii with Malcolm when it happened. I will never forget that. He pulled me aside and asked if everything was okay. If you know me, I can smile through the worst of times. Him still picking up on [my sadness] showed me how emotionally intuitive he is as a person, which carried on in his art. We had a moment out there, and that's part of when a lot of stuff we were doing in the singer-songwriter [realm] hit on-mark with me too.

When we were discovering all these songs and rooting for them to win, it wasn't until we got closer to the summertime where we realized: we can't put all of these songs on *Swimming*. We started sculpting what could be its own separate album, and that's when the first talks of *Circles* being a conjunct thing started happening. I loved the idea. It gave me security in the fact that everything important we were finding with these new songs would be preserved in the right way and got a fair shake to be its own world.

NICK DIERL: The thing that's so interesting about Malcolm is his willingness to embrace the full spectrum of *being*. In some ways, as a result of the lightness about him, it is what made him feel comfortable knowing he had two bodies of work that could be received as being . . . I don't know if *darker* is the right word, but [work] that was willing to engage with aspects of his life that didn't have the lightness at that moment. [*Circles*] was a good outlet for those moments because the actual lived experience at that time was very positive. When you consider his life through recorded music and his life through lived experience, those two things together represented the whole of the spectrum.

There were some *Circles* songs I was familiar with before a number of the songs that ended up being on *Swimming*. There was—not to take away from the intention of *Swimming* and *Circles*—dialogue about some of those songs and whether they fit on *Swimming* versus *Circles*. Malcolm was also cognizant of the fact he was going to a place that was going to be a surprise for his fans, even though his fans were accustomed to being surprised. Even knowing that, *Swimming* intentionally had some of the hallmarks of things he had done before, to sort of bridge that gap.

VIC WAINSTEIN: The oldest one that made the tracklisting for *Circles*, but actually came out on the deluxe, was a song called "Floating." "Floating" was conjunct with "Wings" on *Swimming*. "Wings" was the more rap part of it, "Floating" was the more whimsical, singing part. When we got "Floating" in shape and added a lot of production to make it make sense, and the way we had them together as one track . . . It was probably the most glorified effort, at first, into the *Circles* world. In the end, we decided to take "Floating" off of *Swimming* and let "Wings" be its own track, so that way we could save it for *Circles*.

From that, "Complicated" came next. "Everybody," he became infatuated with covering that because of the piano. He was getting exceptional at piano towards the end there. He was liking the idea of him on piano, singing. This is also before the *Circles* conversation happened—he'd done it before. Then "Good News" came. That was a good four, five in that world. And we were like, "Yo! These are great, together. Fuck, how do we sprinkle them in *Swimming*?" We tried, don't get me wrong. *Circles* became a thing because we ran out of options on how to playlist everything together so [listeners] got it and it made sense. The songs made us make another album for them, they were so good.

After that . . . When we started the album journey to finish *Circles*, we had close to forty songs that were eligible. A lot of them were at different stages of development but were all worthy. "Blue World" was never in the conversation until Jon Brion brought it in; Malcolm recorded "Blue World" with Disclosure in New York in 2016. "I Can

See" was older. "Woods" was older. The only one that became a conscious effort with the *Circles* effort was "Hand Me Downs" . . . He went to Australia and recorded that there. He loved that effort a lot because of how organic it came together and how bare bones it is. Nothing too crazy on the production front. "That's on Me" was also part of it, as well as "Once a Day." Everything else was songs we had stockpiled that we were interchanging.

"Hands," we made that with no intention of it being on *Circles*. "Surf" was a great tune, but it happened early on in the *Swimming* era. "Woods" was great. "I Can See" was pre–*Swimming*. "Circles" was definitely made for *Circles*. Obviously, the lyrics, he was consciously making that world. The other two tunes coming out on the deluxe edition, one of which I wrote, is called "Right." That was done during the same time "Floating" was done. They were literally done in the same week. I produced "Right." Thundercat's playing on both of them, and we had a couple other players here and there. In September 2017, we locked in a month at Conway Recording Studios to work on *Swimming*. Those two songs came about at the same time.

THELONIOUS MARTIN (producer): We were toying with ["Guidelines"] going on Mac's album [*Swimming*], and I couldn't find the session. My hard drive was dropped by an engineer and I had lost, for the time being, about two years' worth of sessions. I'm with the Burns Twins [production team in Chicago] at their crib, replaying a sample, and I FaceTime Mac to show him we're working. He calls me back and he's like, "Yo, can I play you something?" I'm like, "Of course"—it's Mac. He starts playing ["That's On Me"] for me. I'm like, "Alright, this is jazzy. Sounds like nothing else you've ever done before. It's ill!" One of the Burns Twins plays horns and I was like, "Do you want the Burns Twins for the horns?" and Mac's like, "Yeah, yeah." It was a pretty crazy day.

I was blown [by "That's On Me"]. He was sitting at his piano, playing it for me. I was like, "Dog! This is different from the stuff you usually do, Larry Lovestein." When an artist switches up their style and it's still really, really, really good, it's like, *Wow, I didn't know you had this up your sleeve.*

I don't really like posthumous music, but seeing what this was selected from, [having] the family's blessing, and Jon Brion working on it . . . This one, I feel, it's a little bit of a different situation. It's a beautiful situation. Usually, stuff is undone, and the family blessing might not be with good energy surrounding it. That's super important if you're gonna release anything posthumously. I would want Mac's legacy to be carried on in the most proper way possible, and that's what we're getting. We're getting a proper posthumous album. We're getting the family blessing on it. "That's On Me" is on it! This beautiful music . . . It's one last conversation with him.

Nick Dierl: To start, it's important to clarify that there were a lot more people involved in making that decision. There were people not mentioned that were even more vital in making that decision than myself. I don't wanna position myself as being more essential to the process or overlooking anyone else. Ultimately, the reason why the core team felt comfortable was a combination of factors. First and foremost, we knew the body of work was important to Malcolm for people to hear. Two, the extent to which the body of work had already come together. There was a definite template in place and a degree to which a lot of the songs were finished. Had that second point not been the case, that would've changed the landscape in making that decision.

Three, between Jon Brion and Vic, Jeff Sosnow [A&R at Warner], and obviously the family and the Clancys—the extent of their conversations and the degree they felt they understood the directive based on their conversations with Malcolm for how the album should be finished . . . It was really a confluence of those three factors making everyone feel like it was worth proceeding and seeing through.

Vic Wainstein: With *Circles*, there [were] a lot of things I noticed, emotionally and otherwise, that he had finally made peace with. He was able to move forward and grow. That's why I think *Circles* and *Swimming* came together in such an awesome way, without so much grueling effort. Because he was in a mental space where he could be okay with things. Before, that wasn't always the case. Whether there had been actual life events that were putting him in a certain place where he wasn't mentally the healthiest, or it was just growing... He was twenty-six when he passed. I remember being in my twenties and not knowing what the fuck about a lot of things. He was beyond his years, but also, with that, he put a lot on himself mentally and emotionally.

With *Circles*, I saw the Malcolm that finally made peace with a lot of his demons. That opened him up to be able to accommodate this artistic growth and [take] mentally healthy strides. He was able to be genuinely happy. It spilled over into what he did with his time. He enjoyed hanging out with friends again. He didn't have to go get wasted. A lot of people talk about his "addiction," which wasn't one at all. A lot of the weird air that came after his death ... they thought he was an addict or depressed, and it was none of that.

NICK DIERL: On some level, it's an inherently flawed process. You're trying to make decisions in place of not having the one person who should ultimately be making these decisions. In that way, it's never perfect. But, considering the circumstances, I feel like everyone involved treated [*Circles*] with the intention it deserved and made every effort to present it to the world in as respectful a way as possible. Looking around at the way people are engaging with it, it feels like it validates all the decisions that went into the process.

I'm really happy it's providing a sense of closure and peace for a lot of people. I hope people see both sides of this record. Not just for the ways in which it is somber and sobering, in the way it is someone grappling with themselves. I would hope people don't overlook the lightness and the hopefulness on the album, that maybe doesn't reveal itself as immediately as the other aspects. It is an album of hopefulness, and I would hope that people are taking away that aspect as much as, if not more than, the heavier themes of the record.

VIC WAINSTEIN: The accident was purely an accident. He wasn't on a bad streak. He wasn't on benders doing drugs. He was physically the healthiest right before he passed. He was seeing a trainer multiple times a week. He was in great mental shape as well as physical shape. That's what jolted the people who knew him the closest about his untimely death. Every other thing going on in his life was not pointing to something like this. You know? It was also the most annoying fact because we knew he was in such a good place to nurture the next step for himself artistically and as a human. He was robbed of that opportunity. That was the hardest pill to swallow.

UNPACKING THE "CLUTTER"

The release of Mac Miller's *Circles* marked the end of his third and final creative renaissance. With this album, Mac completes the loop of his career, ending with his most unexpected album. Sounding gorgeous, hopeful, bluesy at times, groovy at others, *Circles* still pays much attention to the "clutter" in Mac's head. Damn near every song features imagery that turns Mac's head into a setting, or speaks directly to his unbalanced mental state. These moments are the most human, the most familiar to fans.

Our scene-setting begins with the third verse of "Complicated": "Inside my head is getting pretty cluttered (cluttered, cluttered) / I try, but can't clean up this mess I made." We can imagine the inside of Mac's mind rife with turmoil. When we hear him trying to remedy the mess, we believe him. We've believed Mac Miller has been aiming to feel better since 2012. Never does it sound like Mac is wallowing for pleasure. Always, he is our fighter, even when he struggles to just "get through a day."

Notes on Mac's mental health continue on the following track, "Blue World." Where "Complicated" was all about the internal mess, on the opening of "Blue World," Mac is looking outward to depressing results. We warp back inward on the second verse, back to Mac losing his mind amidst all the "clutter" in his head. "Reality's so hard to find," he admits. This vacillation between the internal and the external gives us the sense that Malcolm is genuinely taking stock of his life and himself.

"I spent the whole day in my head / Do a little spring cleanin'," Mac sings. Here, "Good News" clearly borrows from the imagery of "Complicated." Though "Good News" sounds nothing like Mac as we've come to know him, the writing is familiar. Stepping into his wrought mind is like opening up a favorite novel and being greeted by the familiar voice of a beloved protagonist. It's like coming home.

At home in Mac's head, we find "Good News" to be one of his most touching songs to date. Its candor is disarming. Then, on "Hand Me Downs," Mac passes off the business of working through his mind onto a lover: "And all I ever needed was somebody with some reason who can keep me sane / Ever since I can remember I've been keeping it together but I'm feeling strange." Here, we've once again stepped outside of Mac's head to assess our surroundings. The notion that love provides reason and keeps him stable is one he previously explored on *The Divine Feminine*. We feel a kindred sense of connection with Malcolm as we join him on this journey to better understand himself.

Unlike *Faces*, or even *Swimming*, on *Circles*, Mac does not sound like the underdog in his battle with himself. He sounds like the sure-fire pick for the title belt. Even when things look bleak, we're free of worry; Mac comes out on top.

"You get used to the bullshit, the screws they go missing," Mac sings. To accompany our leading image of "clutter," we now have the famous trope of having a screw loose, suggesting Mac has gone crazy. Repeated several times across "Hand Me Downs," this line serves to remind us of the constant flux Mac Miller found himself in across his career. This tumult is consequently offset by the stunning work of featured artist Baro Sura, who sings a salve of a hook, which eases our worries along with Malcolm's.

"Don't keep it all in your head," Mac advises on "Once A Day." The song both closes *Circles* and the loop of mental health. In the end, as the "hardest working person in the universe," Mac's best bet in life is to create through his pain.

The wizened perspective Mac Miller once had is given new life on *Circles*. By exploring the "clutter," we get to discover a renewed Malcolm. He was simply human, as he always has been, and for that reason, we will never forget him. For that reason, Mac is a part of us.

Remembering Mac Miller

In Loving Memory

SYD: One of the last times we hung out was super random, super-duper random. It was right before he dropped *Swimming*. I hadn't spoken to him in a couple months, maybe, because he was going through a lot with the media and stuff at the time. He's got good people around him, so I knew he didn't need me to reach out—he knew the love was real. We all, over here, decided to give him his space. He hit me up out of the blue like, "Yo, I wanna hang out. We have so much to catch up on." He came to my house. It was me and Matt and our friend Sophia, and he came through and just told us everything that was going on—the truth behind it all, and also another couple things he hid from us that he didn't want us to know.

We spent the first two hours just catching up, chilling on the porch. Then we took him to Mac DeMarco's house. He had been trying to convince me for months, maybe a whole year, to go on tour with him again, but this time it would be The Internet, Mac Miller, Anderson Paak, and Mac DeMarco. He had never been to Mac DeMarco's house, and Mac DeMarco's house is similar to how The Sanctuary was. So we took him over there, sat outside by the fire, and told stories for a couple more hours. That was just how he was. He would pull up on you! He caught an Uber over here by himself. My mom was happy to see him. He hung in the kitchen with my mom for a bit. He was just good energy to be around.

It's not like people don't know how good of a person he was. Thankfully, I don't think I have to mention that. I don't have to really say he was a great person because everybody knows. I think that's the beauty of it: He left his impression. He left a very accurate impression while he was here.

CHUCK INGLISH: I honestly think that if Mac knew he was dead right now, he'd be pissed. If you listen to *Divine Feminine, Swimming, Watching Movies with the Sound Off* . . . That was a musician's musician. If Mac didn't know something, he would figure it out. I honestly think that he was coming to a place where he was going to be the common denominator of all artists. He's an artist's artist. He was about to go on tour with Thundercat! You're not getting too much better at anything than Thundercat with the bass. I think he would wanna be remembered not how the hip-hop media perceived him, but how his peers perceived him.

THUNDERCAT: He was the kind of guy you'd see people make movies about. He was a character, but it was so real. If you weren't tuned in, it could be overwhelming, his ability to bring you in. It was scary. It was like seeing a lion playing with a kitten. There was nothing you could say that he didn't try to—or didn't—comprehend. He was creative, and he exuded a lot of creative energy. He wasn't scared of the unknown, a majority of the time. Him inviting a guy like me into his life, finding a place where I existed in his reality . . . We shared a lot of different things, but as a man, he struck me as my type of guy.

[Our friendship] taught me that everything isn't forever. It taught me to be open. I always talk about this saying he used to have—"Sit down, let it happen." He posted that on the wall at the studio. People would walk in, "What the hell is this paper 'sposed to mean?" But it was like, let real life in. Mac was really, really there. He's another person that taught me what it was to work hard and create, and keep pushing, and let that be the drive. He showed me a different type of work ethic.

I want his music to be remembered as that of an amazing artist of our time, who was taking risks and willing to change and try to find things to make the music better. He made *really* good music. He was a good man. He was a really good man.

Big Jerm: It's not even something I like to bring up . . . I got shot in 2016, and I luckily had health insurance, but somebody set up a GoFundMe for me, and he sent ten grand, which basically paid everything off. That's about as generous as it gets. That's why I went to LA. I just think he wanted to take care of me in a way. He was that type of person, where his friends were just important to him. I think I texted him or something, but him and Ariana [Grande] were some of the first people to come to the hospital too.

Justin Boyd: He always made sure everybody was cool, especially in the studio. That was him 24/7. Obviously, the light was always shined on him, but he made you feel the opposite. You'd walk into a room and he would be more excited to see you than you would be to see him. He'd make you feel like everybody was waiting for *you* to be there.

Josh Berg: He was just the best guy in the studio, because he always had a good attitude and he always just wanted to do stuff! He was clearly obsessed with music and creation and got right to it. There's always music, and he wrote really fast. Or he'd freestyle [the songs]. He was just a—I'm sure this is consistent with every single person that you've talked to—great person to be around, and he was hilarious. That makes the work all that much more enjoyable. For him, it was just music first. One of the things I think we connected on was this exploration of seeing where creativity will take you.

KEHLANI: He was just happy that he was going as far as he was, and people fucked with it. He felt like he was making music that he felt like he loved. He was doing all these tiny shows versus doing giant concerts because, he was telling me, that meant the world to him—having intimate experiences.

He was so grateful all the time. Grateful that there were so many people around him that loved him. Grateful for his family. Grateful for his talent, and not letting it inhibit him or let him be lazy. He let that fuel him and allowed it to inspire his friends. That meant a lot to me. He started having so much fun. A lot of people don't let themselves because they're overthinking everything. He fully enjoyed everything he was doing.

I will always remember him telling me, "It's so cool you have a mini Kehlani in your stomach," and him asking if I knew if my daughter was a boy or a girl yet. He was like, "If it's a boy, I think you should name it Malcolm because I think that's a pretty special name." I was like, "Yeah, I'll think about it because there's plenty of special Malcolms in the world." And he said: "Yeah, and he'll be another special one." I never forgot about that because I found out she was a girl maybe a couple weeks after he passed.

I want people to remember his humanity as they're listening to the music. Also, realize how much bravery and courage it takes to be that honest, be that self-aware, and be that real about things going on internally. He let us witness that entire journey. He let us witness him going from a weed-smoking, school-skipping kid to a grown man who had been in relationships and dealt with substance abuse and depression. He never hid that. That took real courage. That took humanity. Really look at [his discography] as an entirety. Not just, "I heard these big songs, and that's who Mac Miller is to me." Take a second to go and experience the journey from the first tape to the last album. Take in the fact that this man grew up in front of our eyes, in a really beautiful way.

As a man, people gotta remember that he was so much more than the circumstances of how he left the earth. He was so much more than the downfalls and his relationship history, so much more than even his art. How he left us all, it did leave a lot of room for people to judge him, and that's sad because he's so much more than that. Watch an interview, listen to the music. Listen to the way his mom speaks about him. People speak about him in this loving, positive way. That's how they should remember him as a man. So many people are keeping him alive in the best way.

AJA GRANT: For somebody who was at his level, he was a very selfless guy. He made everybody feel loved and welcomed. We didn't deserve somebody like that in this world. He always made everybody smile.

NICK DIERL: One of the things I loved the most about Malcolm: He was goofy. He was having fun at all costs, even if that meant it was at the expense of him not looking cool. I met Malcolm, I must have been twenty-two, twenty-three at the time ... I was still finding myself and finding self-confidence and self-worth. I felt like I had to present this ideal version of myself to the world, and I learned to adore Malcolm. One of the things I liked the most was he wasn't caught up in presenting the cool version of himself and was regularly willing to present a very uncool version of himself when he knew it was funny.

We were in New York for the release of *The Divine Feminine*. He had just taped a late-night show. The album was coming out that night. My fiancée set up my birthday dinner that night. It ended up a much bigger dinner than I could've imagined. There were at least thirty people at the table. At the end of the dinner, Malcolm had to go. He still showed up, got to know all my friends, apologized he had to leave early, and took off.

Forty-five minutes later, the dinner was ending. As happens at big group dinners, you can see everyone starting to work through what the bill is gonna be. Someone asked for the bill and the server's like,

"That guy that took off forty-five minutes ago covered everything already." I was just so impressed at that moment. Not because of the money, at all, but the fact that he wanted to spend his evening getting to know the people that I had known outside of my relationship with him and also then take care of the whole evening.

I hope people remember him for that combination of honesty and aspiration. He's a real testament that you don't have to be the best at every single thing you do, but be honest with yourself and put your best effort forth. He held that above all else, and it shone through in his work. I hope people remember the importance of that and apply it to their own lives.

THELONIOUS MARTIN: I would want Mac to be remembered as a true artist, someone who really cared about his craft and the people around him. I really feel like artists don't just do music, it's about what they embody. For someone to be peaceful, stayin' grounded, [to] offer himself up and shine a light, and be a mirror so people reflect and grow with him and grow on their own, that's an artist. That's a true artist. To be self-aware and to know "I'm going through this; how can I share this musically?" I think he was a master at that—a true artist in every sense of the word, in every fashion.

WILL KALSON: As a human being who cared about his craft and about his fans. As someone who made a major impact on the world. I think that's how he is being remembered. His fanbase is awesome. They're so dedicated, and I know this has been hard on all of them, but they're able to see what he intended. His music is gonna have a lasting impact—forever. Especially with *Swimming* and *Circles*. I think he accomplished what he set out to do. I truly believe that. He's never gonna be forgotten.

SKYZOO: As somebody who cared about the music. He really was about it. He wasn't no vulture in any way, shape, or form. He was about the culture, the music, hip-hop; he respected it and loved it. Everything was real with him. He wanted it. Also, I like the path he started to go on musically with the singing, and I saw where he was gonna go next. You could see him being a sixty-year-old artist, singing instead of rapping. And that's cool! I saw the Billy Joel shit. I saw that shit coming. I was excited to watch that develop, and it sucks we didn't get to see it.

REX ARROW: I don't know that there will ever be a body of work in my life that I'm as proud of, or feels like such a major achievement. What we did, it's hard to compare to anything else. I'm so thankful and happy that we have this body of work I'm incredibly proud of and I knew he was proud of as well. I'm so thankful for that. I'm also so thankful and happy I have all these memories that have nothing to do with the videos we made, that round out the sort of picture of who Malcolm is, [like] living together in Malibu . . . The last time I hung out with him, it was just grabbing a beer. I'm so thankful for Malcolm having come into my life. I don't have words to really articulate that, but I'm so thankful and happy that I met this person.

RAPSODY: I had one bad show. We had a stop in Fort Lauderdale that had like four, five opening acts. You know, nobody trying to have that long of a show. I went on right before Mac, but right before I got on, it starts pouring down rain. I go on, everybody's drenched. By this time, they have ear fatigue, they're wet, and all they really wanna do is see Mac Miller, right? I got twenty, thirty minutes, and it's not going well. The crowd is not receiving it. I'm sure they don't wanna receive it under the circumstances. The show just went left. I ended up walking off. It's the only show I've ever walked off. Mac came out and he was like: "Yo, Rap is my friend and she's gonna finish her set. And y'all are gonna show respect." What had happened was I was performing and people were talking and I was trying to rap through it, and someone threw a brown piece of paper at me. I'm from the South so my mind just went somewhere else when that happened. For him to even do that, that spoke to the person that he was. He didn't have to do that at all. I'll never forget how he stood up for me. How he stood up for all his friends. How he stood up for all people.

KAREN CIVIL: It hurts because it's not just about a musician passing. I lost my friend. I lost one of my closest friends, and I continue to miss him because I just wish one day it's a bad dream and he will just walk into a situation again. But even in life, and in death, he brought us together. And it's so amazing. It's so amazing what he's able to do. I will not stop loving him as a human being, as an artist, and as one of my closest friends. It sucks talking about him in the past tense, but I absolutely loved him as an individual, as a friend, as a brother. He was a lot of things to me, and I miss him.

SAP: If anybody learns anything from Mac, it's live free and be fearless. Get your art out. You just gotta get all your ideas out and not take stuff so seriously. Little shit didn't fuck his day up. He always kept it moving. That's one thing that I definitely learned from him. I only seen Mac get mad, probably, one time. It was this show in Jersey where I guess they messed up his introduction, and he had to start over. I think he, like, punched a wall or broke his hand. He still kept performing. I ain't even know that until after he got off the stage and he had to go straight to the hospital. He gave people everything. He never made too many things about him.

JUST BLAZE: Ultimately, he touched a lot of people. He became a torchbearer of inspiration for an entire generation. It's a beautiful thing to watch that develop. It was happening while he was alive, and he's no longer with us, which sucks, because he had so much more to do and so much more to give. People say that all the time, but if you look at his trajectory and how he was developing as an artist, it's unfortunate. As much as he became his own man, and his own artist, he was on his way to doing so much more.

MARC-ANDRÉ LAUZON: I want Malcolm to be remembered for who he was and not for what demons he had. Malcolm was a talented musician, who was extremely charismatic and down to earth. He would care so much about his fans and his craft. It was very heartwarming to see someone care. On my part, I'll keep pushing his music to the world because I know that's what he would've wanted. He wanted to be heard by everyone. I just hope he found peace with himself and that he could finally be able to rest now.

BENJY GRINBERG: I just know that Mac always cared, and he had to balance a lot of things in his life between his music, his career, his friends, his issues with drugs and other things, and just growing up in this crazy situation. It's just a whole different experience for someone that young to deal with. I think it was a complicated situation for him, and I think that he always kept his friends around from his childhood. They always lived with him. That really helped to keep him grounded.

Aside from that, I think he did his best. He created this amazing music and all the people around him loved him. The outpouring of love that happened after his death was like nothing I've ever seen. Even fans who never got to meet him felt like they knew him. You don't hear that very often when an artist passes. It's not any one story; it's the full thing. How he led his life, how he treated people, the music that he made, and always trying to do the right thing. We all make mistakes, but I think deep down inside he was such a good person and always meant the best, no matter what it was. That's how I remember Mac.

The last time I ever saw him was at his show at Hotel Café. That's usually what I think about the most—him getting off stage, heading towards the green room, and giving me a big hug along the way. That's the last time I ever saw him, and it sort of epitomizes everything. It was him, it was his music, it was his connection with his fans, and him taking a quick second out of his hustle from one place to the other to give an old friend a hug. That's how I think about him. I'm proud to be a small part of his story and to have spent the time that I got to spend with him. I wish that it would have ended differently and that we could still hear all the music that he had to come, and get to hang out more. Just be there. I'm happy that I got to know him at all.

E. Dan: There'll never be real closure for me because I always imagined ten, fifteen, twenty years in the future doing an acoustic folk album that reflected on middle age. I'm just really sad that I'm never going to get to make music with him again. I've never had more fun making music with anyone, and I don't think I will, because I don't know that I'll ever meet anyone who I have that kind of relationship with as a friend and collaborator that I just feel completely open to doing anything. I could do any weird thing in a session with him, and he would find a way to make it work. That's really freeing as a musician. I'm gonna really miss that, just beyond knowing the dude. I'm glad that we were open with each other as far as our feelings.

Our last conversation two days before he died, as most conversations did, ended with "I love you, dude." I'm eternally blessed having known the kid, because not only did he change my life by the music he made, but he changed my life as a person. I never knew anybody so enthusiastic and open to the world around him, which really made me wanna be that way. I saw the value in being excited to be around people. I'm glad that he certainly knew how much respect I had for him musically, because that's what he mostly cared about with anybody he knew. I know that he knew that I loved him.

Song Permissions

All Around The World
Words and Music by Malcolm McCormick, Al Puodziukas, Jesse Keeler, John Stephens, Justin Smith and Nick Dresti
Copyright © 2015 Sony Music Publishing LLC, Blue Slide Park Music, EMI Blakcwood Music Inc., MSTRTRKS Music Inc., Nehrusita Inc., BMG Sapphire Songs, John Legend Publishing, Reservoir Media Music and F.O.B. Music Publishing
All Rights on behalf of Sony Music Publishing LLC, Blue Slide Park Music, EMI Blakcwood Music Inc., MSTRTRKS MUSIC INC. and Nehrusita Inc, Administered by Sony Music Publishing LLC, 424 Church Street, Suite 1200, Nashville, TN 37219
All Rights on behalf of BMG Sapphire Songs and John Legend Publishing Administered by BMG Rights Management (US) LLC
All Rights on behalf of F.O.B. Music Publishing Administered by Reservoir Media Music
International Copyright Secured   All Rights Reserved
Reprinted by Permission of Hal Leonard LLC

Angels (When She Shuts Her Eyes)
Words and Music by Malcolm McCormick, Michael Volpe and Imogen Heap
Copyright © 2013 Sony Music Publishing LLC, Blue Slide Park Music, Clammyclams Music and Megaphonic Limited
All Rights on behalf of Sony Music Publishing LLC, Blue Slide Park Music and Clammyclams Music Administered by Sony Music Publishing LLC, 424 Church Street, Suite 1200, Nashville, TN 37219
All Rights on behalf of Megaphonic Limited in the U.S. and Canada Administered by WC Music Corp.
International Copyright Secured   All Rights Reserved
Reprinted by Permission of Hal Leonard LLC

Best Day Ever
Words and Music by Malcolm McCormick, Eric Dan, Maurice White and Jeremy Kulousek
Copyright © 2013 Sony Music Publishing LLC, Blue Slide Park Music, ID-

Labs Worldwide Sound, EMI April Music Inc., KMR Music Royalties II SCSp and Big Jerm Music
All Rights on behalf of Sony Music Publishing LLC, Blue Slide Park Music, IDLabs Worldwide Sound and EMI April Music Inc. Administered by Sony Music Publishing LLC, 424 Church Street, Suite 1200, Nashville, TN 37219
All Rights on behalf of KMR Music Royalties II SCSp and Big Jerm Music Administered Worldwide by Kobalt Songs Music Publishing
International Copyright Secured   All Rights Reserved
Reprinted by Permission of Hal Leonard LLC

Blue World
Words and Music by Malcolm McCormick, Guy Lawrence, George Forrest and Robert Wright
Copyright © 2018 SONGS OF UNIVERSAL, INC., STAIRCASE WORKS PUBLISHING, UNIVERSAL MUSIC PUBLISHING LTD. and BOURNE CO.
All Rights For STAIRCASE WORKS PUBLISHING Administered by SONGS OF UNIVERSAL, INC.
All Rights for UNIVERSAL MUSIC PUBLISHING LTD. Administered by UNIVERSAL - POLYGRAM INTERNATIONAL TUNES, INC.
All Rights Reserved   Used by Permission
Reprinted by Permission of Hal Leonard LLC

Break The Law
Words and Music by Malcolm McCormick, Bob Wright, Chet Forest and Stephen Bruner
Copyright © 2015 Sony Music Publishing LLC, Blue Slide Park Music, Bob Wright Publishing Designee, Chet Forest Publishing Designee and Stephen Bruner Publishing Designee
All Rights on behalf of Sony Music Publishing LLC and Blue Slide Park Music Administered by Sony Music Publishing LLC, 424 Church Street, Suite 1200, Nashville, TN 37219
International Copyright Secured   All Rights Reserved
Reprinted by Permission of Hal Leonard LLC

Circles
Words and Music by Malcolm McCormick
Copyright © 2018 SONGS OF UNIVERSAL, INC. and STAIRCASE WORKS PUBLISHING
All Rights for STAIRCASE WORKS PUBLISHING Administered by SONGS OF UNIVERSAL, INC.
All Rights Reserved   Used by Permission
Reprinted by Permission of Hal Leonard LLC

Clarity
Words and Music by Malcolm McCormick, Eric Dan, Brent Reynolds, Jer-

Claymation

Come Back To Earth

Complicated

All Rights for YOU CAN'T TAKE IT WITH YOU Administered Worldwide
by KOBALT SONGS MUSIC PUBLISHING
All Rights Reserved   Used by Permission
Reprinted by Permission of Hal Leonard LLC

Donald Trump
Words and Music by Malcolm McCormick and Jonathan King
Copyright © 2011 Sony Music Publishing LLC, Blue Slide Park Music and
Sound Of A Pioneer Music
All Rights on behalf of Sony Music Publishing LLC and Blue Slide Park
Music Administered by Sony Music Publishing LLC, 424 Church
Street, Suite 1200, Nashville, TN 37219
International Copyright Secured   All Rights Reserved
Reprinted by Permission of Hal Leonard LLC

English Lane
Words and Music by Malcolm McCormick, Brent Reynolds and Dominic
Angelella
Copyright © 2011 Sony Music Publishing LLC, Blue Slide Park Music, EMI
Blackwood Music Inc. and Dominic Angelella Publishing Designee
All Rights on behalf of Sony Music Publishing LLC, Blue Slide Park Music
and EMI Blackwood Music Inc. Administered by Sony Music Pub-
lishing LLC, 424 Church Street, Suite 1200, Nashville, TN 37219
International Copyright Secured   All Rights Reserved
Reprinted by Permission of Hal Leonard LLC

Frick Park Market
Words and Music by Malcolm McCormick, Eric Dan and Jeremy Kulousek
Copyright © 2011 Sony Music Publishing LLC, Blue Slide Park Music, ID-
Labs Worldwide Sound, KMR Music Royalties II SCSp and Big Jerm
Music
All Rights on behalf of Sony Music Publishing LLC, Blue Slide Park Music
and IDLabs Worldwide Sound Administered by Sony Music Pub-
lishing LLC, 424 Church Street, Suite 1200, Nashville, TN 37219
All Rights on behalf of KMR Music Royalties II SCSp and Big Jerm Music
Administered Worldwide by Kobalt Songs Music Publishing
International Copyright Secured   All Rights Reserved
Reprinted by Permission of Hal Leonard LLC

Get Up
Words and Music by Malcolm McCormick, Giorgio Moroder and Theo
Rosenthal
Copyright © 2011 Sony Music Publishing LLC, Blue Slide Park Music, EMI
Gold Horizon Music Corp. and Theo Rosenthal Publishing Designee
All Rights on behalf of Sony Music Publishing LLC, Blue Slide Park Music,
and EMI Gold Horizon Music Corp. Administered by Sony Music
Publishing LLC, 424 Church Street, Suite 1200, Nashville, TN 37219

God Is Fair, Sexy, Nasty

Good News

Goosebumpz

In The Air
Words and Music by Malcolm McCormick and Brent Reynolds
Copyright © 2010 Sony Music Publishing LLC, Blue Slide Park Music and
    EMI Blackwood Music Inc.
All Rights Administered by Sony Music Publishing LLC, 424 Church
    Street, Suite 1200, Nashville, TN 37219
International Copyright Secured   All Rights Reserved
Reprinted by Permission of Hal Leonard LLC

In The Bag
Words and Music by Malcolm McCormick, Rupert Thomas Jr., Louis
    Freeze, Brett Bouldin, Eugene Dixon, Bernice Williams, Earl Ed-
    wards and Larry Muggerud
Copyright © 2015 Sony Music Publishing LLC, Blue Slide Park Music,
    Shay Noelle Publishing, Universal Music - MGB Songs, Cypress
    Phuncky Music, Universal Music Corp., 1/2 Bouldin, 1/2 Ince Music,
    Inc., Conrad Music and Larry Muggerud Publishing Designee
All Rights on behalf of Sony Music Publishing LLC, Blue Slide Park Music
    and Shay Noelle Publishing Administered by Sony Music Publish-
    ing LLC, 424 Church Street, Suite 1200, Nashville, TN 37219
All Rights on behalf of Cypress Phuncky Music Administered by Univer-
    sal Music - MGB Songs
All Rights on behalf of 1/2 Bouldin, 1/2 Ince Music, Inc. Administered by
    Universal Music Corp.
All Rights on behalf of Conrad Music Administered by BMG Rights Man-
    agement (US) LLC
International Copyright Secured   All Rights Reserved
Reprinted by Permission of Hal Leonard LLC

Jet Fuel
Words and Music by Malcolm McCormick, Dacoury Natche, Christopher
    Lane, John MacGillivray, Steve Lacy, Philip Thomas and Daniel
    Hardaway
Copyright © 2018 SONGS OF UNIVERSAL, INC., STAIRCASE WORKS
    PUBLISHING, SONY MUSIC PUBLISHING LLC, DAHI PRODUC-
    TIONS, FASHION MUSIC LTD., STEVE LACY PUBLISHING DES-
    IGNEE, PHILIP THOMAS PUBLISHING DESIGNEE and DANIEL
    HARDAWAY PUBLISHING DESIGNEE
All Rights for STAIRCASE WORKS PUBLISHING Administered by STAIR-
    CASE WORKS PUBLISHING
All Rights for DAHI PRODUCTIONS Administered by SONY MUSIC PUB-
    LISHING LLC, 424 Church Street, Suite 1200, Nashville, TN 37219
All Rights for FASHION MUSIC LTD. Administered Worldwide by KO-
    BALT SONGS MUSIC PUBLISHING
All Rights Reserved   Used by Permission
Reprinted by Permission of Hal Leonard LLC

Keep Floatin'

Words and Music by Malcom McCormick, Eric Dan, Jeremy Kulousek, Thomas Allen, Harold Brown, Morris Dickerson, LeRoy Jordan, Lee Levitin, Charles Miller, Howard Scott, Arthur Lee and Cameron Thomaz

Copyright © 2011 Sony Music Publishing LLC, Blue Slide Park Music, IDLabs Worldwide Sound, KMR Music Royalties II SCSp, Big Jerm Music, Far Out Music Inc, Grass Roots Productions, Trio Music Company and Cameron Thomaz Publishing Designee

All Rights on behalf of Sony Music Publishing LLC, Blue Slide Park Music and IDLabs Worldwide Sound Administered by Sony Music Publishing LLC, 424 Church Street, Suite 1200, Nashville, TN 37219

All Rights on behalf of KMR Music Royalties II SCSp and Big Jerm Music Administered Worldwide by Kobalt Songs Music Publishing

All Rights on behalf of Far Out Music Inc, Grass Roots Productions and Trio Music Company Administered by BMG Rights Management (US) LLC

International Copyright Secured   All Rights Reserved
Reprinted by Permission of Hal Leonard LLC

Knock Knock

Words and Music by Malcolm McCormick, Eric Dan, Jerome Kern and Oscar Hammerstein II

Copyright © 2013 Sony Music Publishing LLC, Blue Slide Park Music, IDLabs Worldwide Sound and Universal - PolyGram International Publishing, Inc.

All Rights on behalf of Sony Music Publishing LLC, Blue Slide Park Music and IDLabs Worldwide Sound Administered by Sony Music Publishing LLC, 424 Church Street, Suite 1200, Nashville, TN 37219

International Copyright Secured   All Rights Reserved
- contains elements of "I've Told Ev'ry Little Star" by Jerome Kern and Oscar Hammerstein II

Reprinted by Permission of Hal Leonard LLC

Ladders

Words and Music by Malcolm McCormick, Peter Mudge, Jon Brion, Jeffrey Gitelman, David Pimentel and Kenneth Whalum Jr.

Copyright © 2017 SONGS OF UNIVERSAL, INC., STAIRCASE WORKS PUBLISHING, MUDGEON MUSIC, YOU CAN'T TAKE IT WITH YOU, SPIRIT ONE MUSIC, SONGS OF GLOBAL ENTERTAINMENT, JEFF GITTY MUSIC, HUH WHAT & WHERE RECORDINGS and KENNETH WHALUM JR. PUBLISHING DESIGNEE

All Rights for STAIRCASE WORKS PUBLISHING Administered by STAIRCASE WORKS PUBLISHING

All Rights for MUDGEON MUSIC Administered by BMG RIGHTS MANAGEMENT (US) LLC

All Rights for YOU CAN'T TAKE IT WITH YOU Administered Worldwide

Life

Life Ain't Easy

Loud

Missed Calls

The Mourning After

O.K.

Once A Day

100 Grandkids

Sayezbeatsn At Inc., Michael Clervoix Publishing Designee, Dory Previn Publishing Designee and Jamel Fisher Publishing Designee

All Rights on behalf of Sony Music Publishing LLC, Blue Slide Park Music, IDLabs Worldwide Sound, EMI Blackwood Music Inc., Janice Combs Publishinng Inc., Hoodlife Publishing, Ghost Writers R Us, Me Again Music, Justin Combs Publishing Company, Diamond Rob Music and EMI Music Publishing Italia SRL

Administered by Sony Music Publishing LLC, 424 Church Street, Suite 1200, Nashville, TN 37219

All Rights on behalf of Dors-D Music Administered by Universal Music Corp.

All Rights on behalf of BMG Gold Songs and Big Jerm Music Administered by BMG Rights Management (US) LLC

All Rights on behalf of Sayezbeatsn At Inc. Administered Worldwide by Kobalt Songs Music Publishing

International Copyright Secured   All Rights Reserved

Reprinted by Permission of Hal Leonard LLC

One Last Thing

Words and Music by Malcolm McCormick and Michael Volpe

Copyright © 2011 Sony Music Publishing LLC, Blue Slide Park Music and Clammyclams Music

All Rights Administered by Sony Music Publishing LLC, 424 Church Street, Suite 1200, Nashville, TN 37219

International Copyright Secured   All Rights Reserved

Reprinted by Permission of Hal Leonard LLC

PA Nights

Words and Music by Malcolm McCormick, Benjamin Hazlegrove, Ted Wendler and William Shaw

Copyright © 2011 Sony Music Publishing LLC, Blue Slide Park Music, These Are Pulse Songs, Farmville Publishing, Laser Falcon Publishing and William Shaw Publishing Designee

All Rights on behalf of Sony Music Publishing LLC and Blue Slide Park Music Administered by Sony Music Publishing LLC, 424 Church Street, Suite 1200, Nashville, TN 37219

International Copyright Secured   All Rights Reserved

Reprinted by Permission of Hal Leonard LLC

Perfect Circle/God Speed

Words and Music by Malcolm McCormick, Adam Feeney, Alexander Sowinski, Chester Hansen and Thomas Beesley

Copyright © 2015 Sony Music Publishing LLC, Blue Slide Park Music, EMI Music Publishing Ltd., Nyankingmusic, Shay Noelle Publishing, Alexander Sowinski Publishing Designee, Chester Hansen Publishing Designee and Thomas Beesley Publishing Designee

All Rights on behalf of Sony Music Publishing LLC, Blue Slide Park Music,

Planet God Damn
Words and Music by Malcolm McCormick, Anderson Hernandez, Adam Feeney, Kaan Gunesberk, Njomza Vitia and Aja Grant

Poppy
Words and Music by George Duke, Malcom McCormick and Jeffrey Kirkland

The Question
Words and Music by Malcolm McCormick, Eric Dan, Jeremy Kulousek, Gairy Harris, Dwayne Carter and Zachary Vaughan

LABS WORLDWIDE SOUND, RESERVOIR 416, ROUTE WAY LLC, MUDGEON MUSIC, DEVONTE HYNES
PUBLISHING and TYLER MASON PUBLISHING DESIGNEE
All Rights for STAIRCASE WORKS PUBLISHING Administered by STAIRCASE WORKS PUBLISHING
All Rights for MCNOOTER PUBLISHING Administered by UNIVERSAL MUSIC CORP.
All Rights for DIVINE PIMP PUBLISHING Administered by UNIVERSAL MUSIC - MGB SONGS
All Rights for DAHI PRODUCTIONS and IDLABS WORLDWIDE SOUND Administered by SONY MUSIC PUBLISHING LLC, 424 Church Street, Suite 1200, Nashville, TN 37219
All Rights for ROUTE WAY LLC Administered by RESERVOIR 416
All Rights for MUDGEON MUSIC Administered by BMG RIGHTS MANAGEMENT (US) LLC
All Rights Reserved   Used by Permission
Reprinted by Permission of Hal Leonard LLC

Senior Skip Day
Words and Music by Malcolm McCormick and Gairy Harris
Copyright © 2010, 2012 Sony Music Publishing LLC, Blue Slide Park Music and Songtrust Blvd.
All Rights on behalf of Sony Music Publishing LLC and Blue Slide Park Music Administered by Sony Music Publishing LLC, 424 Church Street, Suite 1200, Nashville, TN 37219
International Copyright Secured   All Rights Reserved
Reprinted by Permission of Hal Leonard LLC

Skin
Words and Music by Malcolm McCormick, Christian Berishaj, Larry Sheffey and Vic Wainstein
Copyright © 2015 Sony Music Publishing LLC, Blue Slide Park Music, Christian Berishaj Publishing Designee, Larry Sheffey Publishing Designee and Vic Wainstein Publishing Designee
All Rights on behalf of Sony Music Publishing LLC and Blue Slide Park Music Administered by Sony Music Publishing LLC, 424 Church Street, Suite 1200, Nashville, TN 37219
International Copyright Secured   All Rights Reserved
Reprinted by Permission of Hal Leonard LLC

Soulmate
Words and Music by Malcolm McCormick, Eric Dan, Damon Riddick and Nikolai Hamedi
Copyright © 2013 Sony Music Publishing LLC, Blue Slide Park Music, IDLabs Worldwide Sound, Damon Riddick Publishing Designee and Nikolai Hamed Publishing Designee
All Rights on behalf of Sony Music Publishing LLC, Blue Slide Park Music

and IDLabs Worldwide Sound Administered by Sony Music Publishing LLC, 424 Church Street, Suite 1200, Nashville, TN 37219
International Copyright Secured   All Rights Reserved
Reprinted by Permission of Hal Leonard LLC

Therapy
Words and Music by Eric Dan, Malcolm McCormick, Jeremy Kulousek and Zachary Vaughan
Copyright © 2013 Sony Music Publishing LLC, IDLabs Worldwide Sound, BMG Gold Songs, Big Jerm Music, Dwayne Carter Publishing Designee, Gairy Harris Publishing Designee and Zachary Vaughan Publishing Designee
All Rights on behalf of Sony Music Publishing LLC and IDLabs Worldwide Sound Administered by Sony Music Publishing LLC, 424 Church Street, Suite 1200, Nashville, TN 37219
International Copyright Secured   All Rights Reserved
Reprinted by Permission of Hal Leonard LLC

Time Flies
Words and Music by Malcolm McCormick, Kehinde Hassan and Taiwo Hassan
Copyright © 2013 Sony Music Publishing LLC, Blue Slide Park Music, Kehinde Hassan Publishing Designee and Taiwo Hassan Publishing Designee
All Rights on behalf of Sony Music Publishing LLC and Blue Slide Park Music Administered by Sony Music Publishing LLC, 424 Church Street, Suite 1200, Nashville, TN 37219
International Copyright Secured   All Rights Reserved
Reprinted by Permission of Hal Leonard LLC

2009
Words and Music by Malcolm McCormick, Jon Brion, James Harris III, Terry Lewis, James Wright, Aja Grant, Chante Moore, George Jackson and Eric Gabouer
Copyright © 2018 SONGS OF UNIVERSAL, INC., STAIRCASE WORKS PUBLISHING, YOU CAN'T TAKE IT WITH YOU, KMR MUSIC ROYALTIES II SCSP, DOWNTOWN DMP SONGS, SUPER RARE CANDY MUSIC, HANTE SEVEN PUBLISHING, GEORGE JACKSON PUBLISHING DESIGNEE and ERIC GABOUER PUBLISHING DESIGNEE
All Rights for STAIRCASE WORKS PUBLISHING Administered by SONGS OF UNIVERSAL, INC.
All Rights for YOU CAN'T TAKE IT WITH YOU and KMR MUSIC ROYALTIES II SCSP Administered Worldwide by KOBALT SONGS MUSIC PUBLISHING
All Rights for SUPER RARE CANDY MUSIC Administered by DOWNTOWN MUSIC SERVICES
All Rights Reserved   Used by Permission
Reprinted by Permission of Hal Leonard LLC

Acknowledgments

Firstly, I want to thank Malcolm for changing my life—all of our lives—for the better. The music, the lessons, the memories, are all invaluable to me and the rest of the MacHeads.

This book would not be possible without the generous people who spoke with me, the blessing from the estate, and the kindness of Karen Meyers, who shot the cover image and reached out to me during the early stages of writing the *Year of Mac* series, and who kept up with my work since. To everyone who took hours upon hours to chat with me about their friend: thank you.

I've been working on this book, both knowingly and unknowingly, since the day Mac Miller passed, and perhaps somehow I've been working on this book since I first heard *K.I.D.S.* in 2010. That said, this book would be nothing without my early champions Z and Brendan, my agent David, and my incredible editor Jacob, who always has time for a lengthy phone call.

Lastly, I'd like to thank my dearest friends, my chosen family, and my wife for supporting me through this work. This book is not, and never was, about me, but you all made me feel whole as I fought to get it done. From the bottom of my heart, thank you.

A portion of the proceeds from this book will go directly to the Mac Miller Legacy Fund.

The Mac Miller Fund

The Mac Miller Fund supports young musicians with resources to help realize their full potential through exploration, expression and community.

Born Malcolm McCormick, Mac Miller was an acclaimed musician and native of the Point Breeze neighborhood of Pittsburgh. A gifted and self-taught musician, McCormick began recording his own music at age fifteen, regularly performing at the Shadow Lounge in East Liberty and other venues around Pittsburgh. By eighteen, he released his breakout mixtape *K.I.D.S.*, before going on to release five studio albums, including his chart-topping, Pittsburgh-referencing *Blue Slide Park* in 2011.

Though unquestionably a formidable creative force that achieved monumental success both critically and commercially in his own career, Miller's legacy might be most defined by his outsized charisma, selflessness and commitment to community-building. From his early days in Pittsburgh to the artistic community that he later fostered in Los Angeles, Miller was endless in the time, energy and effort that he gave to others—not just for their own sake, but for the sake of creating truly beautiful art for the world.

To carry on Miller's artistic and creative legacy, The Mac Miller Fund supports programming, resources and opportunities to youth from underserved communities, helping them recognize their full potential through exploration in the arts and community building.

Additionally, the fund may support organizations that identify and address the problems of substance abuse in the music industry and that directly assist youth aged twenty-seven and under with all stages of addiction-recovery treatment and post-treatment services.

About the Author

Donna-Claire Chesman is a music writer with a deep passion for hip-hop, her pet parrot, and Mac Miller. Currently residing in Philadelphia, Chesman is the Editorial Director of Audiomack by day, and spends her evenings reading with her pet cats.